P9-CCX-026

THE
Pruning
BOOK

THE
Pruning
BOOK

LEE REICH

The Taunton Press

Publisher: Suzanne La Rosa
Associate publisher: Helen Albert
Editorial assistant: Cherilyn DeVries

Editor: Ruth Dobsevage
Designer: Joan Lockhart
Layout artist: Lynne Phillips
Illustrator: Dolores R. Santoliquido
Indexer: Harriet Hodges

Typeface: Minion
Paper: 70-lb. Somerset Matte
Printer: Quebecor Printing/Tennessee Book Operations

Taunton
BOOKS & VIDEOS
for fellow enthusiasts

Text © 1999 by Lee Reich
Illustrations © 1999 by The Taunton Press, Inc.
Photographs © 1999 by The Taunton Press, Inc., unless otherwise noted
All rights reserved.

Printed in the United States of America
10 9 8 7 6 5 4 3 2 1

The Pruning Book was originally published in hardcover in 1997
by The Taunton Press, Inc.

The Taunton Press, Inc., 63 South Main Street,
PO Box 5506, Newtown, CT 06470-5506
e-mail: tp@taunton.com

Distributed by Publishers Group West

Library of Congress Cataloging-in-Publication Data

Reich, Lee.
      The pruning book / Lee Reich.
          p.   cm.
      Includes index.
      ISBN 1-56158-316-2
      1. Pruning.   I. Title.
SB125.R38   1999
635.9'1542 — dc20   96-34301
                                   CIP

ACKNOWLEDGMENTS

A number of people helped bring *The Pruning Book* to fruition. Thanks, first of all, to *Horticulture* magazine's Tom Cooper for sowing the seed of the idea. At The Taunton Press, associate publisher Helen Albert and editorial assistant Cherilyn DeVries nourished that seed as it developed and grew into the book you now hold in your hands. And thanks to my editor, Ruth Dobsevage, for her thoroughness and humor. Also for her pruning—of words—where needed.

I appreciate commentary provided by the following people on selected portions of the draft: Dr. John Barden of Virginia Polytechnic Institute and State University, Dr. Richard Harris of the University of California at Davis, and Dr. William Welch of Texas A & M University. And thanks goes to my father, Joseph Reich, for his part in reading and providing insightful criticism on the draft from beginning to end.

CONTENTS

Plant Lists

INTRODUCTION

Do you wince with pain, as if amputating without anesthetic, when pruning a plant? Or do you ruthlessly attack? Either approach can have good results—provided your cuts are well reasoned, well timed, and well made. These are the three keys to successful pruning, and my aim in writing this book is put them into your hands.

I have attempted to include here nearly every plant that might benefit from pruning. And I use the word "prune" quite literally: "to remove dead or living parts from (a plant) so as to increase fruit or flower production or improve the form" *(Webster's New Twentieth Century Dictionary of the English Language, 1962).* To this end, you will find between these two covers information on how to prune a lilac bush, an apple tree or a maple tree, a hibiscus hedge, a bougainvillea, strawberries, tomato vines, a weeping fig, a wisteria vine, chrysanthemums…as I said, any plant that benefits from pruning. The last section of this book guides you through such specialized pruning techniques as bonsai, espalier, even lawn mowing. (I did say that this book was meant to be comprehensive and fully embrace the word "prune.")

This book is intended for readers as diverse in their interests and skills as the range of plants covered. Too often, directions for pruning are unduly complicated, even for seasoned pruners. I have drawn on my own experiences, in research and in the field, as well as what has been previously written about pruning, to put together a text that is, I hope, both practical and readable.

Information is arranged so that both novices and experts can easily sift out what they need.

This book parts company with other books about pruning in two ways. First of all, I have had no qualms about debunking or at least questioning the value of certain long-held and well-entrenched pruning practices. Cutting back the tops of woody plants when transplanting, flush-cutting limbs from shade trees, and applying wound dressings are all examples of traditional practices that, on the basis of recent research, should no longer be universally recommended (but are still recommended in too many "modern" publications). Let careful and rigorous observation, rather than tradition, be our guides in pruning. The plants will be thankful, and show it.

This book also distinguishes itself in being a book only about pruning. While writing this book, I was often tempted to describe flowers and fruits, to mention site selection, fertilization, and other considerations attendant to growing particular plants listed. But I resisted temptation. Presumably you have done your homework in these matters—now you are ready to prune. What these pages lack in incidentals about plants, I hope they make up for with thoroughness about pruning those plants.

But enough words. As Thackeray observed, approvingly, "One sees him clipping his apricots and pruning his essays." Here, here, and on with both.

New Paltz, New York
May, 1994

HOW TO USE THIS BOOK

Ideally, you will curl up with this book some winter evening—not to prune, of course, but just to read about pruning. The dead of winter is a perfect time to imprint firmly in your mind why a plant might benefit from pruning, what tools you should use, where and when to make the cuts, and how you can generally expect a plant to respond. All this information is offered in Part 1 of this book, "The Basics." With your homework done, you then will be prepared when a break in the weather gives you an urge to prune. All you'll need is a glance at Part 2, "The Plants," for specific information on your particular plant—or plants.

Such a scenario may be wishful thinking, so I've also done my best to accommodate those of you whose initial contact with this book will be as you grab a pair of pruning shears and run out into the garden the first balmy day of the season. A little box entitled "The Bare Bones" at the beginning of each chapter in Part 2 provides you with the essentials for pruning all the plants in that chapter. These instructions will not make you an expert pruner, but will offer sufficient guidance to keep you and your plants reasonably happy.

Part 2, "The Plants," forms the bulk of this book, with each chapter consisting of plants grouped in the categories for which we value them: deciduous ornamental bushes, evergreens, fruits, houseplants, etc. Roses are such a large, popular group that they earn their own subcategory— in the chapter on deciduous ornamental shrubs, of course. These chapters offer detailed pruning instructions in addition to "The Bare Bones" at the beginning.

Use the information in Part 2 by first looking up the appropriate chapter for the plant that you want to prune, then reading over the instructions in that chapter, or a heading within the chapter. Next, check the chapter's Plant List for specifics on the particular plant. If you have trouble assigning a plant to a chapter, look the plant up in the Index.

An advantage of grouping plants the way they have been grouped in Part 2 is that it allows you to prune a plant even if you do not know its name. Or even if the plant has not been included in this book! All you need to do is to decide what sort of plant it is. Even a beginning gardener can differentiate between a deciduous and an evergreen plant—just wait for winter. A year of observation may be needed before you can pigeonhole an unknown plant into an appropriate category, and perhaps subcategory (spring- versus summer-flowering shrub, for example).

Part 3 of this book, "Specialized Pruning Techniques," broadens your pruning skills. Here you will learn about pollarding, pleaching, and topiary; you will find out how to grow a fuchsia as a small tree, how to prune…er, mow… your lawn, how to create a bonsai, and how to espalier an apple tree.

Notwithstanding all the guidance, both general and specific, offered in this book, one caution is in order: No matter how or what you are pruning, couple use of your pruning tool with a keen eye. Plants do not always obey all the rules. Close observation of how a plant grows, and how it responds to your cuts, makes for better—and the most satisfying—results.

PART 1

THE

BASICS

CHAPTER ONE | WHY PRUNE?

There are undoubtedly gardeners who shudder at the thought of putting a blade to a plant. After all, look within the forest and the field at wild plants, their stems untouched by pruning saws and clippers. These plants seem happy enough, living their lives unpruned.

In fact, wild plants are pruned. Large tree limbs on the ground following a wind or ice storm are a dramatic demonstration of "natural" pruning; less obvious are the smaller twigs and branches that litter the ground beneath trees and shrubs. How much natural pruning occurs depends not only upon wind and weather, but also on the plant species. Silver maple and boxelder are frowned upon as landscape trees because of their notorious habit of dropping branches of various sizes. My American persimmon trees save me some pruning work by naturally shedding some of their twiggy branches after they bear fruit.

Animals also contribute to natural pruning. Not only do deer shorten branches, but they also enjoy nibbling along the length of a branch, which results in bare regions of "blind wood." If only deer would browse yews in a more artistic fashion! Rabbits take care of natural pruning near ground level.

Lower limbs of crowded plants also are naturally pruned, dropping off as they weaken and die from lack of light. Foresters encourage this natural pruning by planting timber trees close together, to produce straight, branchless (hence knot-free) trunks.

Whether wild plants, pruned one way or another, suffer or benefit from such pruning becomes a philosophical question. The ragged scar left where wind ripped a large limb off a tree is going to be subject to infection, which is obviously of no benefit to the plant. On the other hand, small plants might benefit from the increased light they receive after a large limb drops from a nearby tree. With natural pruning, individuals may suffer, but the population—the collection of plants in the forest or field—benefits, or at least changes in a natural progression.

Cultivated plants are another story. We prune our cultivated plants both for ourselves and for the plants. Each one has aesthetic, sentimental, even monetary, value, so pruning cannot be left to the vagaries of nature. Deliberate pruning may be necessary.

Most important, before pruning any plant, is to have a clear objective in mind, as well as an understanding of how the plant is likely to respond to whatever cuts are made. Done correctly, pruning will not harm a plant, and may actually help it. Later we will delve into how plants respond to pruning, as well as how to prune without causing them harm.

For now, let's consider the reasons for pruning: to keep a plant healthy; to keep a plant from growing too large; to make a plant more beautiful; to improve the quality or quantity of flowers, leaves, or fruits.

Prune for plant health

Peer into the center of an old, unpruned tree or shrub, and you'll see a jumble of branches rubbing together, many of them weak and dying, some already dead. The wood is weak from lack of light, which, along with poor air circulation, creates the dank conditions favored by disease-causing organisms. This problem is not limited to woody plants. Such conditions might develop within a couple of months even on an herbaceous plant—witness the average tomato plant, carefully pruned early in the season to grow up a stake, then becoming a tangle of stems once summer's heat spurs growth beyond a gardener's enthusiasm for pruning.

Pruning away some branches within that tangled mass of vegetation lets in light and air. The light itself inhibits the growth of certain disease-producing microorganisms, and the combination of light and air circulation promotes more

Natural pruning is fine in the forest, but undesirable in a backyard.

A tangle of branches leads to dead, weak, or diseased wood.

rapid drying of leaves, shoots, and fruits, further reducing the chances of disease. Removing crossing limbs also prevents wounds created by rubbing, another possible entryway for disease.

Let's turn now to a large maple tree, "pruned" naturally by a windstorm. That windstorm does not lop off branches cleanly, or necessarily at a point where the plant can best heal the wound. The ragged, misplaced cut will heal poorly, leaving a large scar through which disease can gain a foothold. Touching up natural pruning with a sharp saw keeps such a plant healthy.

As you look over a plant, no matter what kind of plant it is, be ready to cut away portions attacked by disease or insects. On a dormant plant, look for such problems as bark cankers, which are dark, sunken areas where diseases spend the winter, or tarry, black growths on *Prunus* species, which are indicative of black knot disease (see the photo below). In summer, timely pruning away of stems whose leaves have been blackened by fire blight disease can prevent future infections. Cutting off a raspberry or currant cane below the swollen spot where a borer has entered can stop further damage.

Pruning to promote and maintain plant health begins as soon as you set a new plant in the ground. This is the first and last time you get to view the roots, so take the opportunity to cut off any diseased parts and cut cleanly—for better healing—any ragged ends. Remember that bare-root plants, whether vegetable transplants, shrubs, or trees, are stressed

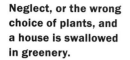

Neglect, or the wrong choice of plants, and a house is swallowed in greenery.

Pruning helps keep certain diseases, such as black knot of plum, in check.

by root loss. Pruning the stems of trees and shrubs, or cutting off some or a portion of the leaves of vegetable transplants, may help these plants recover from the shock of transplanting under dry conditions. With good growing conditions, however, such pruning is unnecessary and results in less growth than if the plant is left unpruned.

Pruning also keeps trees healthy by directing growth while the tree is young, so that limbs are firmly anchored to the trunk, and not apt to break in high winds or under their own weight or when loaded down with fruits.

Prune to keep a plant from growing too large

Pruning dwarfs plants, and is thus a way to control their size. That said, there is a better, or at least an easier, way than pruning to keep plants from growing out of bounds. You need not search far to see homes whose entrances, windows, whose very walls are being gobbled up by the somber yews and junipers planted along their foundation walls. Perhaps the homeowners ignored the plants for a few years, not realizing that the neglected plants would grow into such large, billowing masses of greenery.

Rather than fighting a plant back every year with metal blades, just plant a tree, shrub, or vine that naturally will keep within its allotted space. Dwarf forms exist for many plants, and these eliminate or at least reduce the need for pruning. 'Aurea Nana' arborvitae, for example, never grows higher than 5 ft., as compared with 20 ft. or more for the species. With some plants, most notably fruit trees, size control can be achieved by grafting a stem onto a dwarfing rootstock. Apple rootstocks have been the most studied, and are available for a

Pruning and good plant choice make a well-proportioned landscape.

range of tree sizes, from a full-size tree 30 ft. high down to a 6-ft. dwarf.

For people willing to commit themselves to an annual pruning regime, or in those situations where dwarf plants are not available, pruning is the answer. Many houseplants, for example, are by nature large tropical trees that cannot be allowed to express their full vigor within the confines of a home. Street trees beneath power lines need occasional cutting to keep the lines clear. Peach trees are not naturally very large trees, yet are large enough to put the fruits beyond convenient reach. Left to its own devices, a cultivated grape vine is likely to clamber up a pole or nearby tree to bear much of its fruit at an inaccessible height, as do wild grapes. In all these cases, controlling plant size by pruning does not mean wantonly hacking back branches. Each cut must take into account the plant's needs as well as its response to various types of pruning

This topiary brings another meaning to the phrase 'bear hug.'

cuts. Pruning roots as well as branches may be called for to keep a plant to size.

For many gardeners, and I count myself among such souls, pruning to keep a plant small is not drudgery, but enjoyable and interesting. With only 4 ft. between trees, my apples require dwarf rootstocks *and* diligent pruning to prevent overcrowding—all the while maintaining fruitfulness, of course. Pruning to dwarf a plant is carried to its extreme with the art of bonsai, by which meticulous pruning of both the branches and roots of trees and shrubs creates a picturesque landscape in miniature.

Prune to make a plant more beautiful

When you prune a plant for beauty, your goals may run the gamut. You may want to knit together a view with a uniform hedge or a pleached tunnel of trees. At the other extreme, you may want to shape a plant in a whimsical manner. Topiary animals, carved from shrubs and "scurrying" across an expanse of lawn, are certain to cause a pleasant surprise the first time they come into view. A uniform hedge with "end posts" of shrubs sheared in ornate geometric forms similarly draws your eye. Used on too many plants in a given scene, either extreme in pruning—that which creates harmony or that which creates interest—is unpleasant. The first becomes boring and the second becomes disturbing.

To achieve either effect, a plant's growth can be merely coaxed along in its natural form, or growth can be more radically redirected in a formal manner. No matter how much you prune any plant, however, it will attempt to resume its natural growth habit. And this growth habit will change somewhat as the plant ages. Young plants tend to grow more upright, with longer branches and larger leaves than older plants. A formal shape, being farther from a plant's natural growth habit than a natural shape, usually requires more diligent pruning. So the cordon apple tree—consisting of a single stem—might require pruning two, three, or even more times each year, some in winter and some in summer. A standard apple tree, in contrast, gets along fine with its once-a-year pruning in late winter.

Not all plants trained in a naturalistic way require little pruning: Remember those bonsai plants mentioned a few sentences ago? Their "natural" appearance is actually the result of meticulous pruning of both roots and shoots—all to keep them looking, in miniature, just like their full-size brothers and sisters.

Prune to improve the quality or quantity of flowers, leaves, or fruits

A plant's appeal comes not only from its shape, but also from the individual size or sheer mass of its blooms, its leafy raiment, or its luscious fruits—perhaps all three! Pruning can help coax the best from a plant in any of these respects.

How can pruning have such an effect? Removing stems from a plant removes buds that would potentially have grown into shoots, so more energy gets

Fruit thinning, a type of pruning, results in large and luscious peaches.

The craggy trunk of this bonsai captures the venerability of an ancient tree.

channeled into those buds and shoots that remain. Vigorous new shoots stimulated by pruning are those that are most fiery red on a red-osier dogwood and are what give a pollarded tree—cut back each winter to a mere stump a few feet high—its characteristic headdress of lanky shoots and oversized leaves. (Oversized leaves are often associated with overly vigorous growth.) The more new growth you can stimulate on a woody plant that flowers only on new shoots, the greater the show of flowers each summer. Drastically cutting back such plants in late winter or early spring stimulates an abundance of new shoots.

Some of the buds removed when you lop a branch off a fruit tree are flower buds. Fewer flowers results in fewer fruits, but those fruits that remain get an increased share of the plant's energy. The result is that the remaining fruits are larger and sweeter. An additional benefit of reducing the number of fruits is that a plant might bear moderate crops every season, rather than having alternating seasons of feast and famine. Because of hormones produced in developing fruits, a large crop one year suppresses flower-bud initiation, and, hence, fruiting, in plants whose flowers open a year after the first traces of flower buds are laid down.

Light has a dramatic effect on plant performance, and by cutting off branches to change the form of a plant, you also affect the amount of light reaching the remaining branches. Hedges look their best fully clothed with leaves from head to toe, so they are always sheared at least slightly narrower at their heads than at their feet to allow leaf-nourishing light to reach all surfaces. Fruiting demands abundant sunlight—transformed within plants into sugars—so fruit trees are trained and maintained in such a way that each part of the plant gets as much sun as possible.

Stems are not the only parts of a plant that you can prune to improve plant performance. Removing all but a few flower buds on a dahlia pumps the flowers that do remain into show-quality "dinnerplate" blooms. Similarly, pinching some flowers off a peach tree—yet another form of pruning—redirects the plant's energies to fewer peaches, making them sweeter and larger. (Pinching off flower buds supplements fruit thinning that results from earlier pruning of branches that had flower buds and subsequent pinching off of excess small fruits.)

And one more reason to prune...

Upon coming to the end of this list of reasons to prune, I suddenly realized that there is one more reason, for better or worse, why we prune plants—because we are human. Plants offer us more than mere aesthetic or utilitarian pleasure; they also are outlets for our creativity. We enjoy watching plants respond to our care, reacting to our pinching, snipping, watering, and fertilizing. By this, I do not mean merely watching a plant shrink as we lop off its branches, but, rather, how the plant regrows in response to just how and when it was cut back.

Pruning is just one of many gardening practices, yet it is among the most effective and interesting in terms of what it can accomplish. Depending on how and when you prune, the influence may be evident in a few weeks, in a year, or over the course of years. This book, I hope, will help you to get a response to pruning your plants that both pleases you and keeps your plants happy.

CHAPTER TWO

TOOLS OF THE TRADE

A bowsaw with a sharp blade makes easy work of thick limbs.

Soon after the first human deliberately pruned a plant, ideas for designs of specialized pruning tools may have taken shape. As long ago as the first century A.D., a Roman named Columella wrote of the *vinitoria falx*, a grape-pruning tool with six different functions. Today, you will not find one pruning tool to do six different jobs; depending on your plants and horticultural aspirations, you may not even need six different tools. But if you grow plants, you probably will need at least one pruning tool—in all likelihood a pair of hand-held pruning shears.

More on what tool or tools you will need in a bit; first, a comment on pur-chasing a pruning tool. Better-quality tools cost more and are, in my opinion, well worth the extra money. But be fore-warned that when it comes to pruning tools, "better quality" can have more than one meaning. It may mean a tool manufactured from higher-quality materials, or a tool designed to cut more effectively, or a tool that is more comfortable to use. I have cut branches using stainless-steel pruning shears that were shiny and expensive, but not particularly comfortable to hold or especially effective at cutting, despite the high-quality materials they were made from. If possible, try out a pruning tool once you find one in your price range.

The thumbnail is a useful—and convenient—pruning tool.

Always use a pruning tool appropriate to the size of the pruning cut. Too many gardeners attempt to shimmy and wiggle hand-held pruning shears through branches that are too thick to cut effectively with this tool. Using the wrong size tool makes pruning more difficult—even impossible—and leaves a forlorn-looking plant with ragged stubs. Before purchasing a pruning tool, think about what you will be cutting.

It is sometimes stated, especially in older gardening books, that all pruning should be done with a knife, or with just your thumbnail. The implication is that timely pruning removes any growth before it is beyond the size that can be handled by either of these "tools." (The quotation marks are for the thumbnail.) Perhaps so, in an ideal world, or for a person growing only a half-dozen houseplants in an apartment. But pruning a gardenful of plants with your knife and thumbnail is not practical. And even if it were practical, some limbs do not display their character at an early enough age to signal their need for removal. And how about that wrist-thick limb, dead from disease and now needing removal?

That said, the thumbnail is a fine and convenient pruning tool, ideal for such tasks as pinching out the tips of outdoor chrysanthemums and indoor avocado trees. Do not overlook the rest of your hand as a useful pruning implement. Prune suckers from a tomato plant by just grabbing them, then snapping them off with a downward jerk. Snap off unwanted watersprouts from a tree in the same way way, the minute you notice them. There is no need to trek to the garden shed for any other equipment.

(If you never considered your hand as a pruning tool, stretch your mind and also consider these other specialized "tools:" a shovel, for root pruning; a stream of water from your hose or a broom handle with a piece of hose attached, to thin blossoms from a fruit tree.)

The pruning knife comes highly recommended by those gardeners with the expertise to use it. This knife differs from other knives in having a curved blade, which helps it keep contact with the branch as you cut. If you choose to use a pruning knife, buy one with a folding blade (for safety in carrying it) and a thick handle that is easy to hold without causing blisters.

Personally, I have never been able see the advantage of a pruning knife over a good pair of hand shears, what the British call secateurs. The hand shears will never slip and nick nearby stems, and will cut through wood up to ½ in. thick, which is more than you could ask from a pruning knife. As mentioned previously, this tool is probably the one you will need if you own but one pruning tool.

Because a pair of hand shears is such a useful tool—one which I often drop into my back pocket before I walk out into the garden—check out the style (see the sidebar below), the weight, the hand fit, and the balance of several models before you settle on one. You can buy special shears tailored to fit small hands or left hands. Make sure any pair of shears has a convenient safety catch that does not slip into the "open" position when you want it closed, or vice versa; otherwise, if you carry them as I do, you could end up

ANVIL VS. BYPASS HAND SHEARS

Hand shears fall into one of two categories: anvil and bypass (the latter sometimes called "scissors"). The business end of the anvil-type shears consists of a sharp blade that comes down on top of an opposing blade having a flat edge. The flat edge is made of a soft metal so as not to dull the sharp edge. Bypass pruners work more like scissors, with two sharpened blades sliding past each other.

Anvil shears generally are cheaper than bypass shears—and the price difference is reflected in the resulting cut! Often, the anvil pruner will crush part of the stem. And if the two blades do not mate perfectly, the cut will be incomplete, leaving the two pieces of the stem attached by threads of tissue. That wide, flattened blade also makes it more difficult to get the tool right up against the base of the stem you want to remove.

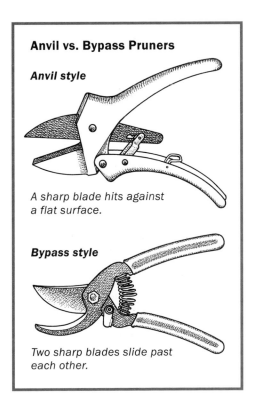

Anvil vs. Bypass Pruners

Anvil style

A sharp blade hits against a flat surface.

Bypass style

Two sharp blades slide past each other.

with a hole in your back pocket. Also take note of how easily the blades of a particular pair of hand shears can be sharpened; some shears have replaceable blades. A bypass pruner should have an adjustable tension screw, so that the blades can be made to close easily, yet be tight enough so as not to bind onto a stem. I particularly like the hooked end of my Pica shears, which prevents stems from slipping free of the jaws as I cut. And for the professional landscaper or orchardist, who is confronted with hours of pruning at a stretch, pneumatic or electrically operated hand shears are available.

For pruning branches larger than ½ in. across, up to about 1½ in. in diameter, you need lopping shears, usually just called a "lopper." This tool is essentially the same as hand shears, except that the blades are heavier and the handle is a couple of feet long. Like hand shears, the lopper's business end may be either of the anvil or bypass type. The long handles of the lopper give you leverage to cut through those larger stems, and allow you to reach into the base of an over-grown rose or gooseberry bush without being attacked by thorns. Some loppers gain extra cutting power with a gear or a ratchet mechanism that allows the blades

The lopping shears slices through stems up to about 1½ in. across.

to sever wood even 2 in. thick. Those extra mechanisms do add weight to the end of the tool, which, with its long handles, may become unwieldy after a few hours of use. Of all the loppers that I have used, I prefer an old pair I bought at a farm sale. The long wooden handles absorb shock and are smoothed from decades of use, and the small bypass blades make a clean cut in spite of the chipped beak on one of the blades. This tool slices through wood up to 1½ in. thick.

If more cutting power is needed than lopping shears can provide, I can always run to the shed and grab a pruning saw. Saws are the next step up in necessary tools as you progress to thicker wood. Do not try to use a saw from your woodworking shop to remove a limb, because such a saw works effectively only on dry wood. The teeth on pruning saws are designed to cope with green wood without clogging or gumming. Larger teeth generally cut quickest, leaving a rougher edge, but the new, so-called Japanese blades (sometimes called "turbo" or "frictionless" blades) cut quickly despite their small teeth. A nice saw for making fast work of limbs up to 3 in. in diameter is a "Grecian" pruning saw, with a curved blade and teeth set to cut on the pull stroke. These small saws squeeze their way into tight places among branches, and, if designed so that the blade folds into the handle, will even squeeze into your back pocket. Where space is not quite so restricted (on the plant, not your pocket), my preference is for the narrow-nosed bowsaw (photo, p. 13), which has a thin, easily replaceable blade that cuts on both the push and the pull strokes. Heavier-bladed, straight-bladed pruning saws look much like carpenter's saws, but with a different set of dentures. Avoid those that are reversible, having a row of coarse teeth

on one edge of the blade and narrow teeth on the other. Such saws inevitably make unwanted cuts on wood near the side of the blade that you are *not* using! Purchase two separate saws instead.

A 'Grecian' pruning saw cuts through moderately thick limbs in tight places, then folds up into your back pocket.

Use a hand shears (the bypass type is shown here) to slice through stems up to ½ in. in diameter.

for the job, or, even better, hire a professional with a chainsaw to do the job for you. Experience with chainsaws breeds respect for this useful, albeit dangerous, pruning tool. If you feel the need to own a chainsaw, purchase one scaled to the thickness of wood you will be cutting. And when you make your purchase, also buy a pair of goggles and, along with a gasoline-powered saw, a set of ear protectors.

If you have formal hedges to take care of, you also need some sort of hedge shears to keep them shapely. Manual shears look like giant scissors with straight handles. Shearing a long hedge of privet by hand can be tiring, so choose hedge shears with care. Recognize that longer blades and handles—which allow you to bite off more and reach farther with each cut—also add to the weight of the tool. Because you constantly bang the handles together as you cut, pay attention to how the handles feel and what kind of shock absorption they have as they come together. My Sandvik shears have padded rubber handles and enough bounce from a rubber shock absorber to make the handles spring apart after banging together, ready for the next cut. Many hedge shears have a notch near the base of the blade for lopping off an occasional, overly vigorous stem that you might come across as you progress down the length of a hedge. Wavy blades on a pair of shears reputedly do a better job by keeping stems from sliding out the mouth of the shears without being cut. I have not experienced that problem because I keep the straight-edged blades on my hedge shears sharp.

Of all power pruning tools used by the average homeowner, probably none is more popular than the electric hedge clipper. The straight bar of this tool, with its oscillating blade, makes it easy to put a

Manual (top) and electric (above) hedge shears are essential for keeping hedges at their best.

We cannot leave the subject of pruning saws without mention of the chainsaw. These gasoline or electric saws make relatively short work of large limbs— even whole trees (but that can hardly be called "pruning")! A chainsaw is overkill where you have only a backyard full of plants to prune. If the size of a cut dictates the need for such a tool, rent one flat top on a hedge. Nonetheless, I still prefer a good pair of manual hedge shears because they are easier to sharpen and require no long extension cord. I can run out and prune a little bit of the hedge at a time, without investing any time or effort in coiling and uncoiling the extension cord. The manual shears, especially if they have high-quality blades, makes a rhythmical and pleasant sound as the honed metal blades slice against each other. If noise does not concern you and extension cords are too much trouble, gasoline-powered hedge clippers are available, but these are mostly heavy-duty models for professional landscapers.

Now we enter the realm of specialized pruning tools, which you may or may not ever require. The first is a shearing knife, useful for keeping a Christmas tree or a large hedge shapely and dense as it grows. This knife has a long handle and a blade that is thin, sharp, and also long. Because it is used samurai fashion, also consider purchasing leg guards along with a shearing knife.

Growers of red raspberries constantly have to remove wayward suckers, and a tool that facilitates this job is a bush hook, which consists of a sharpened hook at the end of a long handle. With this tool, you can walk along the row, hook the blade under a sucker, and jerk it out cleanly without even stooping. I stoop. (Anyway, I have only seen this tool pictured in old gardening books, so if you want one, you probably will have to make it yourself or have it made.)

A lawnmower is, of course, also a specialized pruning tool, one with which everyone is familiar. Reel mowers can be human-, gasoline-, or electric-powered and cut more cleanly than rotary mowers, which must be powered by either gasoline or electricity.

Do not overlook a scythe for "pruning" high grass. The so-called European-style scythe has a straight snath and a light-weight blade that is hammered, then honed, to a razor-sharp edge—all in all a pleasure to use and not to be confused with the heavy, American-type scythe that has a curved snath.

A European-style scythe cuts high grass quietly and efficiently.

Saw or slice high limbs from the ground with a pole pruner.

And then there is the highly specialized strawberry pruner, described in Liberty Hyde Bailey's *The Pruning Book* (1912), for cutting all the runners off a strawberry plant all at once. The tool consists of a 10-in. diameter metal cylinder with one edge sharpened and the other attached to a handle that can be banged with a hammer or stomped upon with your foot. You place the cylinder around a plant, then apply the downward force to cut off the runners.

Of all the pruning tools available, the one that has the least to recommend it is the high-limb chain saw. The chain part of this tool is attached at either end to a rope. You throw the device over a high limb, grasp onto each end of the rope, centering the toothed chain over the limb, then alternately pull down on the ropes. The results can be disastrous: The worst-case scenario has the limb toppling on top of you, tearing a long strip of bark off the trunk on the way down.

A saner way to deal with high limbs is with a pole pruner, an effective pruning tool that admittedly does not reach as high as the high-limb chain saw. With a shearing head seated atop the pole and activated by a handle or rope at the bottom, the tool performs the same job as hand shears, many feet up in the tree. You could also attach a curved Grecian saw on the head of a pole. If you stand slightly to the side when using it, both the curve of the blade and gravity will help you along with your sawing.

Very useful is the pole pruner at whose head is attached *both* shearing blades and a saw. Once you have managed to work this tool up through the tree to the branches that you want to cut, you have a choice of cutting devices. Still, the two-headed pole pruner is not quite as versatile as Columella's six-in-one tool for pruning grapes.

Caring for pruning tools

A pruning tool that you treat with affection will return the favor with years of good service. If the expense of a tool will induce you to give it greater care, then this is one more reason to pay as much as you can afford for it.

Pruning tools do not need to be babied, just cleaned, sharpened, and oiled. Dirt on the blades of a tool may nick or dull its edges, so give the blade—no matter what kind of pruning tool it is—a wipe with a rag each time you finish using it. (I leave a rag hanging conveniently on a nail in my garage near where I keep my tools so that I have no excuse not to use it.) Clean sap off blades with a rag dipped in a solvent such as kerosene. Periodically apply a few drops of oil to the bolt that joins the blades of hand shears, lopping shears, and hedge shears, as well as to the spring that spreads the hand shears' handles. Also oil the wooden handles of tools, unless they are coated with varnish.

You will find it easier and quicker to cut if your tool is sharp. Less immediately obvious will be the beneficial effect on the plant. Plants like sharp pruning tools because clean cuts heal fastest.

You need a whetstone and perhaps a file to sharpen the blades of your pruning tools. (The file is needed for quickly removing metal when a blade has been nicked, not for sharpening.) Before using a whetstone, make sure it is thoroughly wet by soaking it in either lightweight oil or water. Then, when you use the whetstone, keep it wet by applying a few drops of oil or water (whichever you soaked the stone in) to its surface as you use it for sharpening. The liquid floats away particles that you grind off. Hold the blade against the whetstone, or vice versa, maintaining the existing angle on the edge of the blade, then move the blade or whetstone in a motion as if you were shaving a thin slice from the whetstone.

Know your tool before you attempt to sharpen it. On an anvil-type pruner, you need to sharpen only one blade, and you sharpen this blade on both sides. As you sharpen, avoid putting a curve on the edge of the blade. Unless the edge is perfectly straight, it will not rest true against the flat opposing anvil, and stems will cling together with a few threads of plant tissue after each of your cuts. On hedge shears, bypass hand shears, or bypass lopping shears, do sharpen both blades. Because these blades cut as they slide past each other, sharpen each blade only on its outside edge.

Pruning saws need special treatment, depending on the type of saw. Use a special jig and round file to sharpen the blade of a chainsaw. Blades of handsaws are tedious to file, so I would pay to have one of these sharpened. Fortunately, the only saw that I use frequently enough to require sharpening is my bowsaw. When its blade dulls, I just throw it out and snap in a new one. Other types of pruning tools sometimes also have replaceable blades.

When you are not using a pruning tool, store it in a place that is dry and beyond the reach of inquisitive children. An especially good time to go thoroughly over your pruning tools, drying, sharpening, and oiling them, is when you are ready to put them away for the season. Then again, as we shall soon see, there is no season when the avid gardener cannot find something to prune.

CHAPTER THREE

PLANT RESPONSE TO PRUNING

Plants usually respond in a predictable way to pruning. Depending on which part of the plant (stems, flowers, fruits, roots, bark, or leaves) you prune and the degree of pruning, you might get effects on the plant as a whole, as well as right where you make the cut. By understanding how a plant responds, you can get the desired results. Wherever you cut, you wound the plant; therefore you want to prune in a way that facilitates healing.

Overall effects of pruning

Let's get one fact straight: Pruning dwarfs plants. Leaves are what make food for a plant, and the stems are one place in which plants squirrel away food for later use. Cut away a stem or leaf, and you have left the plant with less food. Root pruning decreases the amount of water and minerals a plant can take up. Less food, minerals, or water results in less growth.

The only situations where pruning might not have a dwarfing effect on a plant are when you prune off a dead stem and when you prune off fruits or fruit buds. A plant obviously grows better when removal of a dead stem prevents spread of diseases or insects to healthy limbs. And removing fruits redirects energy that would have nourished fruits into nourishing shoots.

Barring the above two exceptions, many gardeners might take issue with my assertion that "pruning dwarfs plants." Who has not drastically cut back a tree or branch in late winter, only to watch new shoots grow defiantly as compared with more sedate, unpruned counterparts? And the more severely the tree or branch was cut back, the more energetic the response of remaining buds. If you observed even more closely, you would have noticed that new shoots from wood that was pruned back also began to grow earlier in the season, and continued to do so later in the season.

So pruning has stimulated growth, right? Wrong—at least if you consider the plant as a whole. What has happened is that pruning has caused "local" stimulation, that is, stimulation of the buds just below the point where pruning occurred. If you were to tally together the weight of stems pruned off plus the weight of new growth that the tree would have made if it had not been pruned, you would find this total to be significantly greater than the weight of new growth on a pruned tree.

Whether or not you use pruning to dwarf a plant, the local effects of pruning cuts are going to influence plant form as well as the production of fruits and flowers. Often, we may accept some amount of dwarfing as a necessary evil just because we want to prune for other effects. All plants respond to pruning in qualitatively the same manner. By understanding how a plant will respond to your cuts, you can achieve the desired result, whether or not a general dwarfing of the plant is one of your aims.

Localized effects of pruning stems

Pruning a stem can strengthen it, induce flower buds, and/or cause branching, but the effect depends on both the degree and the timing of your cut.

Effect of degree of cutting

Plants show some differences in how they react when their stems are pruned, but such differences are quantitative rather than qualitative, so general rules are useful. For example, picture a young shoot, less than a year old, be it the main stem of a tomato plant or a branch growing off a limb on an apple tree. Unpruned, such a stem will continue to grow from its tip, and side branches may or may not grow out farther down along the stem. The number and the vigor of side branches depend on the vigor of the plant. Those on a tomato plant, for example, may be numerous and strong enough to match or overtake the growth of the main stem. On the apple tree, though, side branches might push out only a few inches of new growth.

Pinching For the least pruning possible on a stem, pinch out the growing point of a shoot with your thumbnail. This pinch causes growth to falter briefly, but also has another effect. The tip of any stem releases a hormone, called auxin, that moves down that stem, inhibiting the growth of lower buds. Remove that stem tip and you stop auxin flow, so lateral buds that were dormant are awakened into growth and existing side shoots now grow more vigorously. Pinching generally is useful for slowing stem growth, to direct the energies of a tomato plant in late summer to ripening fruits, for example. Pinching also is useful when you want to encourage branching (see the drawing on p. 24), as on a potted avocado tree whose single, lanky stem looks ungainly.

Heading You can prune a stem by shortening it with pruning shears or a knife. This type of cut is called a heading cut, and plant response depends on the

Effect of Pinching

Pinching out the tip of a stem encourages branching.

vigorous the response to such pruning. As a general rule, the more vertical the orientation of a stem, the greater its vigor. And a heading cut into one-year-old wood elicits a greater response than does a cut into older wood.

Too many gardeners irreverently hack back their plants in an effort to get rid of unwanted growth, then bemoan the dense and vigorous regrowth from these heading cuts. Nonetheless, in the right situation, a heading cut is a useful pruning technique. There are times when vigorous new growth is needed: to make a strong trunk on a young tree; to create new, bearing wood, if needed, for fruits or flowers; for a decorative effect; to invigorate a frail stem. A heading cut also is the cut of choice where you want branching, such as on a newly planted tree consisting of only a single upright stem. Or when you shear a hedge—making, essentially, hundreds of heading cuts—to create a densely branching visual and physical barrier.

Thinning What happens if, instead of cutting off only part of a stem, you remove it completely, or cut it back to a larger branch? This type of pruning cut is called a thinning cut, and the plant response is: nothing, near the cut. Or, at least, very little. (Remaining shoots on the plant will grow more than they otherwise would have, though.)

So use thinning cuts when you want to remove unwanted growth, such as in the center of a tree or bush, where growth is too dense; reserve heading cuts for situations where you want lush regrowth or branching.

Effect of time of year

"Prune when the knife is sharp" goes the old saying. Not true. (But don't ever prune if the knife—or shears—is not

degree of heading. If you cut a young stem back by one-third, buds that might have stayed dormant on the remaining part of that stem will now be prompted to grow, and they will do so more enthusiastically than if the stem were left alone. Shorten that same stem by two-thirds, and the resulting new growth will be even more vigorous (see the drawing at right on the facing page). (Remember: all this stimulation applies only to the cut stem; the plant as a whole is dwarfed by pruning.) Those buds nearest a heading cut are the ones that make the most vigorous upright shoots; lower down, buds will push out growth that is less vigorous and comes out at wider angles to the cut branch.

The more vigorous a young stem is before it is headed back, the more

sharp.) How a plant responds to pruning depends not only on *how much* you cut off a stem, but also on *when* you do it.

As each growing season draws to a close in temperate climates, trees, shrubs, and vines lay away a certain amount of food in their above- and below-ground parts. This food keeps the plants alive through winter, when they cannot use sunlight to make food because of lack of leaves (on deciduous plants) or cold temperatures. This stored food also fuels the growth of the following season's new shoots and leaves, which, as they mature, start manufacturing their own food and pumping the excess back into the plant for use in the coming winter.

When you prune a dormant plant, you remove buds that would have grown into shoots or flowers. Because food reserves within a pruned plant are reapportioned amongst fewer buds and the roots are all prepared to support growth of more

buds, shoots growing from those buds that remain grow with increased vigor.

As the growing season progresses, response to pruning changes, because shoot growth of woody plants generally grinds to a halt well before leaves fall in autumn. In fact, growth commonly ceases by midsummer. So the later in the growing season that you prune, the less inclined a woody plant is to regrow—the year of pruning, at least.

Traditional theory holds that summer pruning is more dwarfing than dormant

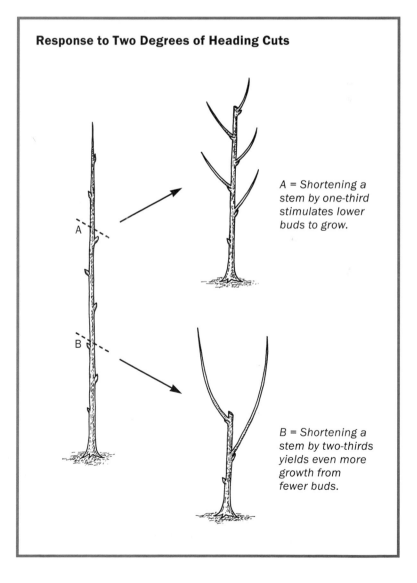

Response to Two Degrees of Heading Cuts

A = *Shortening a stem by one-third stimulates lower buds to grow.*

B = *Shortening a stem by two-thirds yields even more growth from fewer buds.*

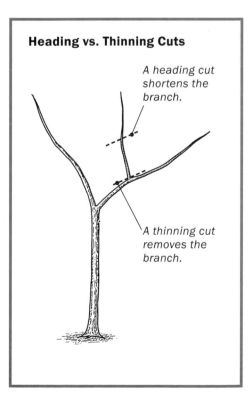

Heading vs. Thinning Cuts

A heading cut shortens the branch.

A thinning cut removes the branch.

pruning, but recent research puts this theory on shaky footing. True, if you shorten a stem while it is dormant, in February, for example, buds that remain will begin to grow into shoots by March and April, whereas if you cut back a shoot in midsummer, no regrowth might occur. Ah, but what about next spring? That's when the summer-pruned shoot, according to this recent research, waits to respond. (Plants have an amazing capacity to act however they please no matter what we do to them.)

What are the practical implications of all this? First of all, if you want to stimulate bud growth, prune a stem when it is dormant. On the other hand, summer is the time to remove a stem to let light in among the branches (to color up ripening apples or peaches, for example), or to remove a stem that is vigorous and in the wrong place. Upright watersprouts, for example, are less likely to regrow if snapped off before they become woody at their bases. Under certain conditions, summer pruning *can* be more dwarfing than dormant pruning, because regrowth following summer pruning can be pruned again. Under certain conditions, summer pruning also can prompt the formation of flower buds rather than new shoots—just what you want for solidly clothing the limbs of a pear espalier with fruits or the branches of a wisteria vine with flowers.

The response to summer pruning depends on the condition of the plant as well as the weather. A weak plant may be killed by summer pruning. A late summer wet spell, especially if it follows weeks of dry weather, might awaken buds that without pruning would have stayed dormant until the following spring. And these responses interact with plant response to various degrees of pruning.

Regrowth and flowering are the dramatic responses to pruning; you also must consider plant health when deciding when to prune. Although immediate regrowth rarely occurs after late summer or autumn pruning, cells right at the cut come alive to close off the wound. Active cells are liable to be injured by cold weather, which is a reason to avoid pruning in late summer or autumn except in climates with mild winters or with plants that are very hardy to cold. Dormant pruning just before growth begins leaves a wound exposed for the minimum amount of time before healing begins. Some plants—peach and its relatives, for example—are so susceptible to infections at wounds that they are best pruned while in blossom. On the other hand, the correct time to prune a diseased or damaged branch is whenever you notice it.

Also consider your own health (your equanimity and your energy) when timing your pruning. Depending on the number of plants you have to prune, as well as other commitments, you may not be able to prune all your plants at each one's optimum moment. I prune my gooseberries in autumn (they never suffer winter damage), my apples just after the most bitter winter cold has reliably passed, and my plums (a peach relative) while they are blossoming.

Plants such as maples, birches, grapes, and kiwis bleed sap profusely if pruned just as their buds are swelling in spring. The way to avoid this loss of sap is to prune either in winter, when the plants are fully dormant, or in spring, after growth is underway. The sap loss actually does no harm to the plants, so rushing or delaying pruning on this account is not for your plant's health, but so that you can rest easy.

Root pruning is a
way to keep potted
plants small.

Effects of pruning parts other than stems

Stems are not the only parts of a plant you might have cause to remove. You might get a desired response by removing flower buds, flowers, young fruits, or even by cutting back plant roots. Less common pruning practices involve cutting into the bark or removing leaves. Let's see how a plant responds to having each of these parts pruned off.

Pruning flowers and fruits

Ripening fruit demands lots of energy from a plant. Flower buds are potential draws for this energy, and whenever you cut, pinch, or otherwise remove either flowers or fruits, you leave the plant with fewer sinks among which to distribute the remaining food. The result is straightforward: bigger flowers and fruits.

In woody plants, the removal of fruits one year has an effect that carries over to the following year. Seeds within fruits produce hormones that inhibit flower-bud formation. Because many plants initiate flower buds a year before the flowers actually open, the hormones from a large crop of fruit one season result in light flowering and a light crop of fruit the following season. Removing some fruits—or flowers or flower buds—each year evens out the production from year to year, eliminating alternating years of feast and famine.

Obviously, to reap benefits from flower bud, flower, or fruit removal, such pruning must be done early in the season. How early depends on how soon a particular plant initiates flower buds. And such pruning must be in the right degree. You won't get the desired effect from inadequate pruning, while excessive pruning of this type reduces the current year's crop too much and results in too heavy a crop the following year.

Ringing the bark, by peeling away a section from between two parallel cuts, can stimulate flowering.

Pruning roots

Root pruning is a centuries-old practice that can reduce water uptake, mineral uptake, and/or the production of certain hormones. Whatever the precise mechanism, root pruning dwarfs any plant. The technique reaches its extreme in bonsai, where, in conjunction with shoot pruning, it keeps a plant that would have otherwise grown to a full-size forest tree small enough to spend centuries in a miniature pot. Less dramatic, but equally useful, is pruning roots to keep a houseplant, or other potted plant, to a manageable size.

Because root pruning temporarily cuts down on a plant's water supply, this pruning should be accompanied by shoot pruning—to remove transpiring leaves—if performed on plants in full leaf. A dormant, leafless plant that has been root-pruned may automatically adjust the number of leaves it grows, when awakening in spring, to the amount of root loss suffered, so it does not necessarily also need its branches pruned.

You don't have to confine your root pruning to potted plants. In the middle of the 19th century, root pruning was used as a way to dwarf fruit trees planted in open ground. In his book, *The Miniature Fruit Garden* (1866), Thomas Rivers described how he root-pruned his trees by either digging them up and replanting them, or by digging trenches around them, then backfilling with new soil. Great judgment, of course, was needed as to how much root pruning a tree could tolerate without excessively enfeebling or killing it. Because of the great labor involved, as well as the somewhat unpredictable response, root pruning fell out of favor. More recently, however, tractor-pulled blades have taken the backache out of root pruning, and there is renewed interest in this technique in commercial orchards.

Besides dwarfing a tree, root pruning also has been used to hasten fruiting; this is another traditional practice that recently has been shown to be of dubious, or no, value. And Mr. Rivers was not the first to recommend root pruning for this effect. Three hundred years previous, Estienne and Liebault (in *Maisons Rustiques*) recommended that young apple trees "loveth to be digged twice," presumably to keep them small and get them to bear fruit. Wisteria vines are notably tardy to flower, and one traditional recommendation for coaxing them along in this direction is to root-prune them. Personally, I'll put my money on summer pruning rather than root pruning to bring any plant to flower. (And, of course, time—every plant must attain a certain age before it can flower.)

Another bona-fide use for root pruning is to lessen the transplant shock of woody plants. An individual root responds to being pruned by growing new lateral roots near the cut. The response is similar to a plant's response to a heading cut on a stem, and, like a heading cut, root pruning is dwarfing even though growth in the region of the cut is stimulated. But if you are going to move a tree or shrub, root pruning a year or more ahead of time reduces transplant shock by inducing the plant to grow masses of roots near enough to the plant to be taken up with the root ball.

Despite the proven uses for root pruning, this practice is somewhat a shot in the dark as compared to the relatively straightforward response of plants to the removal of flower buds, flowers, or fruits. Still, some plants tolerate it and respond more predictably than others. I easily keep my potted fig manageable and fruitful by hacking away of a portion of its root ball each autumn. Response of plants growing in the ground to root pruning depends not only on how much and when you prune, but also on whether or not they receive adequate water during the subsequent growing season. Practice root pruning with moderation and do not forget an important function of roots: to anchor a plant to the ground. Depending on its size and how much you prune, a plant might need a supporting stake until new roots grow.

Removing bark

Removing a piece of bark is a traditional pruning practice that can, in fact, be used to stimulate shoot growth or flowering. Taking out a whole ring of bark—a practice known as bark ringing or girdling—about the time a tree should be in flower often induces the tree to flower the following season. The ring is made by peeling away bark between two cuts scored ¼ in. to ½ in. apart, depending on the severity of the effect desired. For a lesser effect, just make a single cut

around the bark, a technique called scoring. The effect also can be further attenuated by not ringing or scoring completely around a trunk or stem, or by doing either in a spiral fashion, rather than in a closed circle. Cutting out a notch of bark just above or below a bud, a technique called notching, affects only the bud. A notch below a bud slows or prevents its growth; a notch above stimulates the bud to grow. Scoring, ringing, and notching all elicit their responses by perturbing the flow of water, minerals, and hormones within a stem or trunk.

Removing leaves

Leaf removal is rarely practiced, but is another way to induce growth from a bud. Like stem tips, leaves produce the hormone auxin, which inhibits bud growth lower on a stem. Between any leaf and stem is a bud, and auxin produced

Depending on where you make it, a notch can suppress or stimulate growth from a bud.

by that leaf inhibits growth of that bud. So if you want a shoot at a particular place along a growing stem, just pull off the leaf at that point. You could even just cut off the leaf blade—that's where the hormone is made, and the leaf stalk will fall off by itself shortly.

Wound healing: how to cut

Pruning, of necessity, wounds a plant. But this injury need not compromise the plant's health if proper techniques are used.

Plants have an uncanny ability to deal with wounds. Immediately following any wound, whether from the effects of high wind or from the sharp edge of your pruning saw or shears, cells in the vicinity of the wound burst into activity. Their goal: to prevent the spread of infection and seal off the wound. Unless the weather is frigid, rapid respiration ("breathing") and cell division occur, during which time natural antimicrobial chemicals are released and new cells grow to seal off the wound. With little or no microbial growth in frigid weather, the plant can wait to begin repair.

Your job, as a pruner, is to pinch, snip, lop, or saw in such a way as to facilitate your plants' natural healing processes. (To the stickler on terminology, the damaged tissue never actually "heals," but, rather, the damage is overgrown and contained by healthy tissue.) First and foremost in facilitating healing (I've said my bit, so henceforth will dispense with the quotation marks) is to make all cuts clean. Ragged edges leave more damaged cells and more surface area to close over. Sharp prunings tool are a must.

Smaller cuts leave smaller wounds. Try to prune off that tomato sucker when it is 1 in. long rather than when it has shot out to 2 ft. Prune away that misplaced

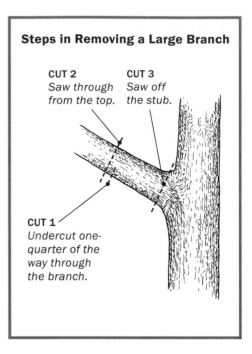

Steps in Removing a Large Branch

CUT 2
Saw through from the top.

CUT 3
Saw off the stub.

CUT 1
Undercut one-quarter of the way through the branch.

maple limb when you can do it with hand shears rather than a chainsaw. Not only will a larger wound take longer to heal over, but new shoots are more likely to sprout up around a larger cut. Pruning away small stems, rather than large ones, also removes less stored food and food-producing tissue of a plant, which is desirable unless you are deliberately attempting to dwarf your plant.

Removing a large branch

Removing a large branch with a single pruning cut can pull off long shreds of bark from a tree as the branch comes toppling down. Avoid this by making three separate cuts. First undercut the branch one-quarter of the way through about 12 in. farther out than your eventual cut. Next, saw through from the top, near the first cut but a couple of inches farther out on the branch. After the branch falls (without tearing any bark), saw off the easily held stub that remains.

Pruning to eliminate disease or insects

Pruning away a diseased or insect-infested part of a plant is pointless unless the whole problem is removed. For this reason, always cut branches back about 6 in. in from where you see the problem. On a large limb that you do not want to cut back, pare away diseased portions of wood back to healthy portions. In either case, healthy wood is evident by its light color and absence of borings. Once you have cut off a diseased or insect-infested portion of a plant, do not just leave it lying on the ground. Disease spores may waft back up into your plant, or insects may make their way back onto your plant or into the soil to complete their life cycle. Thoroughly compost, burn, or otherwise destroy any pest-ridden plant parts that you remove.

Clean tools can be important when cutting away diseased portions of a plant, because some diseases can be transmitted from plant to plant in this way at some point in their life cycle. This is the case, for instance, with fire blight disease, which attacks many members of the rose family during the growing season, but not while an infected plant is dormant in winter. When disease transmission is a hazard, sterilize your pruning tool between cuts by dipping it in alcohol or 10% bleach solution.

Pinching a stem

Young, actively growing tissue heals easiest and quickest, which makes pinching out a growing point between thumbnail and forefinger the least damaging method of pruning. No special instructions here, except perhaps to do this pruning without dirt under your fingernails. (Just kidding. What true gardener has clean fingernails?)

Pruning stems and branches

Shortening a woody stem—a heading cut—must be done with care. Always cut a stem back to a bud, which is where a leaf is growing, or grew the previous season. Most new growth originates from buds, so if you leave an inch of stem beyond the last bud, that inch of stem will eventually die, leaving a stub that will rot away and provide possible entryway for disease. (A few plants—yew and some rhododendrons, for example—can sprout new buds anywhere along their stems; stubs on such plants will not

---

Cutting Back a Stem

INCORRECT
Cut is made too far from bud. Dead stub will remain.

INCORRECT
Cut is made too close to bud. Bud will dry out.

CORRECT
Cut is made just beyond bud and at an angle.

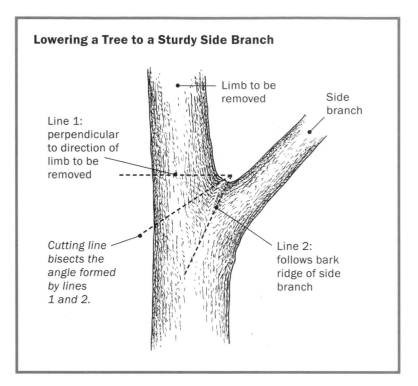

Lowering a Tree to a Sturdy Side Branch

Limb to be removed

Side branch

Line 1: perpendicular to direction of limb to be removed

Cutting line bisects the angle formed by lines 1 and 2.

Line 2: follows bark ridge of side branch

near the origin of a branch for that ridge of bark above the point of attachment, and for a raised collar beneath the point of attachment. Cut the branch just beyond a line from that ridge to that collar. That ridge and that collar will form a natural protection zone, preventing the spread of infection into the trunk when the branch is removed. Removing or damaging the protection zone also can cause sprouts to grow in the vicinity of the wound—just what you don't want when you make a thinning cut!

Avoid erring in the opposite direction and leaving a stub when you remove a branch. The stub will die and decay. Even if decay does not spread into the tree, the dead stub will delay the healing over of the wound and be incorporated within the new growth. If a tree already has a dead stub, do not try to dig out the dead portion from within the branch collar. Just cut the dead branch back to the collar, which will heal by enveloping the stub.

If no branch collar is obvious, as happens with birch and alder trees, you can make an intelligent guess as to its

die back.) On the other hand, if you cut a stem too close to a bud, you might damage the bud or cause it to dry out. The way to shorten a stem is to cut it back a little beyond a bud, at an angle, so that the cut slopes down ever so slightly behind the bud.

If you are shortening part of a tree back to one of its sturdy side branches, begin your cut just above the ridge of bark between the limb to be removed and that branch. Make the angle of your cut midway between a line perpendicular to the limb to be removed and a line that follows that ridge of bark back from the crotch. The resulting cut will angle down slightly, but leave enough wood for continued strong attachment of the branch.

Rather than shortening part of a tree to a branch, you might have occasion, instead, to cut off the branch. Do not cut the branch back flush with the trunk or limb to which it is attached. Look, again,

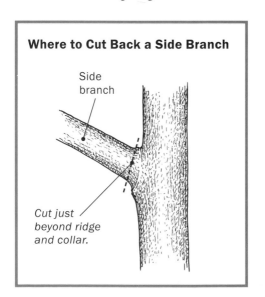

Where to Cut Back a Side Branch

Side branch

Cut just beyond ridge and collar.

location with the help of the ridge of bark between a branch and the limb to which it is attached. The angle that the bark ridge makes with the axis of the branch is about equal to the angle that the bark ridge makes with the branch collar.

Pruning codominant stems

You will not find a branch collar where two stems or limbs are vying to become the "leader," or main trunk of a tree. That's because neither one really is a branch; each is one of two co-dominant stems. Both stems are merely extensions of the main stem below. Maples, especially Norway and silver maples, have a strong tendency to de-velop codominant stems.

Terminology and anatomy aside, what is one to do with such codominant stems? One of them must be removed. The two, nearly parallel stems are weakly attached to each other because of the dead bark that accumulates in the narrow space between them, and because neither is strongly embraced by a branch collar. Although neither stem has a collar, each

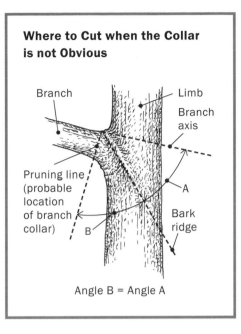

Where to Cut when the Collar is not Obvious

Branch
Limb
Branch axis
Pruning line (probable location of branch collar)
A
Bark ridge
B

Angle B = Angle A

does have a ridge of bark on its upper and lower side. Remove one of the stems with a cut from its upper bark ridge to its lower bark ridge. The wound heals best if you make this cut while the stem is still young (and especially if the ridge is formed with the confluent barks turning out, rather than in, on each other—but you can't do anything about this).

DO WOUNDS NEED DRESSING?

Whether you've cut off a true branch or a codominant stem, do nothing to the bare wound now staring you in the face. Marketing or, perhaps, an innate desire for nurturing has induced humans for centuries to cover wounds with dressings ranging from clay to manure to tar. Such dressings, for the most part, keep the wound moist, maintaining a hospitable environ-ment for disease-causing microorganisms. (Exceptions exist: a particular dressing might be useful because it contains hormones to prevent resprouting, or insecticides to fend off borer attack on susceptible plants such as elm

and pecan.) Because of the way codominant stems are attached, removal of a large one eventually results in a hole in the trunk. No need to fill this gaping hole, either, unless you want to fill it with something merely to keep out water. The water may bother you, but it won't bother the plant.

A good pruning cut—not a poultice—allows a woody plant to seal off the wound and prevent the spread of infection. Take care in how you cut, and appreciate the plant's natural ability to heal itself.

PART 2

THE
PLANTS

CHAPTER FOUR

DECIDUOUS ORNAMENTAL BUSHES

These deutzia bushes (Deutzia gracilis and D. × Rosea) maintain their individuality, yet blend into this shrub border.

A bush is a bushy, woody plant. (Now, that's profound.) Numerous shoots originating at or near ground level are what make a plant bushy. None of these stems ever gets the upper hand over other stems, at least not permanently, so the plant never has a single trunk. Each stem of a bush typically lives just a few years, then dies, its place taken by another stem. On many bushes, stems also branch profusely, clothing the plant from top to bottom with leaves, and perhaps flowers and fruits.

Among bushes, growth habits vary. New shoots on red-osier dogwood, for example, arise from buds on spreading roots and underground stems, making for an ever-widening clump that can fill in an area. At the other extreme is a witch hazel bush, which typically is very reluctant to grow vigorous new shoots. As compensation for this restraint, an individual stem of witch hazel lives for a relatively long time—for a bush.

Because they typically grow densely and not to great height, bushes serve two purposes in the landscape. A bush might be grown as an individual specimen plant, standing alone as a focal point in the landscape, or nestled among other, dissimilar plants, perhaps trees, other bushes, and even herbaceous flowering plants. In either case, bushes grown so that each can express its individuality are commonly—and in this book—called shrubs.

Bushes grown as a hedge, on the other hand, do not stand out as individuals, but meld together into a more or less uniform swathe of greenery (or red-ery, in the case of red-leaved plants), a living wall. Living walls, like those of brick or wood, define spaces and screen out unwanted views or unwanted stares. (Hedges also are cheaper than some built walls, even though they are slower to "erect.")

The natural growth habit of a bush influences its shape. Many short branches clothed throughout with small leaves make billowing mounds of boxwoods. Lanky stems, originating each year mostly from ground level, make forsythia

Whether it is grown as a small tree or large shrub, Kousa dogwood requires little pruning.

DECIDUOUS BUSHES GROWN AS SHRUBS

DO NOT PRUNE at all when the plants are young, but do weed and water.

PRUNE with hand shears and lopper, not hedge shears.

PRUNE AWAY some of the oldest suckers to the ground or to low, vigorous replacement shoots. The more new suckers a plant makes each year, the more suckers that you should prune back each year.

SHORTEN lanky stems arching to the ground, and remove any woody stems that are overcrowded in the center of the shrub, as well as those that are dead, diseased, or crossing and rubbing.

PRUNE shrubs that flower early in the season right after their blossoms fade.

PRUNE shrubs that flower from summer onward just before growth begins.

a fountain of yellow flowers in spring, green leaves in summer, and tan stems in winter. True, the boxwood can be trained to the shape of a vase, and forsythia can be made more formal. As a rule, however, it's best to use your pruning tools to coax a bush along in the direction of its natural inclinations.

Deciduous bushes grown as shrubs

How you should prune a bush depends on when it flowers and what age stems provide the most ornamental effect. Does the shrub flower early in the spring, or later in the summer? Does it flower on old stems, on those that grew last year, or on new shoots? With shrubs grown for their colorful dormant stems, it is often the younger stems that are most dramatic. In the sections that follow, general guidelines for each category are followed by Plant Lists that give specifics. Roses get their own discussion because of the special enthusiasm people have for

Even in winter, this beech hedge defines the landscape with its twigs and dead leaves.

them, and because there are so many types. If you are unsure which category your plant falls into, look it up in the Index, which begins on p. 228. Or, if you do not know the plant's name, categorize it by just watching when and on what age stems flowers are borne.

Pruning at planting time

A shrub may or may not need pruning when you plant it. Bare-root shrubs unavoidably lose roots during transplanting, and the traditional recommendation for such plants is to "cut back the tops to balance the root loss." Over the decades, this recommendation has periodically been challenged with rigorous experiments whose results have been almost universally ignored. Cutting back the top always seemed like the "right thing to do." Of course, none of this applies to balled-and-burlapped or potted shrubs, which lose few or no roots in transplanting.

In fact, if you can ensure a bare-root plant of ideal growing conditions after transplanting, and this mostly means timely watering, then that plant will repay your efforts with better growth the less that you prune it. Cutting back the top of a shrub removes some stored food as well as buds, and buds have been shown to produce hormones that stimulate root growth.

With good growing conditions, prune any new shrub—whether bare root, balled-and-burlapped, or potted—as little as possible. Remove any diseased or dead stems, as well as those that are crossing and rubbing together. Prune away any wayward stems that jut off awkwardly and alone into space, giving the plant an an unbalanced posture. If you plant in autumn, remove some of the top to prevent wind from blowing the

as-yet poorly anchored plant out of the ground.

If you cannot give a newly transplanted, bare-root shrub ideal growing conditions its first season, then go ahead and prune it to put the tops and roots back in balance. Use mostly thinning, rather than heading, cuts.

Maintenance pruning of shrubs that make few suckers

Included within this category are bushes that naturally build up a permanent framework of branches, only rarely sending up new suckers at or near ground level. These shrubs flower directly on older wood, or from shoots that grow from older wood.

The purpose in pruning these plants is twofold. First, build up a picturesque framework. This should require no more than occasional pruning on your part. And second, prune to keep the plant within its allotted bounds.

Grouping plants always entails a certain degree of arbitrariness, and because of their disinclination to sucker, a few plants in this category could also be considered "trees," especially if deliberately trained to one or a few trunks. So if a "shrublike tree" is not listed here, look in the Plant List of deciduous ornamental trees, which begins on p. 80.

When training these young plants, take care to build up an artistic framework of more or less permanent stems. Look at how the stems reach out of the ground, and try to envision them, longer and thicker, years hence. Cut them back if doing so suits your artistic fancy. The nature of any bush is to send up new stems at or near ground level, so if you do not like the stems dealt to you when you planted the shrub, feel free to cut them all down and start all over (at the expense of some growth, of course).

Plant List

DECIDUOUS SHRUBS THAT MAKE FEW SUCKERS

Acer palmatum (Japanese Maple)

Aesculus parviflora (Bottlebrush Buckeye)

Berberis Thunbergii (Japanese Barberry)

Cephalanthus occidentalis (Buttonbush)

Chaenomeles **spp.** (Flowering Quince): Prune when dormant or right after flowering.

Chimonanthus praecox (Wintersweet)

Colutea arborescens (Common Bladder Senna)

Comptonia peregrina (Sweet Fern)

Cornus alternifolia (Pagoda Dogwood)

Corylopsis **spp.** (Winter Hazel)

Corylus Avellana (European Filbert): These plants also can be trained to trees.

Cotinus Coggygria (Smokebush): If you grow this plant for its purple leaves rather than for its flowers, prune severely in winter to stimulate vigorous new growth each spring.

Cotoneaster **spp.** (Cotoneaster)

Cyrilla racemiflora (Swamp Cyrilla, Leatherwood): This bush flowers in whorls at the bases of the current season's growth, but the woody framework grows quite beautiful with age. To enjoy both the framework and the flowers, prune younger shoots back to within a few buds of the framework each spring.

Daphne **spp.** (Daphne): Do not prune.

Dirca palustris (Leatherwood)

Elaeagnus multiflora (Cherry Elaeagnus, Gumi)

Elaeagnus umbellata (Autumn Olive)

Enkianthus **spp.** (Enkianthus): The plants need little pruning, but will sprout readily wherever stems are cut back.

Euonymus alata (Winged Euonymus, Winged Spindle Tree)

Fothergilla Gardenii (Dwarf Witch Alder)

Fothergilla major (Large Fothergilla)

Hamamelis **spp.** (Witch Hazel): When the plant grows as high as you want it to, thin out vigorous stems to keep it at that height. You also can train witch hazel as a tree.

Hibiscus syriacus (Rose-of-Sharon)

Hippophae rhamnoides (Common Seabuckthorn)

Hydrangea paniculata **'Grandiflora'** (PeeGee Hydrangea): Prune in spring. Flowers form on current shoots, so cut back young shoots to ground level or almost to a permanent framework of older limbs, leaving just a few young buds per shoot.

Ilex decidua (Possum Haw)

Ilex verticillata (Winterberry)

Itea virginica (Virginia Sweetspire)

Ligustrum **spp.** (Privet): Privets are usually hedged, but an individual bush does make a nice informal shrub. Prune whenever you want, but if you like the flowers and want as

(continued on page 40)

Good pruning develops the artistic and permanent branching pattern of Japanese maples, whether dwarf or full size.

Once plants in this category mature, they are the easiest shrubs to prune: just don't!

That's the general rule, but admittedly a little pruning may be in order. Remove any dead, crossing, or otherwise poorly placed stems. These plants are hesitant to grow numerous lanky new shoots, but for the plant that does become too crowded, cut away twiggy growth or completely remove one or more older stems. The best approach depends on the growth habit of the particular plant. On those few shrubs that are propagated by grafting, remove any sprouts originating below the graft, preferably with a sharp yank rather than with pruning shears, to reduce the chances for regrowth. Use

your shears artistically, to help a Japanese maple develop its signature, neat, mounded habit, or to help promote the naturally layered appearance of a pagoda dogwood.

Pruning also can rejuvenate an old plant. This is more often needed with flowering shrubs than with shrubs grown mostly for their form or for their leaves. Lightly heading back some branches every few years might be enough to rejuvenate certain plants. On others, rejuvenation will involve occasionally cutting away a major stem completely, allowing it to be replaced by a sucker originating low in the bush. Watch your plants closely to determine their pruning needs, if any.

DECIDUOUS SHRUBS THAT MAKE FEW SUCKERS *(continued)*

many as possible of them (I don't—they have a rank smell), wait until right after flowering to prune.

Lindera Benzoin (Spicebush)

Loropetalum chinense (Loropetalum)

Magnolia **spp.** (Magnolia): Carefully train plants when they are young so that you can avoid having to make large cuts, which heal poorly, on older plants. Prune *M. Soulangiana* (Saucer Magnolia) and *M. stellata* (Star Magnolia) just before growth begins or right after flowering finishes. Deadhead by cutting flowers off rather than by snapping them off, so that you do not injure the growing point just below each blossom.

Paeonia suffruticosa (Tree Peony): Little pruning is needed, just enough to keep the plant tidy and to remove disease.

Paliurus Spina-Christi (Christmas Thorn, Jerusalem Thorn Tree)

Parrotiopsis Jacquemontiana

Poncirus trifoliata (Hardy Orange)

Rhamnus **spp.** (Buckthorn)

Spiraea bullata (Crispleaf Spiraea)

Stachyurus praecox: Occasionally cut away old stems after they flower.

Viburnum acerifolium (Mapleleaf Viburnum)

Viburnum alnifolium (Hobblebush)

Viburnum betulifolium

Viburnum Carlesii (Koreanspice Viburnum)

Viburnum cassinoides (Withe-rod Viburnum)

Viburnum dilatatum (Linden Viburnum)

Viburnum × Juddii (Judd Viburnum)

Viburnum Lantana (Wayfaringtree)

Viburnum macrocephalum (Chinese Snowball Viburnum)

Viburnum plicatum (Doublefile Viburnum)

Viburnum rhytidophylloides (Lantanaphyllum Viburnum)

Zenobia pulverulenta (Dusty Zenobia): Remove spent flowers, with short stems attached.

Maintenance pruning of shrubs that flower on one-year-old wood

You will find many familiar flowering shrubs in this category. Because they all flower only on wood that grew the previous season, as a rule these shrubs require annual pruning to stimulate new growth, each year, for the following year's flowers. Left unpruned, any of these shrubs becomes a crowded mess, with old branches coughing forth few flowers that, in the case of those plants that can grow tall, are beyond nose level and almost out of sight.

The one-year-old shoots on which flowers are borne may grow mainly from older stems up in the shrub, or else mostly from ground level. The location of these flowering shoots determines pruning technique, so I have subgrouped plants accordingly, and follow with instructions for each.

In their youth, the only pruning these plants require is to have some of their youngest stems thinned out during the dormant season. Although I have divided shrubs that flower on one-year-old wood into two subgroups (depending on whether flowering wood grows mostly from ground level or from older branches up in the shrub), three general rules apply to pruning mature plants of both types.

1. On shrubs with variegated leaves, be sure to remove any shoots that have nonvariegated leaves. Such shoots are the most vigorous ones, and will, if unchecked, eventually take over the plant.

2. Prune those shrubs that flower early in the season right after their blossoms fade; prune those shrubs that flower from summer onward just before growth begins for the season. Pruning early-flowering shrubs after they bloom allows you to enjoy their blossoms, but still

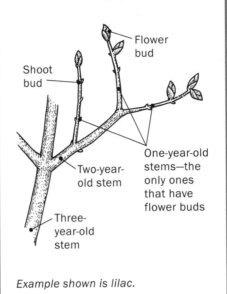

Flowering Habit of Shrubs Whose Flowering Stems Grow Off Older Wood, up in the Shrub

Flower bud

Shoot bud

Two-year-old stem

One-year-old stems—the only ones that have flower buds

Three-year-old stem

Example shown is lilac.

leaves enough time for shoots to grow and ripen wood sufficiently for next season's blooms. Of course, the stems of some of these early-flowering shrubs, cut and plunked into a vase of water indoors, provide cheery blooms to carry you through late-winter garden doldrums—don't hesitate to cut a few for this purpose. The later-flowering shrubs usually bloom on new shoots (that grow off year-old stems), so cutting before growth begins has little effect on the season's flower show. In the following two Plant Lists, I have indicated the flowering season for each shrub.

3. Prune every year, in such a way that the whole shrub is renewed over time. New wood that originates low in the shrub should eventually and annually replace older wood, keeping the plant low, neat, and abundantly flowering.

Now for a few specifics for each subcategory.

Shrubs that flower off older wood up in the shrub can be left for a few years before any wood is removed. Peer in at the base of a mature plant and you will notice wood of various ages growing up from ground level. Begin pruning by cutting away, within 1 ft. of the ground, some of the oldest stems. Those oldest stems are also the tallest ones, so these first cuts quickly lower the plant. If the clump that makes the base of the bush has grown too wide, selectively cut the oldest stems from around the edge of the clump. With early-flowering shrubs, this pruning also has the advantage of removing many spent flowers all at once. The energy that would have gone into seed formation can now be channeled into flowers for next year.

After cutting away some of the oldest stems, move on to detail work. Lower some of the older stems that remain, keeping an eye on the form of the plant and cutting back to a vigorous branch any stem that is too tall or that droops too much. To prevent overcrowding, each year also remove at ground level a portion of the youngest stems. Thin out those within the main clump as well as those that might be spreading, if you want to keep the shrub contained. Finally, higher up in the shrub, head back those stems that have flowered.

It is impossible to give a prescription for how long to leave an older stem, or for how many new stems to leave each year. Such details depend on the nature of the plant as well as how high and how wide you want the plant to grow.

Shrubs that flower on young stems originating at ground level need more drastic pruning. With these shrubs, every year cut away all wood more than one year old, either right to ground level or else to a vigorous branch originating low on the plant. You can tell the age of a stem by its thickness and, on many plants, by the color or texture of the bark.

One of the worst things you can do to shrubs in either subcategory is not to prune it at all. Even worse is to butcher any of these individual plants with a hedge shears.

Maintenance pruning of shrubs valued for their current growth

Here we have shrubs valued only for their new growth. Older stems either detract from the appearance of the plant or else do not survive winter. It is the new shoots that carry the flowers or particularly ornamental leaves that we are after. And yes, in some cases—the young, red stems of red-osier dogwood, for example—we value the plant for the young stems themselves.

This group of shrubs is the easiest of all to prune: simply lop the whole plant down to the ground just as buds are swelling. This annual lopping keeps these shrubs from becoming twiggy at their centers and stimulates vigorous regrowth. For a plant that flowers only on new shoots, the greater the vigor of those new shoots, the more the flowers. With nonflowering shrubs valued for their foliage, very vigorous shoots often bear leaves that are both larger and have a different shape than those that would be borne on more sedate shoots.

When you prune these plants, you do not have to obliterate all above-ground

(continued on page 47)

Plant List

Abeliophyllum distichum (Korean Abelialeaf): Early blossoming. Right after flowering, shorten one-third of the branches so they are about 18 in. long.

Acanthopanax Sieboldiunus (Fiveleaf Aralia): Late blossoming, but the flowers are not all that showy. If you want this shrub to have an upright habit, shorten stems as they age and begin to arch to the ground. Also prune away excess suckers.

Amelanchier spp. (Saskatoon, Juneberry, Serviceberry, Shadbush): Early blossoming.

Amorpha fruticosa (False Indigo): Late blossoming.

Aralia spinosa (Devil's Walkingstick, Hercules' Club): Late blossoming. This plant can spread underground. If disciplined, it can be trained to a tree.

Aronia arbutifolia (Red Chokeberry): Early blossoming. You can train this plant to several trunks, which are permanent unless a borer attacks one. If that occurs, cut back the attacked trunk and let a new one grow.

Aronia melanocarpa (Black Chokeberry): Early blossoming.

Baccharis halimifolia (Groundsel Bush): Late blossoming.

Buddleia alternifolia (Garland Butterfly Bush, Alternate Leaf Butterfly Bush): Early blossoming.

Calycanthus floridus (Common Sweetshrub, Carolina Allspice): Blossoms sporadically from spring into summer, but prune it right after its spring flush of blossoms.

Clethra acuminata (Cinnamon Clethra): Late blossoming.

Clethra alnifolia (Summersweet Clethra, Sweet Pepperbush): Late blossoming.

Clethra barbinervis (Japanese Clethra): Late blossoming.

Clethra tomentosa (Woolly Summersweet): Late blossoming.

Colutea arborescens (Common Bladdersenna): Blooms in early summer, but on new wood, so prune this bush back to older wood while it is still dormant in late winter.

Cytisus scoparius (Broom): Early blossoming. Broom does not regrow from old, leafless wood, so it will die if the bush is cut back heavily. The bush does need pruning, though, or it becomes top-heavy. Prune right after flowering, back to just beyond where old growth ends.

Deutzia spp. (Deutzia): Early blossoming. What little pruning these plants need should be done right after flowering.

Dirca palustris (Leatherwood): Early blossoming.

Edgeworthia papyrifera (Paperbush, Mitsuma): Early blossoming.

Exochorda racemosa (Pearlbush): Early blossoming.

Forsythia spp. (Forsythia): Early blossoming. (photo, p. 44)

Genista spp. (Woadwaxens): Flowering times vary, depending on the species, so follow the general rule about when to prune. Avoid severe pruning, though, or you will excessively weaken these shrubs.

Holodiscus discolor (Creambush, Oceanspray): Late blossoming.

Hydrangea macrophylla (Bigleaf Hydrangea): This plant blossoms late, but the flower buds are formed the previous growing season at or near the ends of branches. Leave old, dry flowers on the plant for winter interest and to protect the coming season's flower buds from winter cold. Prune in spring, cutting stems that have flowered back to the fat flower

(continued on page 44)

buds. Also thin excess twiggy growth to let light and air into the bush.

Hydrangea quercifolia (Oak-leafed Hydrangea): Late blossoming. Prune the same way as Bigleaf Hydrangea (p. 43), unless you are more interested in the decorative leaves than the flowers. For leafy shoots rather than flowers, cut stems back by one-quarter in late spring. Where winters are cold, you may have no choice, because the flowers buds winterkill.

Jasminum nudiflorum (Winter Jasmine): Early blossoming. If you are willing to prune this shrub annually, shorten flowering stems right after they finish flowering each year, occasionally cutting older stems back to the ground. Otherwise, rejuvenate the shrub every few years by lopping the whole thing almost to the ground.

Kolkwitzia amabilis (Beautybush): Early blossoming.

Lagerstroemia indica (Common Crape Myrtle): Late blossoming. Wherever this plant is not reliably winter hardy, cut off winterkilled wood or cut the whole plant to the ground in early spring. Drastic pruning keeps the plant in bounds and results in larger flowers. Where Crape Myrtle is hardy, it requires little pruning, and eventually holds its leaves and flowers high above the ground, showing its attractive bark.

Lonicera **spp.** (Bush Honeysuckle): Early blossoming. When the bush grows large enough, you can thin out the interior and make a vaulted, natural playhouse for a child.

Myrica Gale (Sweet Gale, Bog Myrtle, Meadow Fern): Sweet gale is grown for its fragrant leaves, not flowers, so prune it while it is still dormant.

Neillia **spp.** (Neillia): Early blossoming.

Nevusia alabamensis (Snow-wreath): Early blossoming.

Forsythia in bloom.

Notospartium Carmichaeliae (Pink Broom): Late blossoming. Give this bush little annual pruning, but when the whole plant becomes old and weak, cut everything to near ground level and let it start growing afresh.

Oemleria cerasiformis (Indian Plum, Osoberry): Early blossoming.

Philadelphus coronarius (Mock Orange): Early blossoming.

Philadelphus pubescens: Early blossoming. In addition to cutting away some of the oldest stems, each year also pinch out shoot tips to promote branching. Otherwise, the bush becomes too gawky.

Potentilla fruticosa (Bush Cinquefoil): Late blossoming. There are many ways to approach this bush with pruning shears. Some people suggest removing one-third of the stems in winter, others suggest cutting away weak wood and shortening the strong wood by one-half. I cut everything down to 6 in. above ground each spring, which keeps the bushes short and tidy, although blossoming is slightly delayed.

Prinsepia sinensis (Cherry Prinsepia): Early blossoming.

Prunus glandulosa (Dwarf Flowering Almond): Early blossoming.

Prunus triloba (Flowering Almond): Early blossoming.

Rhododendron spp. (Deciduous Azaleas): Early blossoming. The deciduous species require little pruning other than removal of spent flowers and dead wood. Periodically rejuvenate by thinning out older wood on large plants. Buds form freely along stems, so you can cut them back to wherever you want. Some azaleas tend to grow long, unbranched stems that need to be pinched or cut back to promote bushiness.

Rhus aromatica (Fragrant Sumac): Early blossoming.

Rhus typhina (Staghorn Sumac): Early blossoming. If you are not interested in the flowers and fruits, but want vigorous growth to highlight the leaves, cut the bush back severely every spring.

Ribes alpinum (Alpine Currant): Prune anytime, because this shrub is grown only for its foliage and form.

Sambucus nigra (European Elder): Early blossoming.

Spiraea cantoniensis (Double Reeves Spiraea): Early blossoming.

Spiraea nipponica (Nippon Spiraea): Early blossoming.

Spiraea prunifolia (Bridlewreath Spiraea): Early blossoming.

Spiraea Thunbergii (Thunberg Spiraea): Early blossoming.

Spiraea Vanhouttei (Van Hout Spiraea): Early blossoming.

Staphylea spp. (Bladder Nut): Early blossoming, but blossoms are not spectacular enough to warrant delaying pruning until after they are past.

Stephanandra incisa (Cutleaf Stephanandra): Early blossoming, but flowers are inconspicuous, so there is no need to delay pruning until after they have faded. Prune just enough to maintain a pleasing shape. Watch out for tip rooting of stems that arch to the ground.

Syringa spp. (Lilac): Early blossoming. In addition to following the general pruning guidelines, each year clip or break off spent flowers. *S. Meyeri* (Meyer Lilac) requires little pruning.

Tamarix parviflora (Small-flowered Tamarix): Late blossoming.

Viburnum × *Burkwoodii* (Burkwood Viburnum): Early blossoming.

Viburnum dentatum (Arrowwood Viburnum): Early blossoming.

Viburnum opulus (European Cranberry Bush Viburnum): Early blossoming.

Viburnum setigerum (Tea Viburnum): Early blossoming.

Viburnum trilobum (American Cranberry Bush Viburnum): Early blossoming.

Weigela florida (Old-fashioned Weigela): Early blossoming. Prune weigela heavily to keep it neat.

ANNUAL PRUNING OF LILAC

1. After the flowers fade, start pruning lilac by cutting some of the oldest stems nearly or right to the ground.

2. Next, shorten any very tall stems to a strong branch.

3. Decongest the base of the plant by cutting away some of the youngest stems.

4. Direct the plant's energy into growth, rather than seeds, by snapping off spent flower heads right after bloom.

5. The finished shrub, shapely and ready to prepare for next year's show.

Plant List

Abelia* × *grandiflora (Abelia): Abelia can be grown a number of ways, because it flowers on new wood arising anywhere on the shrub. Where winter cold cuts back the plant, prune it below where wood was killed or to within a few inches of the ground. Where all the stems survive winter cold, merely remove some of the oldest wood at ground level. If you want to limit the plant's height or promote branching, pinch the tips of new growth in spring.

Kerria japonica (Japanese Rose, Kerria): Early blossoming. Wood that has flowered often dies, and that old brown wood also puts on a poor show against the young stems, which stay a vibrant green in winter. Therefore, drastic pruning is needed annually. Cut away wood that has borne flowers.

Physocarpus opulifolius (Common Ninebark, Eastern Ninebark): Early blossoming. Cut out the oldest and weakest wood.

Prunus tenella (Dwarf Russian Almond): Early blossoming. Cut the whole plant to the ground in spring, right after blossoms fade.

Rhodotypos scandens (Jetbead, White Kerria): Early blossoming. Cut oldest stems to the ground and shorten others by about one-half.

***Salix* spp.** (Willow): Early blossoming. Bushy willows require little or no pruning unless you are growing them for their catkins, in which case prune them back hard right after they flower. Of course, also prune in winter—to cut off some stems to bring indoors for forcing. Species grown for their catkins include *S. Elaeagnos* (Rosemary Willow, Hoary Willow), *S. gracilistyla* (Rosegold Pussy Willow), *S. discolor*, *S. caprea*, and *S. melanostachys* (Black Pussy Willow).

Spiraea* × *arguta (Garland Spiraea): Early blossoming.

Spiraea* × *Bumalda (Bumald Spiraea): Depending on the particular variety, flowers appear either on new or old wood. Time your pruning accordingly.

Symphoricarpos albus (Common Snowberry): Late blossoming. Occasionally cut the oldest stems to the ground.

traces of them. But if you do leave a short, woody framework (assuming the plant does not winterkill), this framework will become overcrowded after a few years. Cut off and back some of this wood when that happens, to leave space for new shoots to emerge. For those plants that do winterkill, cut them down to just below the point of winterkill.

Maintenance pruning of roses

Pruning roses need not be complicated. The rose, after all, is just another flowering shrub, albeit one that inspires poets and painters, the formation of societies, and an undue amount of verbiage on "special" pruning needs. Despite the fanfare, roses respond to pruning as do any other shrubs.

Most roses need annual pruning to keep them healthy and shapely,

PRUNING A BUTTERFLY BUSH

1. A butterfly bush in spring, just before growth begins.

2. Lop all the branches to the ground.

3. All that remain are some stubs with new growth starting to poke out.

floriferous, and within bounds. To this end, always cut away misplaced wood on any rose bush, which includes stems that are trailing on the ground if you want the bush growing upright, stems that are rubbing together, and stems that are overcrowded. As you shape your plant, prune to an outside bud where you want a branch to be spreading. Prune to an inside bud where you need to fill in the center of the bush. Also cut away excessively twiggy stems. And cut back any stem that is either diseased or winterkilled until you see white pith, which indicates that you have reached healthy wood.

On any grafted rose, keep on the lookout for sprouts from below the graft union. The leaves, thorns, or, if you let a sprout grow long enough, the flowers, on such sprouts will be different from those of the grafted variety. Remove these sprouts, which are from the rootstock, as soon as you notice them.

You might prune your rose bush in one, two, or all of three different seasons. The first time is in the spring, just as buds are swelling and growth is about to begin. You could have done this pruning while your bush was fully dormant, but differences between healthy and diseased or dead wood are more evident as growth begins. It is also easier to see where to cut to improve the form of a bush while it is still leafless.

Summer pruning usually entails cutting off the flowers, either in their full glory for vases, or after they are spent. Pruning spent flowers saves the plant the stress of forming fruits, called hips. Do not cut spent flowers from roses such as the rugosa rose, the dog rose, and *Rosa Moyesii* because these roses have prominent and ornamental hips. In climates with very long growing seasons, you can cut any everblooming type of

Plant List

DECIDUOUS SHRUBS VALUED FOR THEIR CURRENT GROWTH

Buddleia Davidii, B. Fallowiana, and their hybrids (Butterfly Bush)

Callicarpa japonica (Japanese Beautyberry)

Caryopteris × clandonensis (Bluebeard, Blue-spiraea, Blue-mist Shrub): Cut the previous year's stem growth in late winter to within 1 ft. or so of the permanent framework of branches.

Caryopteris incana (Common Bluebeard)

Ceanothus americanus (New Jersey Tea, Wild Snowball, Mountainsweet) and other deciduous species and hybrids.

Ceratostigma plumbaginoides

Ceratostigma Willmottianum (Chinese Plumbago): Cut back in spring to a point below where stems have been winterkilled.

Clematis heracleifolia var. Davidiana

Clematis integrifolia: Late blossoming

Cornus alba (Tartarian Dogwood): To promote new growth of bright-red stems, prune hard every spring, completely removing one-third or more of the stems. Alternatively, prune less severely and allow the bush to grow larger, with red twigs mostly at its periphery.

Cornus Amomum (Silky Dogwood): Late blossoming. Prune as for *C. alba,* but less severely because the young stems are not as attractive.

Cornus racemosa (Gray Dogwood): The gray color of wood a few years old contrasts nicely with the reddish-brown young wood. Each spring cut away some of the oldest stems and thin out some of the youngest stems to keep the bush open and to stimulate new shoot growth.

Cornus sanguinea (Bloodtwig Dogwood): The young shoots are, unfortunately, not all that "bloody." The bush is by nature unkempt so needs regular pruning to keep it neat rather than to stimulate new growth.

Cornus sericea (Red-osier Dogwood): This species is closely related to *C. alba* and needs the same pruning.

Cotinus Coggygria (Smokebush): If you grow this plant only for its purple leaves, prune it severely each spring. Otherwise, little pruning is required.

Diervilla sessifolia (Southern Bush-honeysuckle)

Elsholtzia Stauntonii (Mint Shrub): Late blossoming.

Eucalyptus Gunnii (Cider Gum, Cider Tree): Grow this plant as a shrub for its juvenile foliage, maintained each year by severe pruning.

Fuchsia magellanica (Hardy Fuchsia): If grown where winters are mild, above-ground portions of the plant survive and can make a permanent framework. In this case, prune the plant back to the permanent framework each spring. Otherwise, prune to ground level.

Hydrangea arborescens 'Grandiflora' (Hills-of-snow)

Hypericum spp. (St.-John's-Wort)

Leycesteria formosa (Himalaya Honeysuckle)

Perovskia atriplicifolia (Russian Sage)

Rhus typhina (Staghorn Sumac): Prune back severely each spring if you are growing this plant mostly for its leaves, rather than for its woody form or fruits.

(continued on page 50)

Pruning Tartarian dogwood produces an annual show of young stems with the brightest color.

***Salix* spp.** (Willow): Bushy willows to prune back hard are *S. irrorata*, to stimulate an annual flush of white, young stems, and *S. purpurea* (Purple Osier Willow), whose young stems are used for baskets. If you are not growing a bushy willow for its decorative young stems or for its catkins (see *Salix* in the Plant List on p. 47), little or no pruning is required.

Sambucus nigra (European Elder): Prune elder back hard each spring if you value it mainly for its leaves, which is undoubtedly the case if you planted one of the varieties with fancy yellow or incised leaves.

***Sorbaria* spp.** (False Spiraea): Late blossoming.

Spartium junceum (Spanish Broom, Weavers' Broom): Prune just before growth begins, cutting back almost, but not quite, into old wood. Eventually try to renovate the whole bush by cutting it down to the ground. Have a new plant ready, though, because this severe cutting sometimes kills an old bush.

Spiraea albiflora (Japanese White Spiraea): This spiraea blooms relatively early, but on growing shoots, so prune while the plant is dormant.

Spiraea* × *Billiardii (Billiard Spiraea)

Spiraea* × *Bumalda (Bumald Spiraea): Depending on the particular variety, Bumald Spiraea flowers on new or old stems. Time your pruning accordingly.

Spiraea japonica (Japanese Spiraea)

Tamarix ramosissima (Tamarisk, Salt Cedar)

Vitex Agnus-castus (Chaste Tree, Hemp Tree): Prune the plant back to where it winterkilled or to within a few inches of the ground.

Vitex Negundo: Prune the same as *Vitex Agnus-castus*.

rose back by about one-third in the middle of August to encourage a good show of autumn blooms.

The third season when you might prune a rose is in autumn. Where winter winds may batter the stems of your bush, perhaps rocking the plant loose in the soil, shorten some stems. And if winter temperatures in your area drop lower than your rose bush can tolerate, you have to bundle up your plant to carry it through the cold weather. In this case, autumn prune to reduce the size of the bush so that it fits into the blanket of straw, Styrofoam "rose cone," or whatever other winter protection you provide.

The growth habit of your bush, and, to a lesser extent, your taste in flowers, dictate pruning from here on. Put simply, an individual rose stem grows, flowers, then gets so old that it flowers little or no more. Prune a rose bush so that the whole shrub is continuously renewed over time. New wood, originating low in the plant, replaces old wood, which you periodically cut away. The number of

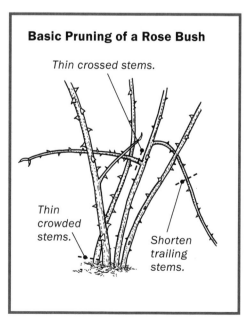

Basic Pruning of a Rose Bush

Thin crossed stems.

Thin crowded stems.

Shorten trailing stems.

young stems might also need to be reduced if they are overcrowded.

The duration of this renewal cycle depends on the growth habit of your rose bush. At one extreme are roses such as the Hybrid Teas, which flower on the current season's shoots. If you cut these plants low every year, you still get flowers—on the new growth. At the other extreme are Climbing Roses, which flower only on old wood, and need little or no annual pruning.

By observing the growth and flowering habits of your rose bush over time, you can apply the general principles above and do a professional pruning job—even if you do not know your rose's name or what type it is. If the plant flowers only on older wood, you will want to leave enough older wood for this year's flowers. Where a bush is overburdened with old wood, remove just some of it to stimulate the growth of, and make way for, new wood. Preserve the graceful, arching growth habit of a bush that is naturally inclined to grow this way by doing most of your cutting at the base, perhaps shortening an occasional gawky stem, just as you would with any other shrub.

More specific recommendations for the various categories of roses are listed in Plant List, which begins on p. 53. But be forewarned: centuries of breeding within and between rose species have made rose nomenclature complicated and inexact. Consequently, there is some variation in growth and flowering habits of roses even within a given category. Also note that the same variety name might be attached to roses in more than one category. For example, 'Lutea' is the variety name for a Climbing Rose and for a Scotch Rose; 'Versicolor' is the name for a Gallica Rose and a Damask Rose. Always couple the information that follows with your own observations.

'Albertine' climbing rose flowers on laterals that grow from older canes.

Renovating an overgrown shrub

You perhaps have inherited, with your property, a neglected, old shrub. This plant presents you with a tangled mass of stems, an awkward posture, and few flowers: not a pretty sight. Can this shrub be brought back to its former glory? Probably.

You have two options in renovating this shrub. The first is the drastic one: you merely lop the whole plant to within 1 ft.

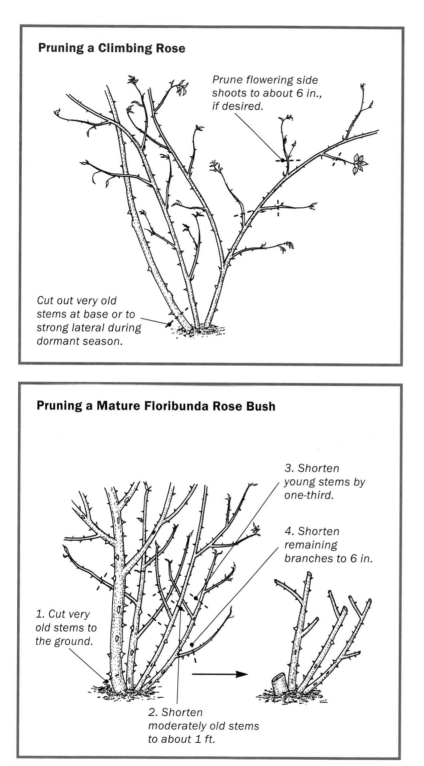

Pruning a Climbing Rose

Prune flowering side shoots to about 6 in., if desired.

Cut out very old stems at base or to strong lateral during dormant season.

Pruning a Mature Floribunda Rose Bush

3. Shorten young stems by one-third.

4. Shorten remaining branches to 6 in.

1. Cut very old stems to the ground.

2. Shorten moderately old stems to about 1 ft.

of the ground just before growth begins for the season. Then cut away any twiggy stems still remaining. Be careful not to cut below the graft union with those few shrubs that are grafted onto a rootstock. Otherwise, the whole renovated plant will grow to become whatever the rootstock is.

Your renovated bush will hardly be worth looking at for a year, perhaps two years. A few very vigorous shoots will grow that first season. The next dormant season, thin out some of these stems, and you're on your way to a "new," shrub, full of blossoms and with a graceful growth habit. You will soon have what amounts to a whole new plant from the ground up.

Your second option is to renovate the shrub over a period of four or five years (see the drawing on p. 60). Although this takes more time, the plant will look decent throughout the recovery period. Each year, just before growth begins in spring, cut out two or three of the oldest stems to ground level or to vigorous branches low on the plant. Also thin out some of the youngest stems, making sure to leave a few as replacement shoots for the old wood you are removing. After a few years—how many depends on how long the shrub has been neglected—you will have cut away all the old wood and replaced it with new wood.

Rather than renovation, you might instead consider capitalizing on your overgrown shrub's age and venerability by transforming the plant into a picturesque small tree. Select as trunks two or three of the oldest stems having pleasant form and growing from ground level to as high as the proposed crown of your tree-to-be. Remove all other growth

(continued on page 60)

Plant List

ROSES

Climbing Roses: Climbing Roses have a mostly permanent framework of older canes on which flowers are borne. Some varieties flower only once per season, while others produce a more modest second bloom. Less vigorous Climbers are sometimes called Pillar Roses.

Climbing Roses require little pruning. If you can reach high enough, right after the flowers have faded cut back flowering branches growing off the canes to about 6 in. Do this immediately if the variety is able to bloom again that season; otherwise, you can wait to prune, if you desire, until the following spring, just before growth begins. Especially on those varieties that flower only once a season, pruning branches is not obligatory.

When a cane becomes very old, cut it away at its base to stimulate the growth of a young replacement. You will have to watch your plant to gauge how long to wait before replacing an old cane.

Some Climbers require even less pruning. Very vigorous varieties, such as 'Kiftsgate', 'Mermaid', and 'Cerise Bouquet', grow so large that there is no hope—and fortunately no need—for pruning them. Bush roses that have mutated to become climbers, such as 'Climbing Queen Elizabeth', 'Gloire de Dijon', and 'Mme. Alfred Carrière', require nothing more than the cutting out of dead wood and heading back of weak wood. (A myth has been promulgated that cautions against severe pruning of the latter varieties for fear that such pruning will cause them to revert to their bush forms. Not so! An equally chance mutation would be needed for a climber to revert back to a bush form, and this is unlikely. A more plausible explanation for the response of such plants to severe pruning is that growing conditions were less than ideal, and severe pruning further weakened already weak plants.)

English Roses: See Shrub Roses

Floribunda Roses: These roses produce clusters of flowers. Individual flowers resemble those of Hybrid Teas, but are smaller.

Floribundas need annual pruning to prevent them from becoming overgrown masses of twigs. Flowers are borne on both new shoots and on old stems, with the old stems bearing the first flowers of the season and the young shoots bearing the later flowers.

Prune to preserve some new and some old stems. While a plant is dormant, shorten older stems to about 1 ft., occasionally removing some of the very oldest ones completely. Prune young stems moderately, shortening them by about one-third. Cut back any remaining branches to 6 in.

To deadhead spent blossoms of Floribundas, cut off the whole cluster rather than individual flowers. Cut back to a leaf with a bud between it and the stem so that you do not leave a dead stub.

Grandiflora Roses: Grandifloras lie somewhere between Hybrid Teas and Floribundas in the size of individual flowers and clusters of blos-

'American Pillar' brings rustic charm to this arbor.

'Impatient', like other floribunda roses, makes up for smaller size blossoms with sheer abundance.

(continued on page 54)

soms. In Great Britain, Grandifloras are considered part of the Floribunda spectrum—which seems reasonable. Floribundas and Grandifloras are pruned in the same way, so refer to Floribunda (p. 53) for details.

Hybrid Perpetual Roses: These old roses are the forerunners of Hybrid Teas, and by comparison are more vigorous and flower twice each season, rather than continuously. Because they flower on growing shoots rather than on older wood, Hybrid Perpetuals can take the same hard pruning as Hybrid Teas. While the plant is dormant, shorten strong stems to about 1 ft., weak ones to about 6 in. Every few years, cut one of the oldest stems to the ground to encourage a young replacement.

'Chicago Peace', a hybrid tea rose.

'Scarlet Meidiland' is a carefree landscape rose.

Some varieties, such as 'Frau Karl Druschki', produce extremely long stems in one season of growth. If you have enough space around such a plant, deal with that lanky growth by pegging it down to the ground. The recumbent posture induces shoots to grow sprout all along the long stem, giving you flowers all over the place. Each spring cut away enough of the old stems to make room for new ones, and shorten branches growing off remaining stems to about 6 in.

Hybrid Tea Roses: Hybrid Tea roses produce long-stemmed, large blossoms, singly or in small clusters, throughout the growing season. The degree of dormant pruning required depends on how much, if any, of the old stems winterkilled, as well as the size of plant, and the number and size of blossoms you desire. To a point, the more drastically you prune, the fewer, the larger, and the later the blossoms, and the smaller the plant.

Begin pruning just before growth begins. Shorten the weakest stems the most, to 6 in. if you want your bush small. Shorten strong stems to 1 ft. or more. Occasionally cut away a stem at its base to stimulate and make room for a young replacement shoot.

Prune away spent blossoms during the growing season. Generally cut back to a bud where the stem meets the stalk of a leaf having five leaflets. If you want especially large blossoms, remove lateral flower buds from a shoot before they open, forcing the shoot to channel all its energy into the remaining central flower bud (drawing, p. 57).

Landscape Roses: This relatively new category of roses consists of low-growing plants that bear masses of small flowers and are used as groundcovers or low shrubs. Pruning a slope covered with established plants is well-nigh impossible—and unnecessary. If you really must, put on some heavy boots so that you can walk right into the planting, and cut back any lanky, vertical stems and dead wood.

Miniature Roses: These roses are low growing, with commensurately diminutive leaves and flowers. Pruning is simple—or is it just that the plants are so small and manageable? Shorten strong growth, thin out weak growth, and occasionally cut away an old stem completely. Keep the plant shapely.

Old-Fashioned Roses: See Shrub Roses

Pillar Roses: See Climbing Roses

(continued on page 56)

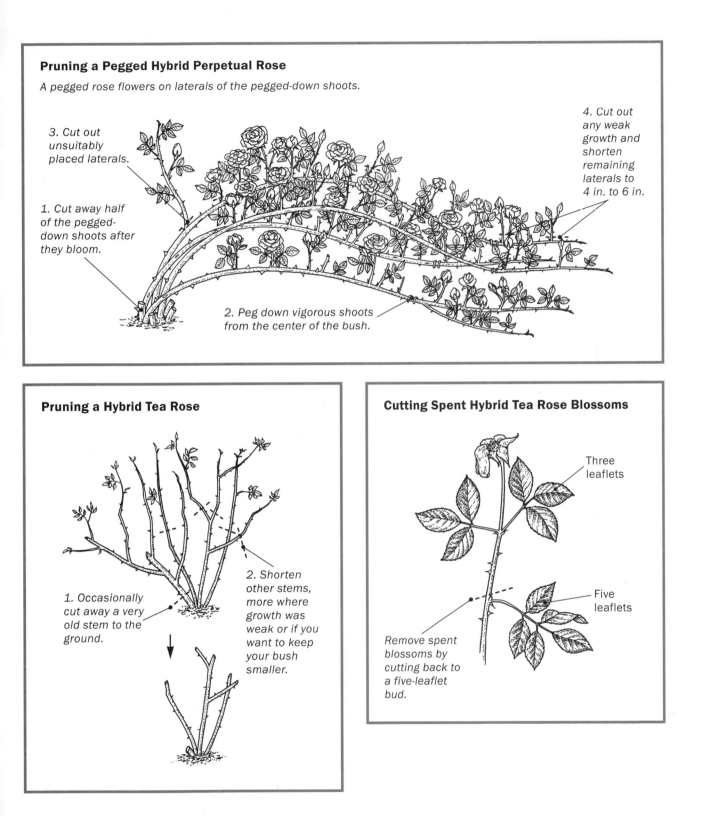

Pruning a Pegged Hybrid Perpetual Rose

A pegged rose flowers on laterals of the pegged-down shoots.

3. Cut out unsuitably placed laterals.

4. Cut out any weak growth and shorten remaining laterals to 4 in. to 6 in.

1. Cut away half of the pegged-down shoots after they bloom.

2. Peg down vigorous shoots from the center of the bush.

Pruning a Hybrid Tea Rose

1. Occasionally cut away a very old stem to the ground.

2. Shorten other stems, more where growth was weak or if you want to keep your bush smaller.

Cutting Spent Hybrid Tea Rose Blossoms

Three leaflets

Five leaflets

Remove spent blossoms by cutting back to a five-leaflet bud.

PRUNING A POLYANTHA ROSE

1. This polyantha rose needs to be pruned before growth gets underway.

2. Stems have been shortened and some old stems cut away.

3. In just a few weeks, the rose again looks glorious.

Polyantha Roses: These old-fashioned dwarfs bear dense clusters of small flowers. Many new stems grow from the base of the plant. Shorten older stems, occasionally removing some of the oldest ones completely to ground level, and cut back younger stems only slightly. Alternatively, prune the whole plant almost to ground level every spring.

Rambling Roses: Ramblers usually flower only once per season, mostly on short branches growing off long stems produced the previous season. Branches on older canes also can bear some flowers.

Prune mostly by cutting away stems that have flowered. The easiest time to do this is right after flowers fade, because then new growth is not yet entangled with old growth, and you can see most easily what has flowered.

In one type of Rambler, typified by 'Dorothy Perkins' and other varieties derived from Rosa Wichuraiana, most new growth arises at the base of the plant, near ground level. If the number of such shoots seems excessive, remove some when you prune. On the other hand, if an insufficient number of replacement shoots is growing from the base, leave some stems that have flowered, but shorten their branches to about 4 in. after the flowers fade. These stems will flower again next year.

On another type of Rambler—'New Dawn' and 'Paul's Scarlet Climber' are examples— new shoots originate higher up along old canes, rather than from the base of the plant. Prune these Ramblers by cutting away stems that have flowered back to new stems growing off along older wood. If there are insufficient new stems, retain some of those that have flowered, but shorten their flowered branches after the flowers fade. Occasionally stimulate new growth near ground level by cutting old wood to within 1 ft. of the ground.

Shrub Roses: Aren't all roses "shrubs," you ask? Yes and no. Yes, they are (even the climbers can be coerced into a more typically shrubby habit); but no, there is actually a specific group of roses commonly called "Shrub Roses."

For the purposes of this book, I have thrown a few other shrubby roses into this category, because of their similar origins and shrubby habits. This mixed bag thus includes Shrub Roses (some of the newer of these are called English Roses), Old-fashioned Roses (sometimes called Old Garden Roses), and Species Roses. For specifics, see the sidebar on pp. 58-59.

Species Roses: See Shrub Roses

Standard Roses: A Standard Rose is a rose grown in the form of a small tree—a straight trunk capped by a mop of flowers. Nurseries make these roses by grafting any one of various types of roses atop a trunk grown from a vigorous rootstock (typically a rugosa or briar rose).

Prune a standard rose according to what type of rose is grafted atop the trunk. Just before growth begins, stub all the branches on a Standard Hybrid Tea back to 6 in., and thin out or shorten any weak or crowded wood that remains. With a Standard Floribunda, also prune just before growth begins, shortening one-year-old wood to 2 ft. and two-year-old wood to 6 in. Drastically shorten any older wood.

Weeping standards are made by grafting Rambling Roses atop a trunk. If the grafted Rambler is the type that sends out most new growth from the base of the plant (now high atop the trunk) rather than along older stems, cut stems that have flowered back to their bases right after flowers fade. If too few new shoots are growing to replace those old stems, leave some stems that have flowered, but shorten their branches to 6 in. right after flowering. If the grafted Rambler is the type that sends out new growth along older stems, just shorten branches to 6 in. right after flowering, and cut away surplus old wood.

Disbudding a Hybrid Tea Rose

Removing small lateral buds makes for a larger central bud.

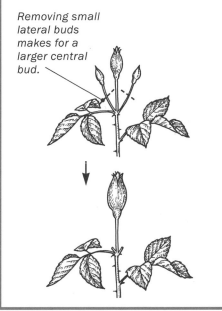

Cut away flowering canes from this rambling rose following bloom to make way for canes that will flower next year.

SHRUB ROSES: A Pruner's Guide

T he roses listed here are all shrubby, but they vary in their vigor and their tendency to send up new sprouts from ground level, as well as in their flowering habits. At one extreme in shrubby roses are those that make few new shoots and flower mostly on older wood (Group 1). Other shrubby roses that flower on older wood send up many vigorous shoots from ground level each season (Group 2). Another type of shrub rose blooms reliably on both new and old wood (Group 3).

GROUP 1

Shrubby roses in this group shrubs need little pruning: only occasional removal of old wood and thinning out of crowded stems just before growth begins or just after flowers fade.

The following roses are representative of this extreme:

> *Rosa gallica, French or Apothecary Rose, represented by 'Pumila', 'Rosa Mundi', 'Belle 'Isis'*
> *Rosa Hugonis, Father Hugo's Rose*
> *Rosa moschata, Musk Rose, represented by 'Plena'; 'Pax', 'Buff Beauty', and 'Penelope' are varieties or parents of Hybrid Musk Roses*
> *Rosa spinosissima, Scotch or Burnet Rose, with 'Andrewsii', 'Fulgens', 'Lutea', 'Sulphurea', and 'Frühlingsgold' as representative varieties*

GROUP 2

Shrubby roses in this group require moderate pruning just before growth begins. Each year take out, at ground level, some of the oldest wood. Also shorten lanky stems that are arching to the ground, or that will arch to the ground once weighted down with blossoms. Do not shorten those stems so much that you ruin the fountainlike growth habit, though. Where branches have grown very long, shorten them to about 6 in.

This category includes:

> *Burgundy Rose, represented by 'Parviflora'*
> *Modern Shrub Roses that bloom only once*
> *Moss Rose, represented by 'Muscosa' and 'William Lobb'*
> *R. × alba, represented by varieties 'Incarnata' and 'Suaveolens'*
> *R. centifolia, Cabbage Rose, represented by 'Cristata'*
> *R. damascena, Damask Rose, including varieties such as 'Celsiana', 'Trigintipetala', and 'Mme. Hardy' (these sometimes bloom repeatedly during the growing season, in which case pruning spent blossoms helps stimulate vigorous regrowth for return bloom)*
> *R. Moyesii*
> *R. rugosa, Japanese Rose, represented by 'Magnifica', 'Rosea', 'Rubra' (these will flower on new shoots growing from ground level, but such blossoms are few and late)*

GROUP 3

Shrubby roses in this group get pruned most severely, to induce vigorous shoots for blooms throughout the season. Just before growth begins, shorten vigorous wood originating near ground level by one-third, and branches to 1 ft. Thin out twiggy growth. And, of course, deadhead religiously to stimulate new growth and to prevent fruit formation.

Some of the shrubby roses that require this treatment include:

> *Modern Shrub Roses that bloom throughout the growing season*
> *R. × borboniana, Bourbon Rose, represented by 'Boule de Neige' and 'Souvenir de la Malmaison'*
> *R. chinensis, China Rose, represented by 'Minima'; Fairy Rose, represented by 'Viridiflora'*

Pruning a Modern Shrub Rose

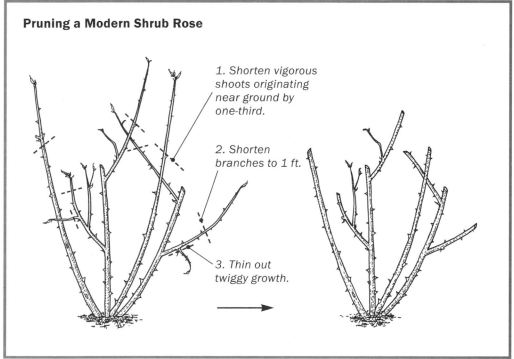

1. Shorten vigorous shoots originating near ground by one-third.

2. Shorten branches to 1 ft.

3. Thin out twiggy growth.

1. 'William Lobb', a moss rose, looks intimidating before pruning.

2. Cutting away some of the oldest wood, at its base, opens the bush quickly.

3. Detail work on stems that remain is shortening laterals and lanky stems.

4. 'William Lobb' now looks healthier and happier.

Making an Overgrown Shrub into a Small Tree

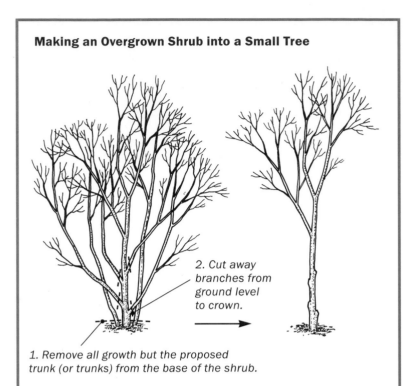

2. Cut away branches from ground level to crown.

1. Remove all growth but the proposed trunk (or trunks) from the base of the shrub.

from the base of the plant. Also cut away any branches growing off those new trunks between the ground and a few feet above the ground—high enough so the plant looks like a tree. Finally, make some heading and thinning cuts to shape the crown.

In subsequent years, new sprouts will grow from ground level and off the trunks; after all, the plant was once a bush. Remove these diligently. With time, the plant will become less rebellious, making fewer such sprouts, and will take the form of a venerable tree.

Sometimes you must consider merely grubbing out an old, neglected shrub rather than renovating it. Surely there is no reason to hesitate with your shovel and saw if you do not like having the plant, perhaps any plant, at the particular location. With a few shrubs, such as woodwaxens and brooms, you

Gradual Renovation of a Shrub

FIRST YEAR
Thin the youngest stems and cut away some of the oldest stems.

SECOND AND SUBSEQUENT YEARS
Repeat the first-year sequence.

New wood gradually replaces old wood, and growth fills in at the base of the plant.

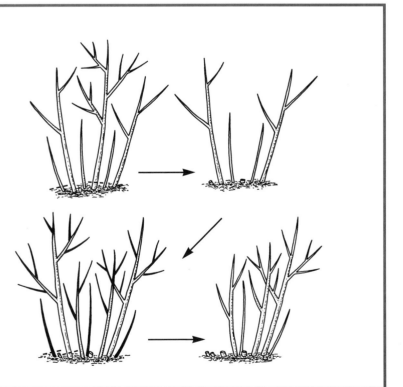

PRUNING A NEGLECTED SHRUB

1. How to begin pruning this neglected lilac bush?

2. First remove any wayward old stems right to the ground.

3. Also cut away some old stems in the center of the bush.

4. Thin younger stems to make room for those that remain.

5. Shorten any branches that droop too much.

Lilac makes a nice hedge, but only if pruned informally.

have to grub them out when they become overgrown. They rarely regrow from old wood, so often die when cut back severely.

If your shrub is a particularly rare species or variety, propagate a new plant before taking any drastic measures at renovation.

Deciduous bushes grown together as a hedge

In order for a hedge to do its job of providing a physical, psychological, and/or visual barrier, each plant making it up must be fully clothed in leaves from head to foot. To create dense and uniform growth, you have to choose appropriate species, plant them correctly,

and—just as important—prune the plants soon after you set them in the ground.

Pruning the young plants

The first pruning is simple but brutal: Cut the whole plant down to within a few inches of the ground. This drastic pruning encourages both vigorous regrowth and low branching.

If the new plants already are well branched right to ground level, it is unnecessary to prune so severely. (The severe pruning recommended is a necessary evil: It temporarily stunts the plant, but does give it the desired growth habit.) Some plants, such as beech, hornbeam, and Nanking cherry, are naturally furnished with branches throughout. Any plants that have been grown in containers may be similarly well furnished if they are old enough and already were pruned correctly as hedge plants in their youth. On these already well-branched plants, head back the main stem and laterals just enough so that they continue to branch further as they grow.

Once you give your hedge plants their first pruning, let them grow unmolested for the rest of their first season.

The second season is as important as the first, with regard to pruning, in the development of a shapely, dense, formal hedge. (Let an informal hedge just grow its second season.) While the plant is still dormant, shorten main stems by about half their length, and branches to just a few inches. Again the goal is to promote dense branching. And again, only a slight

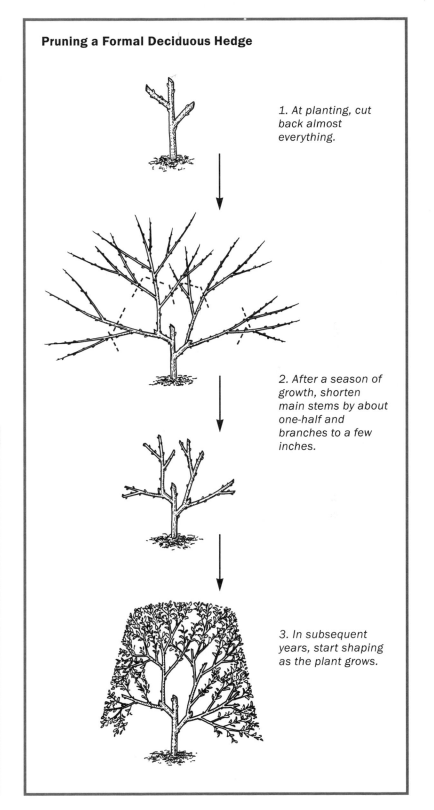

Pruning a Formal Deciduous Hedge

1. At planting, cut back almost everything.

2. After a season of growth, shorten main stems by about one-half and branches to a few inches.

3. In subsequent years, start shaping as the plant grows.

THE BARE BONES

DECIDUOUS BUSHES GROWN TOGETHER AS A HEDGE

CUT BACK plants drastically when you plant to promote low branching and vigorous growth.

FOR A FORMAL HEDGE, shorten main and secondary stems just before the plants begin their second season of growth.

SHAPE formal hedges so that plants are narrower at their tops than at their bottoms.

SHEAR mature formal hedges after the spring flush of growth, almost back to where growth began for the season.

FOR AN INFORMAL HEDGE, prune by removing some oldest stems from the bases of the plants each year and by shortening stems that are too long.

Prune this spiraea hedge, which looks best grown informally, just as you would the individual shrubs. Avoid using hedge shears.

shortening of stems is needed on those plants that already are twiggy from top to bottom.

If your hedge is going to be formal, also start bringing the whole hedge to its desired shape as you shorten growth for this second season. Do this even though the hedge has not yet reached its final size. A formal hedge may take many forms, but whatever the shape, the top should be narrower than the bottom. If the top is wider than the bottom, the bottom will become shaded. Over time,

the shaded portions will die out, leaving gaps in the hedge.

Maintenance pruning

Once a hedge has reached the size and shape that you want, your job is to keep the hedge in that condition. If your hedge is informal—and many bushes (see the Plant List on p. 66) look uncomfortable in formal attire—prune the plants as you would individual shrubs. To wit: prune early-blossoming bushes right after their blossoms fade, late bloomers while they

Shearing a Rigidly Geometric Hedge

are still dormant. Prune by cutting out the oldest stems to ground level or to vigorous young branches, and by shortening stems that are too lanky. The aim is to make the line of arching stems look like a breaking wave advancing across the landscape.

Other plant species will try to invade a hedge, and are easily overlooked amongst the more tangled branches of an informal hedge. As you prune, also cut away—or grub out—unwanted invaders.

Prune the formal hedge with a hedge shears. To maintain its crisp form, a formal hedge needs shearing at least once a year. The frequency of shearing needed depends on just how crisp you want the lines of your hedge, as well as the vigor of the plants. Do your first shearing of the season while the plant is in full leaf,

preferably after the initial growth flush has subsided so that regrowth is minimized. Where winters are very cold or with hedge plants of questionable hardiness, avoid shearing after midsummer, lest you stimulate soft new growth that can be damaged by low temperatures.

When you shear, hold the cutting blades parallel to the surface that you are creating. Shear back almost to the point where you previously sheared. I start low on the hedge and work my way upward, which makes it easier to reach across the top and leaves me less inclined to let the upper portions spread increasingly outward over time. If the hedge is rigidly geometric, especially if its shape inter-locks with other forms in the nearby landscape, stretch a taut line a few inches above the desired cutting line as a guide.

If you want flowers on your formal hedge, you have to accept a more ragged look. With a hedge that flowers early in the season, shear right after the flowers have faded. Depending on the plant species, you may get one more shearing in, but you have to allow sufficient time for regrowth—and raggedness—on plants that flower on stems that grew the previous season. Of course, you can keep shearing back growth on a plant like flowering quince, which flowers on older wood. In this case, though, all the flowers will be buried within the branches. And

that's only if those branches get sufficient light to make flower buds.

With a formal hedge that flowers later in the season, you can cut to your heart's content before growth begins in spring. But soon after growth begins, don't touch those new stems or you won't have flowers.

When you finish shearing any hedge, sweep off the bulk of the clippings, then rake them up. Those few that remain on top or fall within the hedge become inconspicuous within a day or two as they dry and shrivel.

Plant List

DECIDUOUS HEDGES

Abelia × grandiflora (Abelia)

Acanthopanax Sieboldianus (Fiveleaf Aralia)

Berberis Thunbergii (Japanese Barberry)

Carpinus Betulus (European Hornbeam)

Chaenomeles spp. (Flowering Quinces)

Corylus spp. (Filbert): Best as an informal hedge, pruned by selectively removing the oldest stems, rather than by shearing.

Crataegus spp. (Hawthorn)

Deutzia gracilis (Slender Deutzia)

Euonymus alata (Winged Euonymus, Winged Spindle Tree)

Fagus sylvatica (European Beech)

Forsythia spp. (Forsythia): Best as an informal hedge, pruned by selectively removing the oldest stems, rather than by shearing.

Hibiscus syriacus (Rose-of-Sharon): With a coarse texture yet upright growth habit, this bush makes an informal hedge that needs little pruning, except perhaps to restrict its height.

Hippophae rhamnoides (Sea Buckthorn)

Lagerstroemia indica (Common Crape Myrtle): Best as an informal hedge, pruned

by selectively removing the oldest stems, rather than by shearing. Where the tops of the plant are only marginally cold hardy, cut away any winterkilled stems each year before growth begins. If you train the plants as trees, with more or less permanent trunks, cutting the ends of some branches back 1 ft. to 2 ft. will help flowering.

Ligustrum spp. (Privet): As a hedge, privet usually needs two or three shearings each year. Prune anytime.

Potentilla fruticosa (Bush Cinquefoil): Best as an informal hedge, pruned by selectively removing the oldest stems, rather than by shearing.

Ribes alpinum (Alpine Currant)

Rosa rugosa (Japanese Rose): Best as an informal hedge, pruned by selectively removing the oldest stems, rather than by shearing.

Spiraea Vanhouttei (Van Hout Spiraea): Best as an informal hedge, pruned by selectively removing the oldest stems, rather than by shearing.

Symphoricarpos albus (Common Snowberry)

Syringa vulgaris (Common Lilac): Best as an informal hedge, pruned by selectively removing the oldest stems, rather than by shearing.

Renovating a deciduous hedge

With neglect, an informal hedge becomes overgrown, a mass of plants spreading too wide with their bases becoming overcrowded and bare. Renovate such a hedge by crawling inside, to the base of the plants, and cutting away some of the oldest wood near ground level. After you finish that, shorten any overly long stems that remain in order to narrow the hedge.

An alternative, if you have the energy or machinery, is to cut all growth to within 1 ft. of the ground, then go back over the plants and remove any twiggy stems that remain. The hedge will look young, spry, and full within a couple of years.

A formal hedge also can suffer from neglect, and even if you you shear the hedge diligently, it is still going to need periodic renovation. The reason is that when you shear, you always shear *almost* back to where you last sheared so that bare stems are not staring out at you. As a result, the hedge is always slowly enlarging.

A formal hedge with bare areas near ground level probably was improperly pruned when it was very young. Unfortunately, there is little you can do to fill in those bare spots, short of cutting the whole hedge almost to ground level, then pruning the resulting stems as if they were a newly planted hedge. That is, head back the stems to make them branch before they begin their second season of growth. In the third season, start shearing the plant to the desired form, even though it is not yet full size.

To renovate the formal hedge that has grown too tall and wide, but is otherwise full from top to bottom, prune all growth back so that the hedge is 6 in. narrower and shorter than you want for its final width and height. Do this just before

A hedge of burning bush adds a ribbon of color to the autumn landscape.

growth begins in spring, so that the hedge is soon clothed and presentable. Depending on the thickness of the branches, you might need pruning shears rather than hedge shears for this job. The task is not as tedious as it may seem, because a single cut within the hedge will remove a stem with all its attached twiggy growth. As the new shoots grow, shear them back with your hedge shears, at first keeping the hedge a bit smaller than its desired, final size. You now have a "new" hedge.

If you don't like the idea of your hedge being so loose and open—even temporarily—then initially prune back the branches on one side only. Also lower the hedge, if necessary. The following year, prune back the branches on the other side.

CHAPTER FIVE

DECIDUOUS ORNAMENTAL TREES

Neatly formed, dark branches complement the beauty of these cherry blossoms.

In this section we will admire deciduous trees, and prune them for beauty, strength, and long life. For a clear and simple definition of a tree, I consulted my six-year-old daughter. She told me that a tree is big, woody, and has a trunk. I'll add that most new growth on trees arises up in the crown, not near ground level, and that's the difference between a tree and a bush. Both are woody, and some bushes—autumn olive, for example—can grow quite large. After

a few years, though, the archetypal tree puts its energy only into new branches up in the crown, which rises atop a permanent trunk.

Trees vary in their shapes, but all have potentially the same basic parts. There is a trunk, of course, that woody, lower portion of the tree clear of branches. And perhaps leaders, which are extensions of the trunk within the plant. If a tree has one leader, it is called a central leader, and off it grow scaffold limbs, the main side branches of the tree. And then there may be some very vigorous, upright shoots, often growing many feet in a single season. Those that originate up in the plant are called watersprouts; those originating at the base of the plant are called root suckers or root sprouts. The vigor, upright position, and location of watersprouts and suckers generally detract from the beauty of a tree. What's more, such shoots are weakly attached.

Crowns of deciduous trees range from round-headed to spirelike. The spirelike tree—typified by pin oak, sweet gum, and tulip tree—has a single, dominant central leader, which each year pushes higher with new branches growing off it. Although a round-headed tree may have had a dominant leader when young, this leader was soon overtaken by branches, each, in turn, soon overtaken by their side branches. The result (see the photo on p. 70) is the large, spreading crown typical of white oak and sugar maple. Not all trees fit neatly into one or the other category of tree shape, and these shapes can also be influenced by the richness of the soil and the amount of shade in which the tree grows.

Nonetheless, keep in mind the two basic tree forms in the ensuing discussion. They have an important influence on how to handle trees in their formative years. And, as with most pruning, your goal usually is merely to help the tree along. This means building a strong framework on the young tree, maintaining the health and shape of the mature tree, and rejuvenating, when necessary, the neglected, old tree—all the while retaining a natural growth habit.

A note about timing when pruning deciduous trees…with few exceptions, the ideal time is late winter or early spring, just before growth begins. If you cannot bring yourself to sacrifice any

A single dominant leader gives this dawn redwood a spirelike crown.

blossoms from an early-flowering tree, then prune just after the flowers fade, which is not much after growth begins. Pruning while a plant is leafless, or nearly so, offers you an unobstructed view of the branches, making it easier to see what to cut and actually to make the cuts. Wounds also heal most quickly just as growth is getting underway. Some trees, such as maples and birch, bleed sap when cut in spring. Bleeding does the plant no harm, but if it makes you queasy, prune

THE BARE BONES

DECIDUOUS ORNAMENTAL TREES

EXCEPT FOR small trees that develop multiple trunks, allow only one vertical shoot to become the trunk, then central leader. Bend down, cut back, or cut off any competitors.

SELECT scaffold limbs that are thinner than the leader and spaced 1 ft. to 2 ft. apart along the trunk. The height of the lowest one depends on how high a head you want (on your tree!). Keep in mind that scaffold limbs will grow thicker, but their height above ground never changes.

ALLOW weak, temporary branches to remain along the developing trunk and central leader to help thicken and protect them from sunburn. Remove these temporary branches after a couple of years.

PRUNE the developing tree as little as possible!

USE mostly thinning cuts to reduce or maintain size and let light and air into the crown of a mature or overgrown tree.

Lack of a dominant leader gives this oak a rounded crown.

earlier in winter or later in spring, when the plant will not bleed. If you dormant-prune in winter, try to avoid pruning until the coldest part of winter is past.

Definitely avoid pruning late in summer or in autumn. Pruning late in summer is apt to stimulate succulent growth that cannot harden before cold weather arrives. Wounds made in autumn heal poorly, and many fungi are then spreading their disease-producing spores.

Pruning at planting time

Early tree care—and pruning is part of this care—is all-important to the future health and beauty of a tree. When it comes to training the young branches, some pruning may be necessary. But keep this in mind: the less pruning the better.

Let's start with the roots. Little or no root pruning is necessary on a plant whose roots were balled and burlapped after it was dug from the field. If a few lanky roots were tucked in around the ball when the plant was dug, either dig a hole large enough to accommodate those roots as they stretch naturally outward, or else cut them back. It's your choice. Do not just stuff them into the planting hole, or the tree may eventually strangle itself. If your new tree was growing in a pot, slide it out of the pot and then take a knife and slit the root ball in a few places. Tease out the roots at the surface of the root ball with a stick to make sure they grow outwards, into the surrounding soil.

If the tree you receive from a nursery is dormant and bare root, take this last opportunity, before you put the tree into the ground, to inspect the roots. Cut off any that are dead, diseased, or broken. (Be aware that healthy roots of all plants do not look clean and white—healthy persimmon roots, for example, are black.) Cutting frayed ends cleanly reduces the surface area of wounds, so that healing is quicker, reducing the risk of root diseases. As with a balled and burlapped tree, shorten any roots that are too long to splay out into the planting hole—or dig the hole larger.

Slitting the Root Ball of a Potted Tree

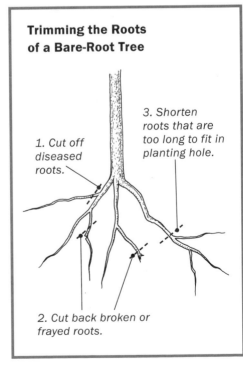

Trimming the Roots of a Bare-Root Tree

1. Cut off diseased roots.

3. Shorten roots that are too long to fit in planting hole.

2. Cut back broken or frayed roots.

Now, let's turn to the above-ground portions of the tree. Most important is to promote the development of a single central leader, the lower portion of which will be the future trunk. (Some trees naturally develop a few main trunks, all originating at ground level, and look quite handsome that way. These plants are usually small trees that never grow large, so developing a strong framework is not as critical as with a massive tree.) If several shoots are competing to become the central leader of your new tree, completely cut away all but one of them. Otherwise, the similar size of such shoots and the dead bark that builds up in the narrow-angled crotch between them creates a weak joint that may well split apart as the shoots and their branches grow heavy. Pruning to a single leader is particularly important on trees whose crowns are round-headed, because of the natural tendency, especially with age, for their leaders to be overtaken by other shoots. Shoots on trees with naturally spirelike growth habits less often misbehave in this way.

If your tree has two central leaders of equal girth and with a narrow crotch between them, cut away one of them. If a side branch has decided to turn its tip upward with loftier aspirations, either shorten that branch or quell its desires by bending it to a more horizontal position with a weight or with a string tied to the trunk or a stake. Or simply remove the offending branch.

Keep to a minimum any other pruning of the above-ground portion of the tree at planting time, and make mostly thinning, rather than heading, cuts (see the drawing at left on p. 25). Cut or pull off any suckers. Cut away any dead, diseased, or broken branches, and remove enough branches along the future trunk so that those that remain are well separated. You

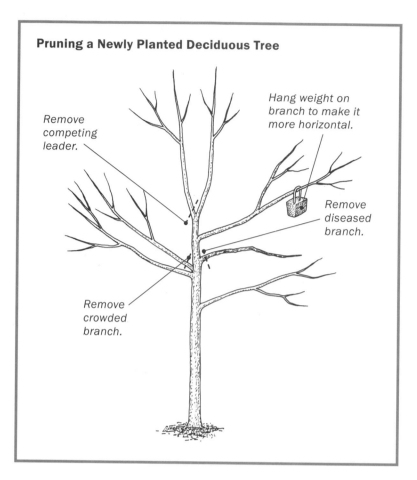

Pruning a Newly Planted Deciduous Tree

Remove
competing
leader.

Hang weight on
branch to make it
more horizontal.

Remove
diseased
branch.

Remove
crowded
branch.

reducing the number of growing points and hence the number of leaves, which transpire water. The traditional recommendation to cut back the top of a tree when you set it in the ground makes sense only for trees that might be expected to suffer from water stress. But do not expect such a tree to grow as much as an unpruned tree getting sufficient water. More leaves mean more photosynthesis, which means more growth. Also, buds awakening at the tips of new shoots produce hormones that stimulate root growth; the more of those buds that remain, the more the roots grow. This is another reason to make mostly thinning, rather than heading, cuts on a new tree—fewer terminal buds are removed.

In summary, if you want maximum growth on your newly planted tree, keep pruning to a minimum, using mostly thinning cuts. Rather than pruning to reduce leaf area, help your young tree along with a stake against wind and with water in times of need.

Pruning while training

The first years that your tree is in the ground, while it is developing branches that will become its main framework, are important to its future strength and beauty. Pruning is one way to direct growth. This pruning is best done while the tree is young, because the small cuts you make on a small tree leave correspondingly small wounds and are less debilitating than the large corrective cuts that are necessary on a large tree. Still, any pruning slows growth, so do only what is absolutely necessary. (In the case of a very windy site, however, pruning specifically to slow growth is beneficial.)

will eventually cut off most, if not all, of these branches, but leave them for now. They help feed the young tree and thicken its trunk.

Two special conditions may necessitate more severe pruning of your newly planted tree. The first is a windy site. In this case, remove enough branches to prevent the crown from acting like a sail and catching enough wind to loosen the tree or even wrench it out of the ground. Use thinning rather than heading cuts.

The second condition that calls for more severe initial pruning is when the tree may experience drought in its first season, either through lack of rain or insufficient watering. Pruning increases the chances for surviving drought by

Your first goal as you train a young tree is to develop a sturdy trunk. You began this process when you pruned the tree at planting time, by selecting a single leader and pruning away, or bending down, any competitors. Continue this process, strictly disciplining the tree to have only a single leader. The trees to watch most closely are those that are naturally round-headed, because their leaders tend to lose their dominance sooner than we would like on a landscape tree.

If you plan to use pruning to restrict the height of your tree, begin such pruning before the tree reaches its desired height. Stop upward progress of the leader by cutting it back to a weak branch. Done early on, not only are the resulting cuts smaller, but the crown's appearance also retains a natural upward flow to gradually smaller branches rather than looking as if it has been stubbed back. Best of all, of course, is to plant a tree that will mature at the desired height.

Your second goal in training a young tree is to build up a framework of permanent scaffold limbs that are strong, well connected, and, of course, good-looking. Depending on the height of clear trunk that you want, some of these scaffolds may actually be semi-permanent—even an old tree with its first scaffold limb 8 ft. above ground needs to retain lower branches when it is young, for nourishment. Do not select permanent or semi-permanent scaffolds starting too low on the trunk, because the distance of any of these limbs from the ground never changes. (Actually, the distance decreases slightly as a limb thickens.)

Gaze up along the trunk to select scaffold limbs, keeping in mind three criteria: The limbs must have adequate spacing along the trunk; the points of

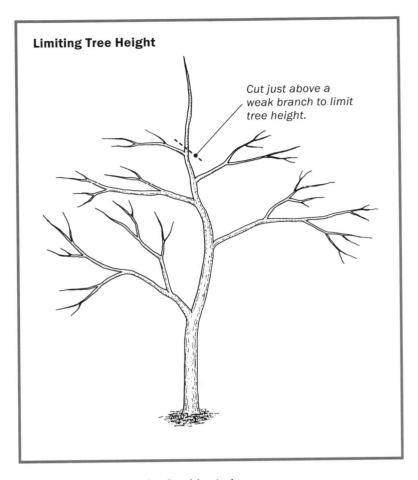

Limiting Tree Height

Cut just above a weak branch to limit tree height.

origin of successive limbs should spiral upward around the trunk; and each limb must make a strong union with the trunk. Just as the distance of a limb from the ground never changes, neither will the distance between limbs. And as the limbs thicken, they will crowd even closer. Select as permanent scaffold limbs side branches that are spaced from 6 in. to 18 in. apart along the trunk (see the top drawing on p. 74), with the smaller distances reserved for trees whose ultimate size is the least.

Choosing for scaffold limbs branches that originate in a spiral up the trunk makes for a prettier tree and allows each limb to be adequately nourished by water and minerals moving up from the roots. For a large tree, no branch should be closer than 3 ft. to the next one directly above it. This way, each scaffold limb will have plenty of space in which to develop.

As you look over branches that are potential scaffold limbs, how do you know which are strongly attached? The most important indicator of a strong union is that the branch is thinner than the leader. This way, the leader will

envelop the base of the branch as they both grow. If a particularly well-positioned branch is too thick in comparison to the leader, you can retain that branch as a scaffold limb by suppressing its rate of growth. Do this by pruning part of the branch off or by bending it to a more horizontal position. If the branch has laterals growing from it, thin some of these, especially those out near the end.

A wide crotch angle between a scaffold limb and the trunk is another sign of a strong union. The problem with a narrow crotch angle is that an increasing amount of dead bark builds up in it over time. Being dead, this bark does not help hold the limb to the trunk. More important, a narrow angle means that the branch is growing more nearly vertical, and the more upright a branch, the greater its vigor. It may be thicker than the leader, or on its way to becoming so. If a narrow-angled branch is particularly well positioned, cut it all the way back when it is only a few inches long, and a wide-angled shoot will often grow in its place (from a latent bud at that node).

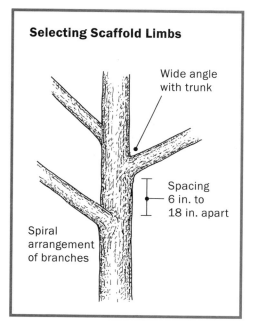

Selecting Scaffold Limbs

Wide angle with trunk

Spacing 6 in. to 18 in. apart

Spiral arrangement of branches

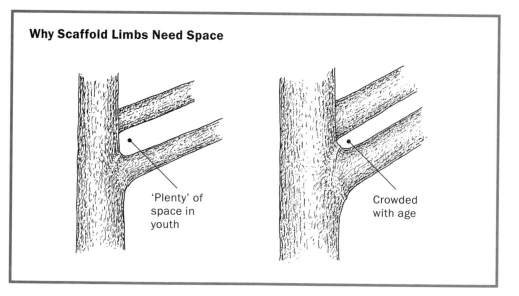

Why Scaffold Limbs Need Space

'Plenty' of space in youth

Crowded with age

Continue to select scaffold limbs over the first few years as your young tree develops. As the main scaffold limbs grow, they will develop their own side branches. For side branches that are strongly attached and have sufficient room to develop, choose those that are thinner than the scaffold limbs themselves and at least 2 ft. away from where the scaffold limb attaches to the central leader. If side branches are well placed but overly vigorous, suppress their growth by bending them down or by pruning them a little. Rarely does a scaffold limb need encouragement to send out branches, but in case it does, use heading cuts. To induce branching on scaffold limbs of deciduous conifers such as larch, dawn redwood, and bald cypress, pinch back shoots as they are expanding.

Some young trees, especially those that eventually become round-headed, develop a lanky leader that is reluctant to make side branches. (Side branches won't grow during the season that the developing leader is growing, that is; the following growing season, the shoot loses control and is overtaken by one or more branches—hence, the round head.) Coax such a lanky leader to branch by heading it back a few inches during the growing season, when it has grown a few inches above where you want a scaffold limb (see the top drawing on p. 76). A shoot from the top bud usually continues growing nearly vertically, as a continuation of the leader, while one, perhaps two, lower buds push out new growth at a wide angle. If necessary, repeat this procedure at each level that you want a new scaffold limb. In contrast to round-headed trees, leaders of trees having a spirelike growth habit are as a rule naturally well supplied with potential scaffold limbs from head to foot.

Above: With dead bark rather than living tissue between them, these two upright limbs are liable to split apart.

Left: A branch that is thinner than the leader and growing out at a wide angle indicates a strong union.

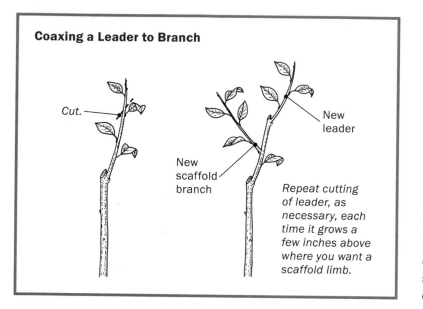

Coaxing a Leader to Branch

Cut.

New scaffold branch

New leader

Repeat cutting of leader, as necessary, each time it grows a few inches above where you want a scaffold limb.

Your young tree will undoubtedly grow many other branches in addition to those that you have selected to become permanent, or semi-permanent, scaffold limbs. Leave most of these for the time being, especially those that are weak or only moderately vigorous. They help feed and thicken the trunk and guard the thin new bark against sunburn. (In the northern hemisphere, this is likely to occur on unshaded south and west sides.) If any temporary branches are growing too vigorously, suppress their growth by pruning them back when they are dormant or by pinching them back in summer, repeatedly if necessary. In any case, do not let any temporary branch

A NOTE ON PRE-PRUNED TREES

I must interject here a short note on pre-pruned trees, as received from nurseries—certain nurseries, at least. Small trees, consisting of only a single whip, are commonly already headed back. Your only recourse, in this case, is to provide good growing conditions and train the tree as described in the text.

Larger trees, already with scaffold branches, also are commonly pre-pruned, giving them what at first appears to be the ideal shape: a length of trunk capped by a nice, full head of branches. But such a tree is really a well-proportioned tree only in miniature. After you plant it out in the landscape, you want a clear trunk longer than 3 ft. And while scaffold limbs 2 in. apart may look nice and full on a miniature tree, they are going to be overcrowded and poorly anchored when each limb is 1 ft. thick. Your recourse with a nursery-butchered tree is to provide good growing conditions and do what pruning is necessary to remove competing leaders and to thin excess scaffold limbs so each has adequate space to develop along the trunk. The real solution, of course, is to avoid purchasing poorly pre-pruned trees in the first place—or you could give the nursery owner a copy of this book.

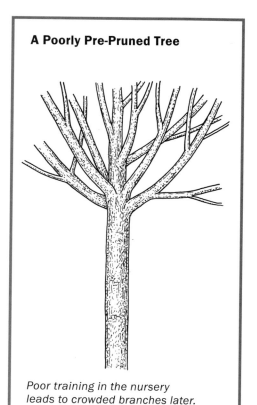

A Poorly Pre-Pruned Tree

Poor training in the nursery leads to crowded branches later.

grow more than 1 ft. in one season. Do not leave any branches—even temporary ones—originating within 6 in. of a scaffold limb.

Remember that those temporary branches are temporary. Never let them grow so vigorously as to overtake either the leader or the scaffold limbs. After a few years, begin removing temporary branches, starting with those that are largest. Do not allow any to grow to the point where their removal leaves a large wound.

Not all trees fall into such neat categories typified by the round-headed white oak or spirelike pin oak. Some trees, such as white birch and alder, naturally form multiple trunks. As you train a tree, you may not always find scaffold branches that are strong, well connected, and well positioned. This is where judgment and ingenuity are needed on your part, which is what makes pruning both an art and a science.

Maintenance pruning

If you did a good job training your tree when it was young, little maintenance pruning is necessary. The grown-up, well-trained tree has large scaffold limbs that are strong and well placed, allowing sufficient light to fall within the canopy to nourish all parts. And the tree looks nice.

Nonetheless, even a mature tree needs periodic pruning. Except in those rare instances where you need to induce branching, limit your pruning to thinning cuts. Remove any limbs that are diseased, dead, or nearly so, as well as one of any two limbs that cross or rub against each other. Remove watersprouts and suckers. These vigorous vertical stems sometimes have the annoying habit of resprouting, even if you—correctly—cut them completely away at their bases.

Red maple welcomes fall with fiery foliage and good form.

Above: Flowering dogwood develops a naturally layered look with little or no coaxing from your pruning shears.

Right: Prune magnolia when young to avoid the need for larger cuts, which heal poorly.

There are two ways to quell this habit. The first way, for the sprout that is still young and tender, is to grab hold of it and rip it off with a sharp tug. The second way, for the shoot that has become woody, is to prune with shears, then paint the wound with a commercial growth regulator (such as Tree-Hold, or other product containing naphthalene-acetic acid).

As any tree ages, it may grow top-heavy and/or develop drooping branches. Limbs higher up in the crown become proportionately more vigorous and increasingly shade those lower down, so the latter grow weak and die. Counteract this tendency by pruning so that the foliage is most dense in the lower half of the tree. Thinning cuts in the crown also help keep the tree open to light and air. Reserve heading cuts for younger branches lower down, to invigorate a faltering stem or shorten a drooping branch.

Not every mature tree received good training in its youth; perhaps you have inherited a misguided tree. Typically, such a tree, besides having poorly selected scaffold limbs, has been butchered by heading cuts. Rampant but crowded and weakly attached shoots sprout from the ends of these limbs. Begin pruning such a tree by dealing with the main scaffold limbs, removing those that are overcrowded or poorly placed (if possible—admittedly, there are trees that are beyond repair). Then thin out the stems growing from the ends of the previously headed limbs, leaving only one if you want to extend that limb. Otherwise, cut the headed limb back to a weaker lateral.

Occasionally, high wind, perhaps in conjunction with snow, ice, or rain, breaks limbs off trees, even trees with sturdy limbs. Repairing such damage may be a job for a professional arborist. Damaged branches need to be cut off cleanly, either at their point of origin or back to a lateral limb. Restore the symmetry of the crown using mostly thinning cuts.

Renovating a deciduous ornamental tree

Eventually, a tree may need renovation because of a combination of age and neglect. Perhaps a tree has grown too large, either in height or width, and the weight of the branches bends the lower limbs too close to the ground. Perhaps a tree is too dense with foliage, creating so much interior shade that inside branches are weakened and humans made gloomy. Letting more air pass through the crown also lessens the stress of wind on the trunk and major limbs.

Lower an old tree by shortening major limbs to vigorous side branches that are at least one-third the diameter of your cut. Stare at the limb structure within your tree before you begin, because you might even be able to pick out a natural lower tier of branches to cut to. Such cuts will suffer less regrowth, and also will preserve the natural form of a round-headed tree even when you remove a lot of wood. Merely lopping off the ends of limbs is a no-no: It looks bad and does little as far as lowering the tree.

Reducing the height of a tree that has a naturally spirelike growth habit usually changes its form. When you lop back that single, stalwart leader, the top of the tree becomes round-headed. Don't feel bad about this. Many spirelike trees undergo this transformation naturally with age. (This is what put the "bald" in bald cypress.)

On trees that have grown too wide, the heavy branches often arch downward. The way to narrow such trees and leave more head space beneath them is by shortening the horizontal limbs to upward-growing side branches.

Open up the crown of a tree to more light and air using thinning cuts, mostly in the top and around the periphery of the crown. The renovated tree will then have most of its foliage in the lower parts and the interior of the crown, giving a well-proportioned appearance to the tree and decreasing the chance that the interior bark, which was previously most shaded, will sunburn.

Be aware that some trees do not tolerate severe pruning, and could die from such treatment. The chart below, from the British Arboricultural Association, lists the tolerance of some trees to severe pruning. When many severe cuts are needed on any tree, spread the job of renovation over a period of two or three years.

TOLERANCE OF TREES TO SEVERE PRUNING

High	Intermediate	Low
Elm	Ailanthus	Beech
Horse chestnut	Alder	Birch
Linden	Ash	Hornbeam
Mulberry	Catalpa	Walnut
Oak	Cherry	
Poplar	Maple	
	Sycamore	

Plant List
DECIDUOUS ORNAMENTAL TREES

***Acer* spp.** (Maple): Young maple bark is susceptible to sunburn, so make sure to leave those temporary branches for shade, even if the tree will eventually be high-headed. You can train some of the smaller maples—*A. Ginnala* (Amur Maple), for example—as large shrubs, but do not cut back old stems because new ones rarely grow up from ground level. As trees, some species require more pruning than others. The weak wood of fast-growing *A. Negundo* (Box Elder) and *A. saccharinum* (Silver Maple) needs frequent pruning to keep limbs strong and to remove dead and broken branches.

***Aesculus* spp.** (Horse Chestnut)

Ailanthus altissima (Tree-of-Heaven): The wood is brittle, so make sure you prune to a strong framework. Pull off root suckers.

Albizia Julibrissin (Silk Tree): The silk tree naturally develops multiple trunks.

***Alnus* spp.** (Alder)

***Amelanchier* spp.** (Juneberry, Shadblow, Serviceberry): The juneberry naturally grows multiple trunks, but can be trained to a single trunk.

***Betula* spp.** (Birch): Grow plants as single trees or as clumps. To create a clump, either plant a few trees together in one planting hole, or cut an established tree to ground level and let a few shoots develop into trunks. Keep an eye out for codominant stems on young plants, and cut away one of them as soon as you notice it. Do what pruning is needed when a stem is small, and keep pruning to a minimum.

***Carpinus* spp.** (Hornbeam)

***Catalpa* spp.** (Catalpa)

***Celtis* spp.** (Hackberry)

Cercidiphyllum japonicum (Katsura Tree)

***Cercis* spp.** (Redbud): Prune as little as possible so that the plant can develop its natural shape.

***Chionanthus* spp.** (Fringe Tree): Grow this plant as either a tree or a shrub. In either case, prune after flowering so that you can enjoy the show first.

Cladrastis lutea (Yellowwood)

***Cornus* spp.:** These plants grow as small trees or large shrubs. In either case, they require little regular pruning, especially if allowed to express their natural growth habit. *C. florida* (Flowering Dogwood) usually grows as a small tree, eventually developing a few feet of clear trunk below its layered branches. *C. mas* (Cornelian Cherry) develops multiple trunks,

---

Pruning is just part of what might be required in tree renovation. Cabling and bracing, for example, might also be needed, but these techniques are outside the realm of pruning, so they warrant no discussion here. Sometimes you can substitute pruning for cabling or bracing—rather than strengthening a weak limb, you can decrease the weight on it by cutting it back.

Renovating an old, neglected tree can be hazardous. Much of the work takes place high above ground, and involves the removal of large limbs. If you have any doubts about your agility, your bravery, your equipment, or your skills (even if you know where to cut, you also have to know where a limb will drop and, perhaps, how to lower it with ropes), call a professional arborist. Offer your knowledgeable suggestions with your feet firmly planted on terra firma. (For a list of arborists in your area who have passed the certification examination of the International Society of Arborists, call 217-355-9411.)

although you can easily train it to a single trunk. *C. Kousa* (Kousa Dogwood) often develops a single trunk, but that trunk remains furnished with branches all the way down to the ground.

Crataegus **spp.** (Hawthorn): Hawthorn is a twiggy tree that also can be planted in masses to shear as a hedge.

Davidia involucrata (Dove Tree): Train the tree carefully when young—with one or more trunks—to avoid later on having to make large cuts, which heal poorly. Prune after flowering.

Delonix regia (Royal Poinciana)

Erythrina **spp.** (Coral Tree): Erythrina includes deciduous, evergreen, and semi-evergreen trees, all of which require little beyond standard maintenance pruning. Some plants have particularly picturesque branching patterns, most evident in winter; prune these to bring out their best form.

Fagus **spp.** (Beech)

Franklinia Alatamaha (Franklinia)

Fraxinus **spp.** (Ash): Ashes are fast growing with brittle wood, narrow crotches, and often few branches. Counteract potential problems by maintaining a single leader, using heading cuts to induce branching, and selecting scaffold limbs with care. With species having two pairs of buds at each node (*F. Uhdei* and *F. velutina)*, the upper pair produces upright growing shoots and the lower pair produces wide-angled shoots. Allow one of the upper buds to to grow when you need to extend a leader or scaffold branch; cut back a shoot from the upper bud to induce a lower bud to grow where you want a wide-angled side branch.

Fremontodendron **spp.** (Fremontia, Flannel Bush): Fremontia does not require pruning. But you can prune to control size, create a single-trunked tree, promote bushiness, and so forth. If you do prune, do so after flowering, and wear long gloves because the hairs on the seed capsules are irritating.

Ginkgo biloba (Ginkgo, Maidenhair Tree): Give this tree time, rather than pruning, to develop an attractive natural form.

The fan-shaped leaves of ginkgo are both unique and beautiful.

Gleditsia triacanthos (Honey Locust)

Gymnocladus dioica (Kentucky Coffee Tree)

Halesia **spp.** (Silver-bell Tree, Snowdrop Tree)

Kalopanax pictus

Koelreuteria **spp.** (Golden-rain Tree)

Laburnum anagyroides (Goldenchain Tree): Train this plant either as a large shrub or as a single-trunked tree. Avoid large cuts, because they heal slowly. Besides regular maintenance pruning, done after flowering, also remove developing seed pods, which are poisonous, messy, and sap the plant's energy.

Larix **spp.** (Larch): To promote bushier growth, pinch the developing shoots in spring. When making heading cuts on older branches, cut back to where the branch still has leaves, or to a side branch.

Liquidambar **spp.** (Sweet Gum)

Liriodendron Tulipifera (Tulip Tree): The wood is brittle but the tree naturally develops a good, strong form. Shorten branches that threaten to break under their own weight, preferably while the tree is young so you can avoid making large cuts. These heal slowly.

Maclura pomifera (Osage Orange): This dense-growing tree can be trained as a thick hedge,

Ginkgo develops good form with a minimum of pruning.

(continued on page 82)

which is an especially good barrier because of its thorns, or as a tree with a single trunk.

Magnolia **spp.** (Magnolia): Do what little pruning a magnolia requires while stems are small, because large cuts heal slowly.

Malus **spp.** (Crabapple)

Melia Azedarach (Chinaberry)

Metasequoia glyptostroboides (Dawn Redwood): To promote bushier growth, pinch developing shoots in spring. When making heading cuts on older branches, cut back to where the branch still has leaves or to a side branch.

Nothofagus **spp.**

Nyssa sylvatica (Sour Gum, Tupelo)

Ostrya **spp.** (Hop Hornbeam)

Oxydendrum arboreum (Sourwood, Sorrel Tree)

Parrotia persica (Persian Parrotia)

Paulownia tomentosa (Empress Tree)

Phellodendron amurense (Cork Tree)

Platanus **spp.** (Plane Tree, Sycamore)

Poncirus trifoliata (Trifoliate Orange, Hardy Orange)

Populus **spp.** (Poplar, Aspen, Cottonwood): Columnar types, such as *P. alba* 'Pyramidalis' and *P. nigra* 'Italica' (Lombardy Poplar) look best branching from the base, so head back young trees after planting and then as shoots grow. No need for anything more than basic pruning on round-headed trees such as *P. deltoides* (Cottonwood). *P. tremuloides* (Quaking Aspen) is commonly grown in groves of several trees, which need no pruning beyond cutting away dead or diseased wood and removing lower branches to expose the attractive bark.

Prunus **spp.** (Flowering Cherries and Plums)

Pseudolarix Kaempferi (Golden Larch): To promote bushier growth, pinch developing shoots in spring. When making heading cuts

on older branches, cut back to where the branch still has leaves, or to a side branch.

Ptelea trifoliata (Stinking Ash, Water Ash): Grow this plant as a large shrub or as a small tree.

Pyrus **spp.** (Pear): Many ornamental pears tend to develop upright, crowded branches. Take special care to train trees with adequate branch spacing, and spread branches for wide crotch angles. Watch for evidence of fire blight disease, pruning it out whenever noted. Avoid too severe pruning on healthy trees or you will stimulate overly succulent shoots, which are especially susceptible to fire blight.

Quercus **spp.** (Oak)

Robinia **spp.** (Locust)

Sapium sebiferum (Chinese Tallow Tree)

Sassafras albidum (Sassafras)

Sophora japonica (Chinese Scholar Tree)

Sorbus **spp.** (Mountain Ash)

Stewartia **spp.** (Stewartia): Train as either a tree or a shrub.

Styrax **spp.** (Snowbell): Snowbells tend to be shrubby trees that need periodic thinning out of weak or crowded branches.

Tamarix aphylla (Athel Tree)

Taxodium distichum (Bald Cypress): To promote bushier growth, pinch developing shoots in spring. When making heading cuts on older branches, cut back to where the branch still has leaves, or to a side branch.

Tilia **spp.** (Linden, Basswood, Lime Tree)

Tipuana Tipu (Tipu Tree)

Ulmus **spp.** (Elm)

Zelkova serrata (Japanese Zelkova): Zelkova makes repeated efforts at multiple leaders, so be diligent in pruning out competitors if you want to maintain a single trunk. Even if you allow multiple leaders, still thin out excess stems so that the crown does not become overcrowded.

Stewartia summer flowers are followed by colorful leaves in autumn, then interesting bark in winter.

CHAPTER SIX

EVERGREEN TREES AND BUSHES

'America' rhododendron in all its glory.

Evergreens provide welcome greenery for northern winters; and even in climates mild enough where almost all woody plants are evergreen, these plants still can provide a verdant backdrop or a focal point in the landscape. We seem to enjoy the view of evergreens more than their use. They are not plants we typically gravitate to for shade or for playing under or climbing in. Form is all-important with evergreens. This emphasis on form and year-round greenery should not diminish the other qualities of evergreens—the texture and glossiness of their leaves, and perhaps their show of flowers.

Trees and bushes are lumped together in this section because with many evergreens the distinction between a tree and a bush is hazy—at least when you stand back and look at the plant. It's often a question merely of size, since trees and bushes are both commonly clothed with leafy branches right down to ground level, hiding a single trunk even if it is present. In this chapter I have divided evergreens into functional rather than botanical groupings: conifers, broadleaf evergreens, palm trees, and bamboo.

As a general rule, evergreens require little pruning—unless you insist that a plant conform to your desires rather than to its natural growth habit. In that case, it's better to choose a plant that will mature to the size and shape that you want. Otherwise, you create unnecessary work for yourself. And although plants never give up trying to grow, you may slowly lose the enthusiasm to keep a plant in check. You do not have to look

Just a bit of pruning and this bird's nest spruce rises to the occasion.

far to find a home whose doorways or windows are engulfed by evergreens that were once small but grew beyond the energy of the homeowner. To reiterate: Form is all-important. And if the plant naturally adopts the desired form, so much the better.

A couple of other generalities apply to this very diverse group of plants. First of all, they need no special pruning at planting time. Because they are usually sold either balled and burlapped or potted, evergreens do not suffer transplant shock. (Unless they are very small and quickly moved, evergreens cannot be transplanted bare root, because they continually lose water through their leaves.) Prune as needed when transplanting, only to develop strength and beauty.

Many evergreens can be grown as either informal or formal hedges. For a formal hedge, the plant should have small leaves, or at least small in proportion to the size of the hedge, and be able to tolerate shearing. The more rigid the form, the more shearings that are required (for more on hedges, see pp. 60-65).

Coniferous trees and bushes

Cones are the giveaway for conifers ("cone-ifers"), but are not always all that obvious. The cones of yew, which look like small brown seeds peeking out of their scarlet, fleshy covering, are hardly cone-y, but are botanical cones nonetheless. Conifers also have narrow or needlelike leaves. But "narrow" is a matter of degree, and the leaves of a conifer such as podocarpus are actually broader than those of a "broadleaf" evergreen such as heather. Still, you identify most conifers by their cones and narrow leaves.

THE BARE BONES

CONIFEROUS TREES AND BUSHES

TO CONTAIN GROWTH or make a plant smaller, prune just before growth begins, cutting stems back to side branches within the plant. Conifers vary in their ability to regrow from old wood, so be careful.

TO MAKE A PLANT DENSER, shorten new growth in spring as it is expanding.

ON TREES, maintain a single central leader with well-placed, weaker scaffold branches growing off it.

GENERALLY, coniferous evergreens need little pruning when being trained or after they mature, especially if you plant one suited to the site.

Growth habits and timing of pruning

Conifers have two types of growth habits; random branching and whorled branching. Recognizing them is a matter of importance when it comes to pruning.

Branches on random-branching conifers arise anywhere along the trunk and branches. Typically, random-branching conifers grow in spurts through the season. These plants vary in their capacity to resprout when cut back into older wood. Shear any of these conifers to make growth more dense. How much you can shear depends on whether the particular species can sprout new growth from either old or young wood, or just from young wood.

Branches on whorled-branching conifers arise in whorls at discrete intervals along the trunk or stems. Whorled-branching conifers generally have few latent buds or dormant growing points on the leafless parts of stems, so the stems do not regrow when cut back. And, as growth begins, each bud is already programmed for all the growth

Growth Habit of Conifers

Random branching pattern (e.g., juniper)

Whorled branching pattern (e.g., pine, spruce)

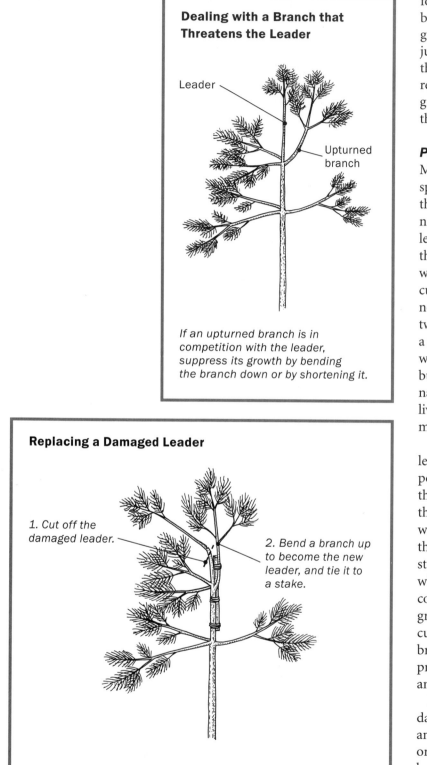

Dealing with a Branch that Threatens the Leader

Leader

Upturned branch

If an upturned branch is in competition with the leader, suppress its growth by bending the branch down or by shortening it.

Replacing a Damaged Leader

1. Cut off the damaged leader.

2. Bend a branch up to become the new leader, and tie it to a stake.

for that season. To make a whorled-branching conifer bushier or to slow its growth, pinch back new growth in spring just as the buds are expanding, but before they are fully expanded. The best time to remove branches, however, is just before growth begins, so that new foliage hides the cuts.

Pruning while training

Most coniferous trees have a naturally spirelike habit, at least when young, so they need little pruning beyond that necessary to maintain a single central leader, or extension of the trunk within the plant. Rarely do any shoots compete with the developing leader, but if they do, cut them off completely as soon as you notice them. Otherwise, you will have two shoots developing into leaders, with a narrow angle between them. Not only will this upset the symmetry of the tree, but old, dead bark will build up in that narrow-angled crotch, and, with no living tissue to join them, the two leaders may split apart with age.

All branches growing off the central leader should be subordinate to it in position and in growth rate. As long as the diameter of the branches remains less than the diameter of the central leader, wood of the central leader can envelop the branches where they meet, leading to strong unions. In the rare instances where a branch is growing too fast in comparison with the leader, slow its growth by shortening it. Do this by cutting one or more laterals on this side branch back to other laterals, thereby preserving the natural beauty of the plant and avoiding dead stubs.

If by chance the developing leader is damaged or broken off, replace it with another leader. In whorled conifers, one or more of the topmost branches will bend upward of their own accord to attempt leadership. Select one of these as the leader, and help it along by temporarily tying it to a stake either set in the ground or lashed to the remaining portion of the previous leader. The other branches will droop back to their subordinate position. If a stub was left where the old leader was lost, a latent bud at the base of that stub may grow into an upright shoot. This shoot will be more vigorous and in a better position to serve as a leader than any side branch, so give it preference. In any case, do select and encourage a new leader, or else vigorous new shoots will poke up along the tops of the upper branches—not a pretty sight!

A central leader may not be forever or for all conifers. Conifers that grow as low or sprawling shrubs do not naturally form central leaders—nor are they supposed to! And with age, some conifers that were spirelike in their youth develop a rounded head. Prune the major branches that form the rounded head of such a conifer so that they are unequal in vigor. This makes the top both stronger and prettier.

Direct growth on young plants of whorled conifers by shortening or removing elongating shoots as they are expanding. Because growth for the season is preordained and contained in the expanding shoots on these conifers, you generally cannot prompt the growth of side branches by heading back existing branches. You can control the size of a pine tree or make it denser by shortening the "candles."

Random-branching conifers are more accommodating when it comes to pruning, because the location of their buds and the time of their growth are not so rigidly programmed. Train these plants by cutting wayward branches off or back to side branches, and promote

denser growth and branching with heading cuts. Limit plant size by shortening branches before growth begins each season. To reduce the size of a random-branching conifer more drastically, shorten branches back to side branches within the plant, so that pruning cuts are hidden from sight.

Conifers have fine-textured leaves and are clothed with leafy branches from top to bottom, so they make ideal hedges. Depending on the natural size of the particular conifer and the desired size of the hedge, an informal coniferous hedge may need little pruning beyond the removal of occasional wayward limbs.

Below: Make growth more bushy on whorled conifers by pinching back new growth just as it is expanding.

Left: Shorten pine 'candles' by breaking off a portion—cutting would leave ragged ends on the leaves.

1. How can you deal with this branch jutting out of place?

2. If you shorten it just as much as needed, you'll be left with an ugly stub staring you in the face.

3. Instead, prune off the branch with a cut well down within the bush.

4. The offending branch is gone without a trace.

The amount of cutting back tolerated depends on the ability of the particular plants to send out new growth from old wood. No matter what kind of evergreen is involved, shape the hedge correctly from the start, giving it a slightly wider base than top. If the hedge's sides are vertical or, even worse, if the hedge is top-heavy, the lower branches will become shaded, lose their leaves, and die.

Maintenance pruning

Despite the preceding verbiage, conifers chosen to suit their site require only minimum pruning. Keep an eye out for overcrowded limbs, which can lead to the shading and death of light-starved branches. Periodically thin out laterals where they are overcrowded. Also prune away any dead or diseased wood.

As a conifer ages, its lower limbs may start to die, the amount depending on the degree of shading and the plant's tolerance for shade. Even if they don't die, you may want to remove lower limbs as a plant ages. An old tree might look nicer with its crown up off the ground (although many conifers do not) or, in the case of a plant such as lacebark pine, with its decorative old bark in full view. Perhaps you want to be able to sit or walk beneath the canopy. If you are going to remove older limbs, spread this job over a period of years, rather than stressing a tree by doing it all at once.

Your aim with a mature coniferous hedge is to keep the plants full and within bounds. Shape whorled conifers, and make growth dense, by clipping back new growth (the candles, in the case of pines) before it is fully expanded. You can use hedge shears on whorled-branching

3

4

conifers like firs because of their naturally dense growth. Hedge shears also work fine on random-branching conifers— they will send out new growth from branch tips as well as from random points along branches. Shear just before growth begins for the season so that new growth will hide the cuts. If necessary, shear again later in the season, but less severely. Later cuts are less likely to be hidden by new growth (definitely not with a whorled-branching conifer), and you should avoid shearing severely enough or late enough in the season to stimulate soft, new growth that may not harden off before winter. Where more radical shaping on either type conifer is necessary, use hand shears or a lopper to shorten branches to their point of origin or to side branches within the plant.

There is one basic problem with shearing conifers to size. (Actually two, the first being that the practice is too pervasive.) Inevitably, when you cut back

branch tips you always leave at least a little of the earlier growth. The result is that a sheared plant keeps growing larger and larger. Eventually, such a plant outgrows its bounds, and then the choices are limited to digging out the plant—or the whole hedge—or to renovating by drastic pruning of all the wood. Few conifers regrow when severely cut back. The way to avoid this problem and produce a more natural-looking hedge (admittedly not always desirable) is to shorten branches selectively each year with pruning shears. Better yet, choose the right size and shape of plant at the outset.

Plant List

CONIFERS

***Abies* spp.** (Fir): Firs have a whorled branching pattern with few dormant buds. Because they have such short spaces between leaves along a stem, firs are dense and need little pruning. If necessary, pinch developing shoots in spring for more bushiness, and cut wayward branches back to laterals. Unless you want to restrict height, do not pinch the topmost whorl, because regrowth from there is usually poor. For hedging, shear after growth hardens in midsummer.

Agathis robusta (Queensland Kauri): This whorled-branched conifer develops a naturally symmetrical shape so it needs little help from you. Occasionally these trees try to develop two leaders; remove the weaker one when you notice it.

Araucaria heterophylla (Norfolk Island Pine): This symmetrical tree with whorled branches rarely needs pruning. Laterals never turn upward, so protect the leader—it is irreplaceable. Pinch side shoots if you want more branching.

Calocedrus decurrens (California Incense Cedar): This tree needs little pruning. Let it grow naturally or shear it as a hedge.

***Cedrus* spp.** (True Cedar): True cedars have a random branching habit. Short growths, called spurs, form on branches, and these have some latent buds. To control size, cut branches back to laterals, although sometimes this will cause a vigorous new shoot to grow from a spur. To make the plant fuller, pinch back developing shoots. Generally, these plants require little pruning. You can shear *C. Deodara* (Deodar Cedar) as a hedge.

***Cephalotaxus* spp.** (Plum Yew): These random-branching trees and shrubs need little pruning beyond the removal of dead, diseased, and misplaced wood. Old wood will make new growth if cut back, so you can grow this plant as a tree or a shrub, sheared or clipped informally.

***Chamaecyparis* spp.** (False Cypress): To shorten a branch of this random-branching conifer, cut it back to wherever it still has leaves, and new growth will push out. Redirect growth by cutting a branch back to a lateral. Prune the ends of branches to make the plant grow more densely. False cypress is a good plant for hedging.

Cryptomeria japonica (Japanese Cedar): Cryptomeria has a random branching habit. To shorten a branch, cut it back to a live lateral shoot (some naturally die and fall off) or to a tuft of foliage. Make growth more dense by pinching back expanding foliage.

Cunninghamia lanceolata (China Fir): China fir has a whorled branch arrangement. Remove misplaced, dead, and diseased branches as well as suckers growing from the roots.

× ***Cupressocyparis Leylandii*** (Leyland Cypress): This randomly branched conifer rarely needs pruning unless you want to shear it as a hedge, and even that is rarely necessary except to control size.

***Cupressus* spp.** (Cypress): Cypresses are randomly branched conifers that can push out new growth wherever there are leaves. So if you want to shorten a branch, cut it back either to a lateral or a point where leaves persist. Cypresses tolerate being sheared for hedging. To make a specimen tree denser, prune back the tips of the branches. Following pruning, cypresses are slow to begin growth.

***Juniperus* spp.** (Juniper): Junipers have a random branching pattern, with some growing points even where there is no foliage. Therefore, these plants can be cut back more severely than many other conifers. Plants have either needlelike or scalelike leaves. Species with scalelike leaves, such as *J. chinensis* (except when juvenile), *J. horizontalis* (Creeping Juniper), *J. occidentalis* (California Juniper), and *J. virginiana*

(Red Cedar), regrow following pruning better than do those with needlelike leaves, such as *J. Sabina* (Savin Juniper) and *J. squamata*.

Cutting back the stem tips makes the plants denser. Junipers take well to shearing, for hedging. Two or three shearings a year might be needed for a tight, formal hedge.

To remove larger branches without leaving a mangled look, shorten them to weaker laterals within the plant. This pruning is a way to make a plant smaller and to open up the interior to light, where shaded branches often die out. Shortening individual limbs in this manner is also the way to contain the growth of a prostrate form of juniper while preserving the natural form of the plant.

Libocedrus **spp.** (Incense Cedar): Prune stems on this randomly branched conifer back to wherever leaves persist, or back to laterals. Promote dense branching by pruning back the stems tips. Incense cedar tolerates shearing as a hedge.

Picea **spp.** (Spruce): Spruces have a whorled branching pattern with a few dormant buds. To make a plant smaller or to shape it, prune back to side branches or to visible dormant buds. To make a plant denser, pinch lateral shoots when they are about half-grown in spring. Or shear just before growth begins, shearing a second time, if necessary, in late spring or early summer. Generally, spruces need little regular pruning. Even old plants look best with their oldest branches retained, gracefully sweeping the ground.

Pinus **spp.** (Pine): Pines have a whorled branching pattern and, with few exceptions, almost no latent buds or dormant growing points. Exceptions include *P. nigra* (Austrian Pine), *P. resinosa* (Red Pine), and *P. sylvestris* (Scotch Pine), which are capable of resprouting from buds on two-year-old wood where needles are retained.

Make a pine tree smaller by cutting branches back to secondary branches within the canopy while the plant is dormant. Pruning the "candles," which are expanding new growths, can keep a tree from growing large or make a tree fuller and bushier. New shoots generally arise only from buds within candles.

Completely breaking off a candle discourages further elongation at that point. Shortening a candle, instead, decreases the distance at which the next whorl of branches develops, making for a denser tree. Snap the end of a candle off with your fingers rather than cutting it back with pruning shears to avoid also cutting off expanding leaves, which would then brown at their tips.

(continued on page 92)

This Norfolk Island pine has naturally good form. It requires little or no pruning.

A couple of tricks sometimes fool mature pine stems to grow side branches. The first trick is is to cut away a ring of bark ⅛ in. wide around the stem where you want branching to occur. The other trick is to remove needles 1 in. to 2 in. beyond where you want branching to occur. Both tricks are most successful the younger the tree and the closer to the end of the stem you can cut bark or remove needles.

Platycladus orientalis (Oriental Arborvitae): This randomly branching conifer can regrow wherever there is foliage, so you can cut wood back either to side branches or to where foliage persists. To make the plant denser, cut back the tips of the stems.

Podocarpus macrophyllus (Southern Yew, Japanese Yew, Buddhist Pine): This randomly branching conifer resprouts even if cut back into old wood, so shape the plant with heading and thinning cuts. To make the plant denser, pinch or shear the tips of growing shoots during any of its growth flushes through the season.

Pseudotsuga menziesii (Douglas Fir): Douglas fir rarely requires pruning. The tree has a whorled branching habit with few dormant buds, so limit pruning to shortening to side branches, for size control and cutting back new growth as it expands for a denser tree. You can shear Douglas firs as a hedge plant. Do not cut out the top of an old tree or it will decline.

Sciadopitys verticillata (Umbrella Pine, Japanese Umbrella Pine): This whorled conifer has an attractive natural symmetry so it needs little pruning. Watch for, and eliminate, any competitors with the central leader.

Sequoia **spp.** (Redwood and Sequoia): *S. sempervirens* (Redwood) is randomly branched and well supplied with latent buds throughout. Head or thin stems to shape a tree and control its size. Promote denser growth by pruning branch tips. Allow only a single leader to grow. *S. Wellingtonia* (Giant Sequoia) is also random-branching, but has few live buds on leafless wood. Shorten a branch either to a live lateral (some naturally die and drop) or to where there is a tuft of foliage. Promote branching by pinching back expanding shoots.

Sequoiadendron giganteum (Giant Redwood): This random-branching giant has such a pleasing natural growth habit that it rarely requires any pruning. That's good, because it grows to a height of 250 ft. or more!

Taxus **spp.** (Yew): Yew is random branching and well supplied with dormant growing points, so will return to life even if cut back brutally. Control size and shape the plant with heading or thinning cuts. Pruning the ends of stems makes growth denser. For a formal hedge or bush, shear yew as needed just before growth begins for the season, then shear again one or two times during the season. Training yew as a tree shows off its beautiful reddish bark.

Thuja **spp.** (Arborvitae): This randomly branching conifer can regrow wherever there is foliage, so cut wood back either to side branches or to where foliage persists. To make the plant denser, cut back the tips of the stems, or shear.

Tsuga **spp.** (Hemlock): Hemlocks are randomly branched conifers that are full and graceful without any pruning. Grow hemlocks as trees or hedge plants. Clip or shear hedges just before growth begins, repeating, if necessary, in midsummer. Hemlock will resprout from bare wood, so you can rejuvenate a plant by cutting it back severely.

Broadleaf evergreen trees and bushes

Generally, do what little pruning is necessary to bring out the natural form of a broadleaf evergreen. The right plant in the right place needs minimal pruning. Techniques for pruning evergreen trees and shrubs are similar to techniques for pruning their deciduous counterparts (see chapters 4 and 5). Because evergreens are clothed in year-round greenery, though, the arrangement of their branches is never prominent, so we prune these plants for pleasing three-dimensional form, as well as for plant health, strength (in the case of trees), and perhaps flowers.

When needed, direct growth just as you would on any other plant. To remove a wayward stem without causing regrowth, cut it away at its point of origin or back to one of its side branches. Where you want denser growth, shorten a stem while the plant is dormant or pinch a shoot as it is growing. Wait to prune early-flowering plants until after their blossoms fade if you do not want to miss their show. Other specifics with respect to timing of pruning are noted in the Plant List, which begins on p. 96.

Except where otherwise indicated, do most pruning of these plants around the time that growth is beginning. Dormant pruning can be done anytime that a plant is dormant, but if you wait until just before growth commences, new growth will quickly hide the pruning cuts. Also, winter damage is more evident once new growth begins, and it is less likely to occur with marginally cold-hardy plants pruned at this time.

THE BARE BONES

BROADLEAF EVERGREEN TREES AND BUSHES

EXCEPT FOR bushes or small trees with multiple trunks, allow only one vertical shoot to become the trunk, then central leader. Bend down, cut back, or cut off any competitors.

TO CONTAIN GROWTH or make a plant smaller, prune just before growth begins, cutting stems back to side branches within the plant. Broadleaf evergreens vary in their ability to send out new shoots from old stems that are cut back.

TO MAKE A PLANT DENSER, pinch the tips of growing shoots.

GENERALLY, broadleaf evergreens need little pruning when being trained or after they mature—especially if you plant one suited to the site.

Just a little pinching and thinning keeps this Mexican orange shrub shapely and florific.

Training

Prune a bush to give a pleasing form and sufficiently dense growth.

Most important with a broadleaf evergreen tree is to train the branches to a sturdy framework when the plant is young. Begin as soon as you plant by allowing only a single main stem, which will become the future trunk and central leader of the tree. If two or more shoots are competing for the role of central leader, cut away all but one. If a branch is turning upward and threatening the leader's dominance, slow growth on that branch by pruning it back partially or by bending it down, with weights or string, to a more horizontal position (see the top drawing on p. 86). Throughout the early development of your tree, keep that central leader upright and dominant.

This single-leader "rule" is not hard and fast. Because the distinction between trees and shrubs is vague with evergreens, many plants that are naturally bushy can be trained to small trees (and many of the trees can be bushlike). Small trees are not threatened by collapse, and many of them look attractive with multiple trunks originating from ground level. Develop this form by selecting two or three trunks as the plant grows; alternatively, let the plant grow as a bush, then reduce the number of stems growing from ground level and trim off branches from the stems that remain to make them into trunks.

Small branches growing off the central leader of a developing tree will, in time, become main scaffold limbs of that tree. Begin selecting future scaffold limbs when you put the tree in the ground. Choose branches that are spaced far enough apart along the developing leader so that they will not be crowded even when the tree reaches old age. A distance of 6 in. to 18 in. is adequate, with the closer distances reserved for smaller trees. Successively higher branches should arise in a spiral fashion up the trunk so that each has adequate space to develop and is not being starved by another branch directly and closely beneath it. So that the trunk can envelop and firmly hold the base of a branch, that branch must be thinner than the trunk. If a well-placed branch is too thick in proportion to the trunk, slow its growth by pruning part of it away, especially near the end of the branch. Strength that comes from good scaffold-limb choice and development becomes increasingly important with larger trees.

Selecting Scaffold Limbs

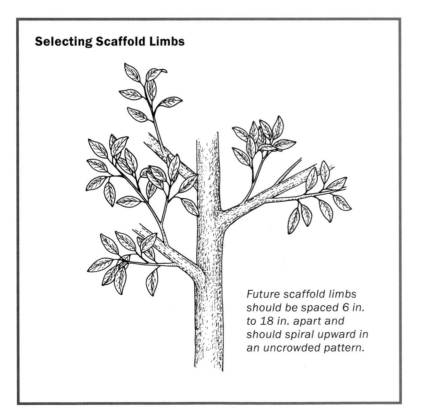

Future scaffold limbs should be spaced 6 in. to 18 in. apart and should spiral upward in an uncrowded pattern.

Leave any other branches growing off the leader as temporary branches. These branches will help strengthen the developing leader and trunk. Only remove those branches that are crowding the permanent scaffolds. Leave temporary branches only for about three years, and prune them back in the meantime if they start getting too big.

Choose side branches growing off scaffold limbs in a similar way as you chose the scaffolds themselves. Retain side branches that are not crowding each other or growing too near the central leader, then prune to suppress the growth of any that threaten to grow thicker than the limb from which they spring.

Maintenance pruning

With good early training, neither trees nor bushes in this category require much pruning. As with any plant, remove dead, diseased, and misplaced wood. Some of the plants look nicer if their faded flowers are removed. A few of the bushes require heavy annual pruning for a good show of flowers or to keep the plants from growing scraggly. Aside from consulting the Plant List, which begins on p. 96, another way to tell how much pruning is needed to keep your bush happily flowering is to watch the plant for a season or two and note how old the wood is when it bears flowers. The younger the flowering wood, the more severe the annual pruning required.

Renovation

Major renovation of any broadleaf evergreen must be done with caution, because some of these plants do not regrow from old wood and some do not heal large wounds well. Consult the Plant List that follows for specific directions. Or determine how well your plant resprouts from old wood by heading back a branch to an older, leafless portion and watching its response. Merely shearing the top of a plant is not a good way to lower it—the plant will look horrendous right after pruning and even worse when it sends out new sprouts along the tops of the branches. Instead, cut an individual tall limb back either to its point of origin or to a branch low within the canopy. Do not make too many major cuts in a single year, or you will overly stress the plant. Only certain bushes tolerate severe cutting back in the name of renovation. To make a renovated plant less of an initial eyesore, spread the job over a few years, shortening some of the decrepit, old wood to the ground or to low, vigorous branches each year.

Plant List

BROADLEAF EVERGREEN TREES AND BUSHES

Abutilon spp. (Flowering Maple): Regular pruning is needed to stimulate shoots, on which blossoms form. Either cut the whole plant back in late winter or, in mild climates, cut a different portion of stems back periodically throughout the year.

Acacia spp.: Little pruning is needed, whether these plants are grown as bushes or as trees. Beyond training, just cut away dead wood and twigs.

Acalypha spp. (Copperleaf): Prune as needed, to shape plants. If you grow copperleaf as a hedge, shorten stems with pruning shears and pinch shoot tips. Using hedge shears mutilates the large, decorative leaves.

Aralia japonica. See *Fatsia japonica*.

Arbutus spp. (Manzanita, Strawberry Tree): The strawberry tree tolerates severe pruning.

Arctostaphylos spp. (Bearberry, Manzanita): Prune to make these shrubs shapely, removing stems completely or shortening them to side branches. Do not cut back to bare wood, because it may not send out new growth. Pinch back shoots to make them grow more bushy. These plants normally need little pruning.

Aucuba japonica (Japanese Laurel): This plant will tolerate severe pruning needed to rejuvenate or shape it. Cut stems to the ground or back to leaves or buds. Pinch shoots to promote bushiness.

Azara microphylla (Boxleaf Azara): Pinch and shorten shoots on young plants to promote bushiness. Cut off stems that have flowered after the flowers fade. Provide for renewal by occasionally cutting away the oldest stems at ground level.

Berberis spp. (Barberry): Prune evergreen species right after flowers fade in spring.

Bougainvillea spp. (Bougainvillea): Prune in summer and early autumn, depending on how vigorously the plant is growing and how firm you want to be about controlling that growth. Thin crowded wood and shorten lanky stems just before growth begins. If you want to, you also can limit the number of main trunks sprouting up from the ground. Grown with one or just a few stems, bougainvillea becomes a nonclinging vine.

Brachychiton spp. (Bottle Tree): This tree needs little pruning beyond basic training.

Brassaia actinophylla (Australian Umbrella Tree, Queensland Umbrella Tree): Prune mostly to make a plant full, by heading back stems and pinching new growth. The plant will resprout if cut to the ground for renovation.

Brugmansia spp. (Angel's-trumpet): Prune back stems to a couple of buds to stimulate new flowering shoots. Do this periodically through the growing season or, where winter weather is cool or cold, just before growth begins for the season.

Buxus spp. (Box): Box requires little pruning, unless clipped as a formal hedge. Prune whenever needed, but where winters are cold, do the job at least a month before the average date of the first autumn frost. To renovate, cut the plant to ground level just before new growth begins.

Caesalpinia spp.: Prune or don't prune *C. Gilliesii* (Bird-of-paradise Shrub), as you like, to make the plant shrublike or treelike, or to reduce its height if it has grown too tall. *C. pulcherrima* (Barbados-pride, Dwarf Poinciana) needs no regular pruning. Cut it to the ground every year if it is damaged by frost or if you want to keep it small.

Callistemon spp. (Bottlebrush): Follow general pruning directions, but do not cut back to leafless parts of stems because they will not send out new sprouts. Direct the shape and size of the plant with small cuts; cuts over 1 in. in diameter do not heal well.

Calluna spp. (Heather): Older wood does not resprout readily, so shorten the previous season's growth by one-half to keep heather compact. If you shorten stems with hedge shears, vary the angle at which you hold the shears so that the finished surface is rolling rather than flat-topped.

***Calothamnus* spp.** (Net Bush): Cut older stems back right after flowering to keep the plant invigorated.

***Camellia* spp.** (Camellia): Little pruning is required beyond that needed to shape a plant. Thin flower buds on young plants to channel energy into growth, and on older plants if you want to increase the size of remaining flowers. The best time to prune stems is just after the flowers fade.

Camellias vary in their growth habits. If your plant is too spreading when young, cut back some side branches to divert energy into vertical growth. Similarly, if your plant is too gangly, head some stems to the bases of previous years' growth to induce branching. (Only one bud will break from cuts on the youngest wood.) With camellias such as *C. reticulata*, which are reluctant to sprout from older wood, promote bushiness by merely pinching the growing tips.

Renovate an overgrown camellia by cutting the whole bush to bare stems, either all at once or over the course of a couple of seasons. You cannot do this with *C. reticulata*, because it may not regrow.

Cantua buxifolia (Magic Flower, Sacred-flower-of-the-Incas): Prune this sprawling shrub, which grows almost like a vine, by removing or shortening misplaced stems after the flowers fade. For a neat plant, tie the stems to a trellis or a post.

Carpenteria californica (Tree Anemone): Despite the common name, this plant is bushy—and requires little regular pruning.

Casuarina equisetifolia (Horsetail Tree, South Sea Ironwood): This tree needs little pruning. Shear, if desired.

***Ceanothus* spp.** (Redroot): As soon as the flowers fade, prune the flowering shoots of evergreen species so that they are only two or three buds long.

Chamelaucium uncinatum (Geraldton Wax Plant): Train this plant as a tree or shrub.

Prune the mature plant after the flowers fade, but do not cut back into leafless wood.

Choisya ternata (Mexican Orange): Pinch growing tips to control plant size and thin out older stems to stimulate new growth.

***Chorisia* spp.** (Floss-silk Tree): These plants require little pruning.

Cinnamomum Camphora (Camphor Tree): Little pruning is necessary.

Camellia in bloom.

***Cistus* spp.** (Rock Rose): Rock rose does not take kindly to pruning, but looks unkempt if left alone. New shoots do not break from older wood, so keep a plant low and bushy by pinching or lightly shearing new growth as it develops. Periodically cut back the oldest stems right after the flowers fade, either to the ground or to branches. Cuttings root readily, so it is easy to have a replacement ready in case of disastrous response to pruning.

***Clerodendrum* spp.** (Glory-bower, Kashmir-bouquet): *C. Bungei* and *C. philippinum* are vigorous and spreading. Keep them in check by cutting them back severely in spring, pinching back new growth, and cutting off or digging up suckers from wandering roots. The lanky stems of *C. Thomsoniae* (Bleeding Glory-bower, Tropical Bleeding-heart) could

(continued on page 98)

make this shrub a vine. Prune it lightly right after blossoms fade, shortening some stems and disentangling and removing some others.

Clethra arborea (Summersweet, Sweet Alder): This tree needs little pruning.

Cleyera japonica: This shrub needs little pruning.

Clianthus puniceus (Glory Pea, Parrot's-beak, Red Kowhai): After flowering, completely cut away some of the oldest and most spindly stems. Then head back some of the stems that remain. Vigorous new growth will blossom the following year.

Codiaeum variegatum (Croton): Prune mostly to keep the plant thick with leaves. Head back leggy stems, then pinch growing shoot tips. If the whole plant is overgrown, first cut back one part of the plant, then cut back the other part after growth is well underway on the first part.

Coprosma spp.: *C.* × *Kirkii* grows low and spreading; keep it dense by shearing it back in spring or summer. *C. repens* (mirror plant, looking-glass plant) grows larger and needs periodic pruning, whenever you wish, to keep it from becoming straggly.

Cordyline spp. (Dracaena): These plants are closely related to dracaena (the plant with this botanical name), even to the point of sharing their common name. Both plants need little pruning. If a stem grows too tall, lop it back and it will send out one, perhaps two, new shoots—probably. Or cut an old stem completely to the ground to make room for younger replacements. Prune while the plant is actively growing.

Corokia cotoneaster: Prune as needed with an eye to accentuating the picturesque form of the branches.

Correa spp.: Pinch shoots to promote branching, then shorten stems right after the flowers fade. But do not cut back to the leafless parts of stems or you may not get regrowth.

Corynocarpus laevigata: Once trained as a shrub or small tree, this plant needs little pruning.

Cotoneaster spp. (Cotoneaster): Like the deciduous species, the evergreen species require little pruning. Do what little pruning is necessary in winter, or wait until old leaves are falling and new buds are just beginning to grow. Keep an eye out for branches blackened by fire blight and cut them back 1 ft. into healthy wood.

Crassula argentea (Jade Tree): Prune just before growth begins. The plant resprouts readily from old nodes.

Crinodendron Patagua: Little pruning is needed for this plant, which can be grown as either a shrub or small tree.

Daphne spp.: For these evergreen species, prune back flowering shoots right after the flowers fade.

Dendromecon rigida (Tree Poppy): Prune back ungainly shoots after flowering ceases, but avoid cutting back to wood more than 1 in. thick.

Diosma ericoides (Breath-of-Heaven): Keep this shrub compact by shearing branches back right after the flowers fade. Thin out excessive growth. Do not, however, cut the whole branch back severely, because it may not recover.

Dodonaea viscosa (Hop Bush): This versatile plant can take on many guises. You can leave the upright stems to grow into a billowy mass or you can shear them into a formal hedge. Remove most of the stems and the plant will grow into a small tree with single or multiple trunks.

Dombeya spp.: No special pruning is needed to keep these trees and shrubs neat and healthy. Prune in early spring or, in tropical areas, in summer.

Cotoneaster berries add a touch of color in fall.

Dracaena spp. (Dracaena): Dracaenas need little pruning. If a stem grows too tall, lop it back and it will send out one, perhaps two, new shoots—probably. Or cut it completely to the ground to make room for younger replacements. Prune while the plant is actively growing.

Drimys Winteri (Winter's-Bark): Train to a single trunk or to multiple trunks. From then on, just basic pruning is needed, which can be done at any time.

Duranta repens (Pigeon Berry, Skyflower): Prune away stems that have borne berries, cutting them either to the ground or to low side branches that have not yet flowered. Prune enough to prompt a good supply of new shoots, which will flower the following year.

Elaeagnus spp.: Evergreen species need only basic pruning in late spring.

Eranthemum pulchellum (Blue Sage): Pinch shoot tips to make this sprawling shrub more compact. Lop all stems down to the ground in spring to get an overgrown plant back in order quickly.

Erica spp. (Heath): Clip back spring-flowering heaths to the bases of flower stalks right after flowers fade. Prune summer-, fall-, and winter-flowering heaths the same way, except wait until just before growth begins in spring. Do not prune into old wood, which will not resprout. And if you use a hedge shears, vary the angle of cut so that you leave a wavy, rather than a flat-topped, surface. *E. arborea* (Tree Heath) needs no pruning except to shape the plant and remove damaged wood.

Eriogonum spp. (Wild Buckwheat, Umbrella Plant): Encourage dense growth on young plants by pinching shoot tips.

Escallonia spp.: Prune escallonias annually, either shearing them as hedge plants or keeping them shrubby by cutting away the oldest stems at ground level. Also cut back wayward branches.

Eucalyptus spp.: Eucalyptus trees and shrubs require little pruning. When a bushy type gets too gangly, cut the plant to the ground and allow a few of the new sprouts to grow for a new framework. The small and large tree types of eucalyptus need little or no pruning beyond their training stage. To make multiple trunks on a small tree, cut it down to within 2 ft. of the ground and select new trunks from the sprouts at the base. Bending a small trunk to the ground, and holding it down with rope, will stimulate new sprouts near ground level if none are already there. Some types of eucalyptus are grown for their juvenile leaves. On these plants, cut the stems back heavily each year to stimulate vigorous regrowth of juvenile wood.

Euonymus spp.: The evergreen species need little more than corrective pruning, or you can shear them as hedge plants.

Euphorbia pulcherrima (Poinsettia): Prune poinsettia in spring, after blossoming finishes. The more severely you cut back the plant, the more spectacular the flower display—this is not necessarily all-important if you also want leafy mass from a poinsettia nestled among other plants in a shrub border. Shoots allowed to grow unchecked on severely pruned bushes will have lanky stems with large flowers at their ends. For a bushier plant, and more, albeit smaller, flowers, head back the stems every two months until September. As a houseplant, cut back poinsettia stems to 6 in. in April or May. Depending on the particular variety, pinching may or may not be needed to promote bushiness. At any rate, cease pinching in September; a period of long nights is then needed in order to induce flower buds that will open by Christmas.

Eurya emarginata: This relative of camellia needs little pruning.

✕ **Fatshedera Lizei** (Aralia Ivy, Tree Ivy): This plant displays its hybrid heritage of a bush and a vine as its vertical stems collapse under their own weight. Train the plant either as a loose bush or as a bushy vine. If you need to start again, just cut the stems to the ground and the plant will regrow.

Fatsia japonica (Japanese Fatsia, Paper Plant): Fatsia (sometimes listed botanically as *Aralia japonica*) typically sends up new shoots from

(continued on page 100)

ground level. Thin them out if they are too numerous, and when a stem grows too tall or too old, cut it back to a branch or to the ground, to be replaced by a young sprout. Prune in spring or summer.

***Ficus* spp.** (Ornamental Figs): No special techniques are required for pruning ornamental figs. Prune in spring and summer; where winters are frost free, prune anytime.

***Fuchsia* spp.** (Fuchsia): Pruning stimulates the growth of new shoots, which, after six to ten weeks of growth (and cool night temperatures), bear flowers. Prune according to how large you want your bush to grow; the more severe the pruning, the smaller the bush. Where winters are cold, wait to prune until just before growth begins. Pinch the tips of the stems as they grow to promote more bushiness.

Galphimia glauca: This shrub tends to get leggy, so pinch out the tips of growing shoots to promote bushiness, or clip with hedge shears.

Gamolepis chrysanthemoides: Unpruned, this vigorous shrub has most of its leaves out near the ends of the stems. For a fuller look, regularly pinch back growing shoots, beginning after the flowers fade. For a quick renovation, cut the whole bush back severely, either in late winter or during the growing season.

***Gardenia* spp.** (Gardenia): Outdoor shrubs need little pruning. Just before growth begins, shorten some stems and thin out twigs. To promote further branching, pinch the tips of growing shoots, but not later than August. Stems will regrow if you have to cut them back severely to renovate the bush. Prune a potted gardenia the same way as an outdoor shrub, except more frequently and severely, to keep it pot size.

***Garrya* spp.** (Silk-tassel Bush): These bushes need little pruning, whether grown as shrubs or as informal hedges.

Grevillea robusta (Silk Oak): Because of its inherently weak wood, silk oak needs to be trained to an especially sturdy framework. Shorten lanky stems and thin out dense wood enough to allow wind to pass through the canopy. Avoid leaving large pruning wounds, which heal poorly.

Grewia occidentalis (often sold as *G. caffra):* This shrub is adaptable in the landscape. Shear it as a hedge, pinch it to promote bushiness, or let it grow with abandon as a fountain of green. For maximum flowers, reserve major pruning for autumn, after flowering stops.

***Hakea* spp.** (Pincushion Tree): These plants need little pruning and can be trained either as bushes or as small trees.

***Hebe* spp.:** These vigorous shrubs tolerate heavy pruning. To promote bushiness, shorten stems that have flowered by half their length. To renovate a bush, cut away the oldest stems to the ground, then shorten those that remain so they are each 1 ft. or so long.

Heteromeles arbutifolia (Toyon, Christmas Berry): Toyon tolerates various types and degrees of pruning, so do what is necessary to grow it as a shrub, an informal hedge, or a small tree, or to renovate it. Prune just before growth begins.

***Hibbertia* spp.** (Button Flower, Guinea Gold Vine): Prune *H. cuneiformis* in spring, after blossoms fade. *H. scandens* stems are more trailing, like those of a vine, and the flowers appear throughout the growing season. Prune before growth begins, untangling and cutting back stems that are congested or too old.

Hibiscus Rosa-sinensis (Chinese Hibiscus): Blossoms form on new growth. Stimulate new growth on mature plants by shortening stems, before growth begins, by about one-third. If needed, pinch the growing tips of young plants to promote branching. Renovate overgrown shrubs by periodically cutting back the oldest stems to well-placed side branches lower down. Do this periodically through the growing season until August. Do not shear hibiscus if you grow it as a hedge. Prune branches selectively instead.

Hoya carnosa (Wax Plant): Prune this trailing shrub as needed. The only caution is not to disturb the stalks of old flowers, because new flowers will also be borne on them.

Hymenosporum flavum: This tree naturally makes few branches, but you can change its ways by pinching growing shoots. On isolated plants, shorten long, weak stems if they need strengthening. Trees planted together in groves do not need pruning.

Hypericum calycinum (Rose-of-Sharon, Aaron's Beard): This low shrub gets straggly unless you prune it back severely almost every spring.

Ilex spp. (Holly): Prune as needed for good structure and form, but avoid cutting back into leafless portions of the plant if you want regrowth. Prune while the plant is dormant.

Illicium spp. (Anise Tree): These plants need little pruning and can be grown as shrubs, hedges, or small trees.

Ixora coccinea (Jungle-of-the-woods, Jungle-flame): This bush needs only occasional basic pruning.

Jacaranda mimosifolia (Green Ebony): Train this tree to a single trunk or to multiple trunks. Little pruning is needed beyond training. New sprouts grow readily from near ground level, and are useful for changing the form of the plant or for replacing wood damaged by cold.

Jasminum spp. (Jasmine): All jasmines flower on growth that is one year old, so prune them just after they finish flowering. Shorten scraggly stems, thin out overcrowded and old stems, and pinch growing tips where you want branching.

Justicia spp. (Water Willow): Pinch stem tips of *J. Brandegeana* (Shrimp Plant) as they grow to encourage branching. Once the plant is sufficiently bushy, stop pinching and let flowers form at the ends of branches. After the flowers fade, cut back the flowering stems. Severely cut back stems of *J. carnea* (Brazilian-plume) in spring every two or three years, then pinch the stems as growth progresses to encourage bushiness. Just cut away the oldest wood at ground level on *J. californica* (Chuparosa), *J. Leonardii,* and *J. spicigera.* Also pinch new shoots a couple of times during the growing season on the latter two species.

Kalmia latifolia (Mountain Laurel): Mountain laurel needs little pruning beyond what is necessary to keep the plant shapely and remove dead or diseased wood. Prune right after flowers fade. If necessary, make drastic cuts to promote young growth to replace a leggy branch, or even to renovate a whole, overgrown shrub.

Lantana spp. (Shrub Verbena): Prune these shrubs regularly to remove old wood and keep them tidy. Cut just before growth begins, as much as you like, because flowers form on new wood. If you have the time and the inclination, also pinch out the tips of developing shoots to promote bushiness.

Laurus nobilis (Laurel, Sweet Bay): Prune in spring and, as needed, through the growing season to shape the plant any way you like — as a formal or informal hedge, or a tree.

Lavandula angustifolia (Common or English Lavender): Prune in spring to keep the plant neat and to remove winterkilled wood. Later in the growing season, clip off spent flower heads as they form. Lavender is not usually long-lived.

Be careful not to damage the flowering spurs of hoya, because they also bear next year's flowers.

(continued on page 102)

Leptospermum spp. (Tea Tree): Prune these shrubs right after the flowers fade. Grow the plants as informal or formal shrubs, or as small trees. Because old wood will not send out new growth, cut back stems to side shoots.

Leucophyllum frutescens (Ceniza, Barometer Bush): Prune ceniza while it is dormant. Little pruning is needed, but if you want to renovate an unkempt plant, just cut it back almost to the ground.

Leucothoe spp. (Fetterbush): Prune fetterbush just before growth begins in spring, cutting away the oldest stems and shortening lanky stems. If you prune off spent flower heads after blossoming ceases on *L. Davisiae* (Sierra Laurel), the bush may bloom again in autumn.

Ligustrum spp. (Privet): Privets are adaptable plants. Prune as much or as little as needed, and whenever you want, all depending on what you want the bush to look like.

Lithocarpus densiflorus (Tanbark Oak): This tree needs little pruning.

Loropetalum chinense: This shrub needs little pruning.

Lyonothamnus floribundus (Catalina Ironwood): This tree needs little pruning beyond the removal of unsightly spent flowers.

Magnolia spp.: Magnolias need little pruning beyond that necessary to develop good form and remove diseased, dead, and misplaced wood. Wounds are slow to heal and susceptible to disease, so make cuts in summer, completely removing some stems or shortening others to branches. Avoid creating large wounds.

× **Mahoberberis spp.:** These bushes need little pruning. Shorten scraggly stems, or cut old ones to the ground, as necessary.

Mahonia spp. (Oregon Grape Holly): The species vary in their growth habits and pruning needs. Generally, prune right after the flowers fade. Upright stems of *M. Bealei* and *M. Fortunei* have a bold visual effect, which should not be disrupted with heading cuts. When a stem grows too old or too tall, just cut it away at ground level to make room for new stems. Bushier species such as *M. Aquifolium* and *M. pinnata* benefit from having their stems shortened to give the plants more fullness and better shape. Periodically cut away the oldest stems. Maintain colonies of plants that spread by underground stems (*M. Aquifolium* 'Compacta', *M. nervosa,* and *M. repens)* by shortening the stems to whatever height you desire.

Malvaviscus arboreus (Wax Mallow, Turk's-cap): Prune anytime during the growing season to keep this vigorous bush tidy and contained. You can also clip wax mallow as a formal hedge.

Maytenus Bouriu (Mayten): Prune just before growth begins. Train mayten as a tree with a single trunk or with multiple trunks. Remove suckers at the base of the tree, and thin branches to keep the crown open.

Melaleuca spp. (Honey Myrtle, Bottlebrush): Prune honey myrtle anytime, bringing out its character as a shrub, developing a single trunk as a tree, or, in the case of *M. hypericifolia* and *M. nesophylla,* shearing the plant as a hedge. Do not expect regrowth from cuts back into old wood.

Michelia spp.: These plants need only corrective pruning to develop a desirable shape. *M. Figo* (Banana Shrub) is happy as a shrub, a clipped hedge, or a tree with multiple trunks. *M. Doltsopa* grows to become a large tree, but is content to look like a shrub in its youth.

Murraya paniculata (Orange Jasmine): Orange jasmine requires no special pruning, and you can grow it as an informal shrub, as a tree, or as a clipped hedge.

Myoporum spp.: These bushy plants, some species of which grow to tree size, need little pruning other than removal of wayward stems and, if trained to trees, lower limbs.

Myrica spp.: These plants are adaptable. Let them grow unrestrained, except for occasional tidying, as informal bushes. Or shear regularly for a formal look. Or prune away lower branches to make a small tree with multiple trunks. Apart from regular shearing as a hedge, prune just before growth begins.

Myrsine africana (Cape Myrtle, African Boxwood): Shear this dense shrub for a formal appearance, or selectively clip wayward stems for a more billowy, informal look.

Myrtus communis (Myrtle, Greek Myrtle): Myrtle is a naturally dense plant even without pruning. Shear for a formal look, or selectively remove branches for an informal look. You can also remove branches to bare the trunk and make a small tree. Selective removal of some upper branches gives the plant a more open look.

Nandina domestica (Heavenly Bamboo): Clean up and make way for new growth by cutting away old, ragged stems at ground level.

Neopanax arboreus (Five-fingers): This tree needs no special pruning beyond the removal of wayward or unhealthy stems.

Nerium Oleander (Common Oleander, Rosebay): This large bush sprouts freely from its base. Prune just before growth begins, limiting plant size by cutting the oldest wood at ground level and shortening overly long stems to side branches. Pinch shoot tips to promote bushiness. You can cut a long-neglected shrub to the ground and it will send up new shoots. By removing lower branches and root suckers, you can train oleander to be a small tree. Be careful of how you dispose of prunings. All parts of the plant are extremely poisonous, and even burning produces an irritating smoke.

Nothofagus spp.: No special directions are needed to prune this genus.

Olmediella Betschlerana (Costa Rican Holly, Puerto Rican Holly, Manzanote): This versatile plant needs little pruning, and can be trained as a shrub or tree, or grown as either a formal or informal hedge.

Osmanthus spp. (Osmanthus, Devil-weed): These plants require little pruning.

Paxistima spp.: *P. Canbyi* (cliff-green) and *P. Myrsinites* (Oregon Boxwood) both are trailing shrubs that require little pruning.

Pernettya mucronata (Pernettya): Pernettya requires little pruning other than removing wayward stems, and occasionally shortening old stems to stimulate new growth. It can be pruned anytime.

Phillyrea decora: This bush has a dense and neat growth habit, so requires no pruning beyond cutting back occasional wayward stems just before growth begins in spring.

Phlomis fruticosa (Jerusalem Sage): To keep this bush from becoming ragged, each year prune stems back by about one-third. Also cut away any thin stems. Plants bloom through spring and summer, and will keep up the pace better if you shorten flowering stems after each flush of flowers.

Photinia spp.: Train the young plant to a few stems. On mature plants, cut stems frequently to stimulate the growth of new red leaves.

Pieris spp. (sometimes mistakenly called Andromeda): Pieris requires little pruning. If necessary, shorten a stem to shape a bush. Cutting back to a group of leaves results in several new sprouts; cutting back into bare wood usually produces only one. Prune right after flowering.

Pittosporum spp.: Pittosporums are adaptable and can be trained as trees, shrubs, or hedges. Cut back wayward stems for an informal look, or shear as needed for a more formal appearance. These plants withstand the heavy pruning needed to remove excess old stems and to bring a plant back into bounds. The species *P. floribundum* grows neither large enough for a tree nor dense enough for a hedge; grow it as a specimen shrub.

Plumbago auriculata (Cape Leadwort): Grow cape leadwort as an informal mound or as a compact bush. Prune after flowering. On informal plants, just cut back lanky stems. For a more compact plant, shorten the youngest stems by about one-third each year; occasionally cut away old stems completely.

(continued on page 104)

Below: The rhododendron bud at right is a terminal growth bud; pinch it off just before growth begins to encourage branching. The fat bud at left is a flower bud.

Right: Branching can also be encouraged by pinching young rhododendron shoots before their leaves fully expand.

Prunus **spp.:** Evergreen species grow as trees or as bushes, with no special pruning needs.

Pyracantha **spp.** (Firethorn): Unpruned, firethorn bushes grow a bit too wild, with their light-starved interiors bearing few berries. Firethorn does tolerate severe pruning, except to leafless stubs, so always prune back to a side branch or to a leaf, or remove a branch completely. Regular pruning, done after the berries drop in winter, consists of shortening wayward stems and thinning dense growth. If you want a more compact bush, pinch the tips of new shoots. If renovation of the whole plant is needed, cut the oldest wood right down to the ground in late winter.

Pyrus Kawakamii (Evergreen Pear): Prune this tree when young to develop a strong framework of branches. Mature trees need periodic pruning to remove dead, diseased, crowded, and old wood.

Quercus **spp.** (Oak): Tree species that develop round heads with age need help in getting their heads up off the ground. Maintain a single, central leader and a framework of subordinate scaffold limbs. Eventually, the leader will lose dominance and the head will spread, high above the ground. From then on, the tree needs little pruning.

Quillaja Saponaria (Soap-bark Tree): A mature soap-bark tree needs little pruning. Branches clothe the trunk all the way to the ground; remove them if you want a clear trunk. In exposed sites, thin branches to let the wind pass through the crown.

Rhododendron **spp.** (Azalea and Rhododendron): Young rhododendrons tend to be leggy. Encourage branching by pinching off terminal growth buds just before growth begins and by pinching growing shoots before their leaves fully expand. (You can recognize terminal growth buds by their slenderness, in contrast to the fat stubbiness of flower buds.) On younger or smaller plants and, where practical, on older plants, remove spent flower heads by bending the stalks over until they break away from the stems. Be careful not to damage the growth buds at the base of each flower stalk.

Mature rhododendrons need little pruning beyond that necessary to shape or renovate the plant, as well as to remove diseased and dead wood. Generally, prune right after flowering. An exception would be *R. maximum* (Rosebay), which flowers late, after shoots have begun growth.

If a rhododendron overgrows its bounds, you can cut the whole bush back drastically as soon as it finishes flowering. Ideally, prepare the bush a year or two before such surgery with mulch and a good supply of moisture and food. Select new main stems from among those that grow after you prune. Rhododendrons do not always push out new growth from old stubs, so play it safe with gradual renovation, cutting back a few old branches each year. Rhododendrons that are particularly reluctant to sprout from old wood include the Falconeri and the Thomsonii series, "tree" rhododendrons, and those with smooth bark. Train these plants by pinching their shoots while the plants are young so that they never need renovation.

In contrast to rhododendrons, azaleas are well supplied with leaves and growth buds all along their stems. Shape and renew azaleas by shortening and removing stems, and promote bushiness by pinching growing tips. If you grow azaleas in a greenhouse, stop pruning by June if you want early flowers. Flower buds usually take eight to ten weeks to develop with temperatures greater than 65°F. The buds then are ready by September (although sometimes plants need to be exposed to long nights also).

Rhus spp. (Sumac): The evergreen sumacs are bushes or bushy trees that need little pruning other than that necessary to shape the plants. Prune them in spring.

Ribes spp. (Currants and Gooseberries): Little pruning is need on either *R. speciosum* (Fuchsia-flowered Gooseberry) or *R. viburnifolium*. Occasionally cut away the oldest stems on the former species.

Rondeletia spp.: Pinch growing tips and shorten stems, right after flowering, to promote bushiness.

Rosmarinus officinalis (Rosemary): Upright varieties such as 'Tuscan Blue' need more pruning than do prostrate varieties such as 'Prostratus' and 'Lockwood de Forest'—but only for the sake of appearance. Rosemary does not sprout new growth from the bare parts of stems, and old wood eventually becomes bare, so you cannot head back an old plant to renovate it. Instead, train the plant when it is young, shortening leafy

young stems right after the flowers fade and pinching the growing tips to promote bushiness.

Salvia spp. (Sage): To keep these bushes neat, cut stems back by half and thin out twigs, or just let the plants grow willy-nilly.

Santolina Chamaecyparissus (Lavender Cotton): This bush is apt to become scraggly, so prune it—severely, if necessary—right after it finishes flowering. If grown as a hedge, prune early in the season, then again after a flush of blooms.

Sarcococca spp. (Sweet Box): Prune these shrubs anytime, occasionally cutting the oldest stems to the ground. *S. Hookerana* and *S. saligna* (Willow-leaf Sarcococca) spread slowly underground, so also remove stems growing out of bounds. You can renovate the shrub by cutting all the stems to the ground.

Schinus spp.: Train both *S. Molle* (California Pepper Tree) and *S. terebinthifolius* (Brazilian Pepper Tree) carefully to a sturdy framework of branches when the trees are young. This is important for *S. Molle* in order to avoid large pruning cuts later, which heal poorly. The wood of *S. terebinthifolius* is brittle, so shorten rangy branches and thin the crown to let wind through the branches. You can also grow *S. Molle* as a sheared hedge.

Severinia buxifolia (Chinese Box Orange): Do any pruning needed in spring to grow this plant as a small tree. Otherwise, shear during the growing season for a hedge.

Simmondsia chinensis (Jojoba): As a specimen shrub, this plant needs little pruning. Shear regularly for a more formal hedge.

Skimmia spp.: Skimmias are naturally slow-growing and dense, so they need little regular pruning.

Sparmannia africana (African Hemp): To tidy up this plant, prune out the oldest stems at ground level and shorten those that are overly long. Another approach is to remove almost all of the stems and grow the plant as a small tree.

(continued on page 106)

Spathodea campanulata (African Tulip Tree, Flame-of-the-forest): When mature, this tree needs little pruning. The wood is brittle, so train a young tree to a strong framework.

Stenocarpus sinuatus (Firewheel Tree): Give this tree good basic training when young, and only occasional maintenance pruning will be needed when it matures.

Stransvaesia Davidiana: Prune Stransvaesia while it is dormant, emphasizing the plant's natural lines and growth habit.

Streptosolen Jamesonii (Fire Bush, Orange Browallia, Marmalade Bush): Prune heavily to contain the plant and to stimulate new growth on which blossoms are borne throughout the growing season. Do this pruning right after flowering ceases or just after frosty weather ends.

***Syzygium* spp.** Neither *S. Jambos* (Rose Apple, Malabar Plum) nor *S. paniculatum* (Australian Brush Cherry) needs extensive or frequent pruning. Just shorten misplaced stems in spring. You can shear or clip Australian brush cherry as a formal or informal hedge.

Tecoma stans (Yellow Bells, Yellow Elder): Yellow bells is a bush that needs only basic maintenance pruning just before growth begins in spring. You can also train the plant as a small tree with one or more trunks. Remove faded blossoms to prolong the flowering period.

Tecomaria capensis (Cape Honeysuckle): Unchecked, cape honeysuckle turns into a sprawling bush. If this is the form that you want, just remove wayward branches right after blossoms fade. To grow it more like a vine, allow the plant to grow only a few stems; cut all others to the ground.

Tetrapanax papyriferus (Rice-paper Plant): Each stem of this plant is capped by flowers, with two shoots angling up and out from beneath each flower like the letter Y. Periodically thin out the stems, at ground level, to restrict their number, or remove all but one trunk. Also shape the plant by shortening stems up in the plant. Side branches will grow when you cut back to the middle of a stem, but regrowth rarely occurs when you cut back to a side branch. Avoid touching new growth to bare skin, because it is highly irritating.

***Teucrium* spp.** (Germander): Prune regularly only if you want your plant to look neater. Do so by shortening shoots in late winter, then again one or two times during the summer. To renovate the whole plant, cut it almost to the ground in late winter, and thin out any remaining twiggy growth.

Thevetia peruviana (Yellow Oleander): This large bush sprouts freely from its base. Prune just before growth begins, limiting plant size by cutting the oldest wood to the ground and shortening overly long stems to side shoots. Pinch shoot tips during the growing season to promote bushiness. You can cut a long-neglected shrub to the ground and it will send up new shoots. By removing lower branches and diligently removing root suckers, you can train the plant as a small tree. If you do so, thin out the crown to keep it open or else wind is liable to topple over this shallow-rooted plant.

Tibouchina Urvilleana (Glory Bush, Lasiandra, Pleroma): Pinching shoots and shortening lanky stems keep this plant bushy and compact. Quickly revitalize an overgrown bush by lopping everything to the ground. New shoots will sprout.

Trichostema lanatum (Romero, Woolly Blue-curls): Pinch shoot tips to promote branching. Also cut back stems after they flower to promote additional flowering and branching.

Triphasia trifolia (Limeberry): Little pruning is needed.

***Tristania* spp.:** None of the commonly cultivated species needs much pruning.

Pruning *Tetrapanax* (Rice-paper Plant)

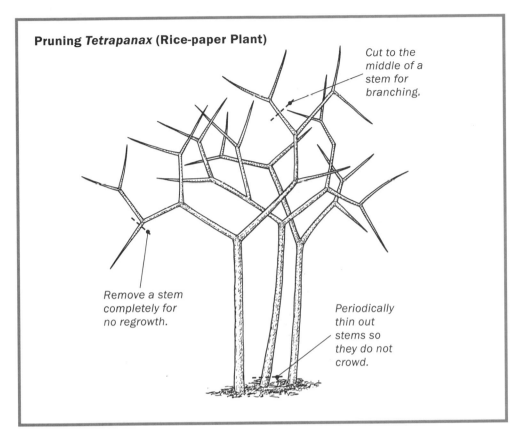

Cut to the middle of a stem for branching.

Remove a stem completely for no regrowth.

Periodically thin out stems so they do not crowd.

Turraea obtusifolia (South African Honeysuckle): Prune this bush anytime that suits your needs.

Umbellularia californica (California Bay, California Laurel, Pepperwood): California bay needs little pruning beyond initial training if allowed to develop as a tree. You can grow this plant as a hedge, in which case prune in spring and again, if necessary, in summer. If you want to renovate or dramatically reshape this plant, cut it back severely.

Viburnum **spp.:** Prune an evergreen viburnum just before growth begins only as needed to give the plant a pleasant shape.

Vitex lucens (Pururi): Train pururi when young to have either a single trunk or multiple trunks. Subsequent pruning needs are minimal, just the removal of misplaced, dead, and twiggy wood.

Xylosma congestum: Xylosma is a most adaptable plant—you can prune it to be a single or multi-trunked small tree, an espalier, a creeping ground cover, a formal or informal hedge, even a living sculpture. Whatever your goal, prune as severely as necessary just before growth begins. Or don't prune xylosma at all, and let it grow as an informal shrub.

Yucca **spp.:** Prune flower stalks back to the whorl of leaves after flowering ceases. At that time, also thin out offshoots to prevent overcrowding. On treelike species, cut out-of-place branches back to where they meet other branches or the trunk.

Palm trees

Palm trees, although broadleaf evergreens, warrant a special section because there are so many genera and species, and they can all be pruned in essentially the same manner. Palm trees grow from their tips, rarely branching, so there is little that you can do to shape a plant. (*Hyphaene thebaica*, Gingerbread

THE BARE BONES

PALM TREES

CUT AWAY excess or dying trunks at ground level.

CUT OFF old leaves and fruits if they present a hazard.

As this palm grows taller, its older leaves should be pruned off.

Palm, is a notable exception.) Some palms grow new trunks at ground level. If a cluster of various-aged trunks becomes overcrowded or too wide, cut unwanted trunks down to the ground. With some species, old trunks die after fruiting—remove the dead trunk at ground level. Still other palms have one major trunk, but occasionally send up one or more new ones from the ground. These palms look best with single trunks, so remove upstarts when they appear.

Beyond trunk removal, other pruning of palms consists of removing old flower clusters, fruits, and dead fronds, mostly to clean up the trees. A heavy fruit such as a coconut does not look bad, but is a hazard if it drops onto someone's head. Dead fronds can similarly present a hazard of dropping on an unsuspecting passerby, or can harbor rodents. Fronds with spiny leaflets can cut skin, and dry fronds present a fire hazard. And anyway, dead fronds spoil the look of a plant.

Remove dead fronds in two stages. First hack back the leaf stalk almost to its base, using a machete to make two cuts that leave an upside-down V. A year later, the remaining base of the dead stalk will be easy to pull off, or the base will have fallen off by itself.

Prune fruits, fronds, and stems from palm trees whenever needed.

Bamboo

Bamboos warrant their own section here because, although they represent many genera and species, their pruning needs are essentially uniform. Pruning bamboo consists of cutting away old canes to the ground. Do no cutting for the first three years after the plants are set in the ground, to allow the planting to establish itself. After that, a general rule is to remove canes that are three years old (or

older, if you have been remiss) to make room for new canes. Thin out two-year-old canes also if you want new canes to grow thicker, but avoid excessive thinning of a grove or plants will not be able to create the shade they need.

To emphasize the vertical look of a clump or a grove of bamboo, cut off lower side branches if they appear.

Also prune to control growth, if needed. For hedging, lop off the tops of the plants when they reach the desired height. Never cut off the top of a bamboo cane below where it has leafed out or that cane is liable to die. Limit the underground spread of "running" bamboos by cutting down all canes at the boundary of the grove. A lawnmower is effective against young shoots. Sinking a barrier of metal, concrete, or other impenetrable material 2 ft. into the soil will keep the roots from spreading.

A grove of yellow-groove bamboo is mysteriously inviting.

THE BARE BONES

BAMBOO

CUT to the ground canes that are three years old, or older.

KEEP running types of bamboo from spreading beyond their allotted space.

CHAPTER SEVEN

ORNAMENTAL VINES

Honeysuckle festoons a wall.

Vines are long-stemmed plants that grow skyward, but only if they get help. To get themselves up off the ground, they borrow the support of nearby trees or bushes, walls, posts, pergolas, wires, fences, even (unfortunately) downspouts and gutters.

The mere proximity of a plant with long stems to a support does not get those stems skyward. The vine needs a way to grip. Along the stems of English ivy are aerial rootlets that insinuate themselves into tiny holes in mortar and bricks and hold the plant as it grows upward. Grape tendrils are actually modified leaves that quickly close around whatever they touch, pulling the plant upward hand over hand (tendril over tendril). It is the leaf stalks themselves of clematis that twine, in a similar manner, around any available support. At the tips of the tendrils of a vine such as Virginia creeper grow little discs, called holdfasts, that both look and act like suction cups. And finally there are those vines that whose stems simply flail around in space until they touch a suitable object thin enough to twine around. Each twining vine's upward mobility starts with an innate twist. Japanese wisteria, for

THE BARE BONES

ORNAMENTAL VINES

CUT newly planted vines almost to the ground in order to force new growth into just one or a few shoots.

PRUNE OUT tangled or dead stems.

TO CONTROL SIZE, cut the oldest stems back to their bases or to low, healthy side shoots.

PINCH OR CUT BACK unruly growth in summer.

DO the bulk of pruning on early-flowering vines right after flowers fade. With vines flowering from summer onwards, or with vines whose flowers and fruits are inconsequential, prune just before growth begins for the season.

example, is a clockwise twiner, while Chinese wisteria twines counterclockwise.

The long stems of a few plants have no means for clinging to a support. Such plants—bougainvillea, aralia ivy, and *Forsythia suspensa*, for example—are perhaps best considered as sprawling bushes, and are treated as bushes in this book. Planted against a wall, they may press upward for a distance, lacking anywhere else to go. These plants can be grown like bona-fide vines if they are restricted to only a few stems, and those stems are tied to some support. Then again, some of the self-climbing vines included in this chapter could be grown as sprawling bushes if their stems were headed and pinched to encourage low branching and discourage lanky growth. With even stricter pruning, a clinging vine such as wisteria can even be trained as a tree, with a trunk that eventually supports the head.

Pruning while training

All perennial vines need pruning as soon as they are planted. Channel the plant's energy into one or a few stems to induce a rapid climb up the support. Do this by cutting away extraneous shoots or by pinching their tips to slow their growth.

Depending on the plant's growth habit and the plant's support, you may opt for a single permanent stem, a few permanent stems, or a permanent stem with permanent side arms growing from it (see the drawing on p. 112). The permanent stems to which a vine is cut back to each year are called cordons. A plant such as silver lace vine or a late-flowering clematis, which grows vigorously and flowers only on new

'Heavenly Blue' is the variety name and color of this morning-glory; no pruning is needed.

Three Ways to Train a Woody Vine

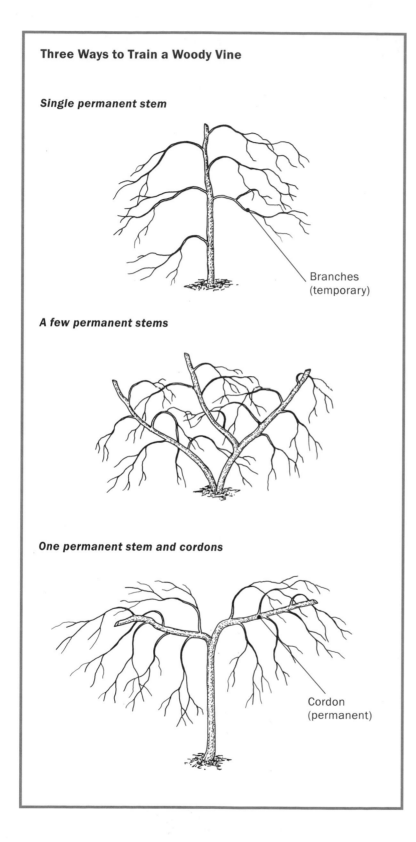

Single permanent stem

Branches
(temporary)

A few permanent stems

One permanent stem and cordons

Cordon
(permanent)

growth, does not need any permanent stems or cordons, because you prune each year by lopping all growth nearly back to the ground.

Maintenance pruning

A few kinds of vines need little or no regular pruning. Examples are annual vines, such as morning-glory and cardinal climber, on which you want maximum growth from the start to the end of the growing season. Other examples include some vines that are allowed to ramble over the ground, like bittersweet, which is naturally unruly and looks right at home billowing over low mounds of earth and enveloping old tree stumps. (Even so, a vine used as groundcover may need drastic mowing every few years to prevent the buildup of an increasingly thick mat of old stems.) And yet another example is any vigorous vine permitted to express its full vigor using a living tree as support. *Clematis montana* or climbing hydrangeas are sometimes grown this way, unfettered. But the tree and the vine must be well matched, or one will suffocate the other.

Aside from the above exceptions, most vines, once they have climbed their support, need at least a little annual pruning—and some vines will need more than a little. Cut away dead and diseased stems, as well as those that are spindly. Depending on what the vine is climbing on, annual pruning may be necessary to control growth. In the wild, many ornamental vines clamber into trees, so that eventually only birds can appreciate the parts of the vine with leaves and flowers. For most ornamental uses, we want leaves and flowers in sight and, in the case of fragrant flowers, near nose level; periodic removal of old stems keeps leafy and florific younger stems low on the plant.

Pruning is also needed to keep an ornamental vine looking ornamental. Periodically cutting away old stems low in the plant not only brings leaves and flowers low, but also disentangles stems. Without pruning, the plant eventually becomes an unsightly mass of dead, diseased, and weak stems because of shading and crowding.

Regular pruning also helps those vines that are grown for flowers to put on their best show. Plants whose blooms appear on vigorous growth of the current season benefit most from the stimulation of new growth by pruning, and such vines can be lopped clear down to the ground just before growth begins each season. These vines also can be allowed to use a nearby shrub for support (a late-flowering clematis returning the favor on an early-blooming lilac, for example), because a yearly lopping back prevents the vine from engulfing the shrub. Pruning has less effect on the flowering of vines whose blooms appear on shoots growing from older wood.

Generally, the time for pruning a vine is just before growth begins, while the plant is still dormant. With vines that flower early in the season, you can wait to prune until after flowers fade so that you do not sacrifice any of the show. Summer pruning, in addition to dormant pruning, helps keep an overly rampant vine in check, and results in tighter growth on other vines when a more formal effect is desired.

Renovation

A vine whose growth is out of hand—or an inherited monster—is easy to renovate. Just cut the whole plant almost to the ground. Then, from among the new sprouts, select one or a few stems with which to rebuild the plant anew.

Left: An oak tree provides support for a wisteria vine.

Below: Bittersweet can be trained, but also looks good left to its own whims.

Plant List

ORNAMENTAL VINES

Akebia quinata (Five-leaf Akebia): Control growth by thinning out stems just before growth begins or just after flowering. Remove stems that are spindly or tangled, and, if you prune after flowering, stems that have flowered.

Allamanda cathartica (Allamand, Golden-trumpet): Prune lightly just before growth begins.

Ampelopsis **spp.:** The twining stems of some species are very vigorous *(A. brevipedunculata* var. *Maximowiczii,* for example) and can be left to climb up trees without restraint. On an arbor or pergola, keep growth in check by shortening some stems each year. Or, even neater, train one or more stems as permanent cordons, then cut back the stems each year to within a few buds of the cordons while the plants are dormant. Over the years, picturesque knobby stubs will build up where you keep shortening the stems. Other species, including *A. arborea* (Pepper Vine) and *A. humulifolia,* similarly need their stems shortened and thinned out. In addition, dig out unwanted suckers from spreading roots of *A. arborea.*

Anemopaegma Chamberlaynii: Prune this tendriled vine lightly in spring to keep it in bounds, then again after the flowers fade, removing spindly stems and overly rampant growth.

Antigonon leptopus (Coral Vine): Shorten and remove stems, when and as needed, to control growth and avoid a dense tangle of living and dead stems.

Aristolochia **spp.:** Prune these vigorous twiners to keep them in bounds. They flower early and on one-year-old wood, so cut out excess growth right after the flowers fade.

Beaumontia grandiflora (Herald's-trumpet, Easter-lily Vine): Depending on where this plant is grown, flowers appear either on current shoots (in Florida) or on shoots two years old and older (in California). Prune severely in the latter case, lightly in the former.

Berberidopsis corallina: Prune this twining vine lightly just before growth begins.

Bignonia capreolata (Cross Vine, Trumpet Flower): Just before growth begins, remove suckers and shorten shoots that flowered previously to a few buds. If more growth control is needed, cut back stems as they grow.

Celastrus scandens (Bittersweet): When the plant is dormant, cut off tangled branches and those that have fruits—they are decorative indoors. Also shorten the previous season's growth. Pinch shoot tips in summer to promote branching.

Cissus **spp.** (Grape Ivy, Treebine): These vines require little pruning. Prune only to control growth, disentangle stems, and remove weak, diseased, or dead stems.

Clematis **spp.:** Cut all clematis vines to within a few inches of the ground when you plant them in order to force new shoots from the base of the plant and from below ground. From then on, the pruning method depends on the growth and flowering habit of the particular plant (see the sidebar on pp. 118-121).

Clytostoma callistegioides (Argentine Trumpet Vine, Love-charm): Tendrils of this rampant grower cling to almost anything. Cut the plant back whenever needed to keep growth in check.

Cryptostegia **spp.** (Rubber Vine): Prune after the flowers fade.

Distictis **spp.:** Depending on the vigor of the vine and the space allotted, prune as needed to control growth. Species vary in their vigor, from the weak-growing *D. laxiflora* to the stronger-growing *D. buccinatoria* (Blood-trumpet) to the strongest grower, *D.* × *Riversii.*

Euonymus Fortunei: Varieties of this plant run the spectrum, from those that are shrubby to those that are vining, climbing with aerial roots. Prune vining plants as needed to keep them in bounds. Do most of the pruning early in the season, then prune more lightly, as needed, as the plant grows. When grown as a groundcover, the vines need to be severely cut back every few years to prevent the buildup of an increasingly thick mat of old stems.

Ficus pumila (Creeping Fig, Climbing Fig): Prune whenever and to whatever degree necessary to control growth. Eventually, the ends of stems become mature, producing larger leaves and bearing fruit. Periodically shear the plant back if you want to retain its smaller leaves and prevent its maturing.

Gelsemium sempervirens (Yellow Jessamine, Carolina Jasmine; Trumpet Flower): Prune after flowering to get rid of dead and broken stems, then shear back remaining growth.

Hardenbergia spp.: Prune these twining vines after flowering to control growth and to remove tangled and old or weak stems.

Hedera Helix (English Ivy): Prune English ivy as needed to keep the vine within bounds. Do major pruning in the spring, then follow up through the season. Severely cut down English ivy used as a groundcover every few years to prevent a mat of old stems from building up. With time, ivy may take on a mature growth habit. It then grows as a bush rather than a vine, has unlobed leaves, and bears flowers followed by berries. You can prevent your plant from becoming mature by pruning it severely. The basal portion of even a mature plant always remains juvenile.

Hibbertia scandens (Snake Vine, Gold Guinea Plant): Prune early in the season, before flowers open, removing overcrowded and tangled stems.

Holboellia spp.: Prune lightly, as needed, to get rid of weak stems and contain rampant ones.

Hydrangea anomala petiolaris (Climbing Hydrangea): Prune just before growth begins by cutting back overly vigorous stems and shortening flowering stems that are growing too far out from the wall or other support. Pruning also stimulates the growth of new shoots, on which flowers are borne.

Ipomoea spp. (Morning-glory): Cut perennial species of this twining vine to the ground before growth begins for the season. Annual species require no pruning.

Jasminum spp. (Jasmine): Jasmine is a twining vine that flowers on old stems. Each year, right after flowering, cut back one-third of the old stems to make way for, and stimulate the growth of, new ones that will flower the following year.

Lapageria rosea (Chilean Bellflower, Chile-bells): This twining vine needs little pruning, which can be done whenever necessary.

Lonicera spp. (Honeysuckle): Depending on the species, flowers are produced early in the season on short branches growing off previous year's stems, or later in the season on longer, current growth. Prune those plants that flower early—which include *L. Periclymenum* (Woodbine), *L. × Tellmanniana*, and *L. tragophylla*— right after flowering. Cut back some flowering wood and thin out weak growth. Prune late-flowering vines just before growth begins, shortening old stems and removing those that are overcrowded. More vigorous species, such as *L. japonica* (Japanese Honeysuckle) need more ruthless cutting back than moderate growers, such as *L. Hildebrandiana* (Giant Burmese Honeysuckle, the "giant" being the leaves and flowers) and *L. sempervirens* (Trumpet Honeysuckle).

Macfadyena Unguis-cati (Cat's-claw, Funnel Creeper): Just before growth begins remove suckers and stems that flowered previously. Cut low in the plant to keep it full from the ground up.

Mandevilla spp.: Prune just before growth begins, removing enough twining stems so that they are not too tangled. Mandevilla blooms on new growth so you can lop the whole plant back severely if necessary. Pinch shoot tips if you want to promote further branching.

Mandevilla in all its tropical splendor.

(continued on page 116)

***Muehlenbeckia* spp.** (Wire Plant): Masses of wiry stems give wire plant its common name. Prune them back as much as needed whenever they grow out of bounds.

Oxera pulchella (Royal Climber): Prune to contain growth and remove dead stems, right after the flowers fade. Unpruned, the stems pile together to form a shrublike plant.

***Pandorea* spp.:** Prune as needed to retain healthy growth and to keep the plant within bounds.

***Parthenocissus* spp.** (Woodbine): All woodbines require similar pruning. Just before growth begins, cut away stems growing out of bounds. With *P. quinquefolia* (Virginia Creeper) and *P. tricuspidata* (Boston Ivy), which cling to surfaces by holdfasts, also cut away stems whose holdfasts have come loose—they cannot grip a surface again. Cut back wayward stems on all species throughout the growing season.

Pileostegia viburnoides: This vine, which clings by aerial roots, needs little pruning apart from shortening the flowering branches in spring if they become so long and heavy that they threaten to pull the plant off its support.

Polygonum Aubertii (Silver Lace Vine): Just before growth begins each season, heavy pruning will stimulate an abundance of new shoots, on which flowers are borne. You can even prune the plant down to the ground each year to get it started.

Pyrostegia venusta (Flame Vine, Golden-shower): Flame vine is a rampant grower that flowers on new shoots, so prune heavily in winter to keep the vine in bounds and to stimulate new growth.

Rhoicissus capensis (Cape Grape, Evergreen Grape): Pinch growing tips and cut away stems as needed during the growing season.

Schizophragma hydrangeoides (Hydrangea Vine): Prune just before growth begins by cutting back overly vigorous extension shoots. Shorten flowering shoots where they grow out too far out from their supporting wall or fence. Pruning also stimulates the growth of new shoots, on which flowers are borne. Plants allowed to ramble over the ground or to climb naturally up trees need no pruning.

Solandra guttata (Goldcup, Trumpet Plant): Promote new growth and branching by heading stems severely and pinching the growing shoots. The stems are thick for a vine, and if you prune severely and frequently enough through the season, you have a goldcup shrub—somewhat wild—rather than a goldcup vine.

***Solanum* spp.:** Prune these vines just before growth begins to untangle their stems, limit size, and stimulate new flowering shoots. Through the growing season, cut back wayward shoots. Species vary in vigor, so different species require different degrees of pruning. With more severe and frequent pruning, many species become shrubby.

Sollya heterophylla (Bluebell Creeper, Australian Bluebells): Prune early in the season to direct and control growth.

Stauntonia hexaphylla: Flowers are borne in the axils of new shoots, so prune the stems almost to the ground or to a permanent framework each year, just before growth begins.

Tetrastigma Voinieranum (Chestnut Vine, Lizard Plant): Cut back the vining stems whenever necessary.

Trachelospermum jasminoides (Star Jasmine, Confederate Jasmine): Lightly prune this vine, which clings by means of aerial roots, just before growth begins.

***Wisteria* spp.:** Wisteria is a naturally twining vine that can take many forms—a two-dimensional covering against a wall, a three-dimensional blanket over an arbor, or a freestanding (with the initial help of a stake) tree or shrub. Whatever the form, in new plants encourage the strong growth of shoots that will comprise the main framework of the "finished" plant. This framework consists of a trunk and one or more main arms. To encourage side shoots in the developing plant, head back stems intended to become the permanent framework to about 3 ft. each winter until they have grown as long as you want them to. Subsequently, head them back each year, in midsummer, to where they started growing for that season.

Wisteria often is reluctant to settle down and flower. Sometimes this is the fault of the gardener, and sometimes it's only a matter of time (especially if plants have been grown from seed). Flowers are borne near the bases of growing shoots, but not if a plant is growing too vigorously. Avoid severe annual pruning, which stimulates excessively vigorous growth. If a plant continues to grow too vigorously despite your non-efforts, try root pruning too slow it down.

An even better way to slow growth and coax the maximum number of blossoms from wisteria is with a combination of summer and winter pruning of side shoots. About midsummer, prune each side shoot back to it about 6 in. long. This will only temporarily check growth; the plant soon will grow new shoots. Go over each of these branches again in winter, shortening them to two or three buds. This is also a good time to remove any stems that are too tangled.

There are other variations on pruning wisteria: pinching out the tips of all side shoots a few times during the growing season; cutting side shoots monthly to two or three buds; or shortening side shoots to 6 in. every two weeks throughout the summer. Any of these methods is especially useful when you want the tighter and more florific habit needed for a tree wisteria or more formal espaliered wisteria. Nonetheless, many people are disinclined to pay any attention to their wisteria vine once bloom is past, and are willing to sacrifice some bloom. They can follow the advice of Liberty Hyde Bailey, writing in 1927 in his *Standard Cyclopaedia of Horticulture:* "There are several ideas about

training wisteria. A good way is to let it alone. This produces rugged, twisted, and picturesque branches and gives a certain oriental effect, but is not the best method for covering a wall-space solidly or for making the best display of bloom."

Left: Detail pruning puts the dripping lavender-colored wisteria blossoms where you want them.

Below: Minimum pruning produces a rugged old wisteria.

CLEMATIS: A Pruner's Guide

The numerous species and hybrids of clematis can be lumped into one of three pruning groups based on whether flowers form on new wood, (Group 1) on old wood (Group 2), or on a little of both (Group 3). Plants within each group can be pruned similarly. If you are not sure which group a plant belongs to, let the plant grow freely for a year or two, and watch how it flowers.

Following the description of each group and instructions for pruning is an alphabetical listing of species and varieties in the group. (Varieties may represent a species or hybrids of two or more species— hence the separate listings of species, then varieties.) Where a variety name is assigned to more than one species, or hybrids of species, the species or hybrid origin is listed in parentheses after the variety name.

**PRUNING A
GROUP 1
CLEMATIS**

1. *Clematis paniculata*, a Group 1 clematis, in late winter.

2. Begin by cutting the stems loose from the building.

3. Next start pulling the vine down.

4. A quick tug gets most of the vine all at once.

5. Thin out stems near ground, leaving about 1 ft. of growth.

6. The completed pruning job.

GROUP 1

Clematis in this group bear their flowers late in the season, from summer through autumn, toward the end of new shoots.

Group 1 is the easiest to prune. Just before growth begins for the season, lop all stems back to strong buds within 1 ft. or so of the ground. There is no need to cut back so severely if you are going to let the plant ramble high into a tree. Certain plants in this category, such as *C. orientalis* and *C. tangutica*, start blooming earlier and then continue longer if they are not cut back so hard.

The following species and varieties are included in this group:

C. Addisonii
C. aethusifolia
C. akebioides
C. apiifolia
C. × aromatica
C. brachiata
C. Buchananiana
C. campaniflora
C. chiisanensis
C. chinensis
C. connata
C. crispa
C. × cylindrica
C. Douglasii
C. Drummondii
C. × Durandii
C. × eriostemon
C. Fargesii soullei
C. finetiana
C. Flammula

C. fusca
C. gentianoides
C. glauca
C. heracleifolia
C. × huldine
C. integrifolia
C. × Jouiniana
C. ladakhiana
C. ochotensis
C. ochroleuca
C. orientalis
C. paniculata
C. Pitcheri
C. recta
C. Rehderana
C. serratifolia
C. songarica
C. speciosa
C. stans
C. tangutica
C. tangutica var. obtusiuscula
C. ternifolia
C. texensis
C. thibetana
C. tosaensis
C. triternata
C. uncinata
C. versicolor
C. Viorna
C. Vitalba
C. Viticella

'Abundance'
'Alba' (C. integrifolia)
'Alba Luxurians'
'Allanah'
'Anna'
'Ascotiensis'
'Bill MacKenzie'
'Blue Boy'
'Campanile'
'Cardinal Wyszynski'
'Carmencita'
'Comtesse de Bouchaud'
'Davidiana'
'Drake's Form'
'Duchess of Albany'
'Edward Pritchard'
'Elvan'
'Étoile Rose'
'Gipsy Queen'
'Gravetye Beauty'
'Hendersonii'
'John Huxtable'
'Kermesina'

'King George V'
'Lady Betty Balfour'
'Ladybird Johnson'
'Little Nell'
'Mme. Baron Veillard'
'Mme. Édouard André'
'Mme. Grangé'
'Mme. Julia Correvon'
'Margaret Hunt'
'Margot Koster'
'Mary Rose'
'Minuet'
'Mrs. Robert Brydon'
'Olgae'
'Pagoda'
'Pastel Pink'
'Perle d'Azur'
'Peveril'
'Pink Fantasy'
'Prince Charles'
'Purpurea'
'Purpurea Plena Élegans'
'Rosea' (C. douglasii and C. crispa)
'Rouge Cardinal'
'Royal Velours'
'Rubra' (C. viticella)
'Rubro-marginata'
'Sir Trevor Lawrence'
'Star of India'
'Tango'
'Tapestry'
'Princess of Wales'
'Twilight'
'Venosa Violacea'
'Victoria'
'Voluceau'
'Warsaw Nike'
'Wyevale'

GROUP 2

Clematis in this group bear their flowers early in the season, in the leaf axils of the previous year's stems.

Group 2 is also relatively easy to prune. Prune severely as soon as the flowers fade, cutting the whole plant to within 1 ft. or so of the ground. You have to be a little careful, because very old stems may not resprout following severe cutting. Either do not cut the plant back into very old wood (in which case the plant gets larger and larger each year), or at least do not cut back all of the stems, or have a young replacement stem ready in case the plant dies. You can also train these plants to cordons. Then, each year right after flowering, cut back stems that bore flowers to within a few inches of the cordon.

No matter which way you grow plants in this group, the new shoots that appear following pruning are those that will bear flowers the following season. To some degree, the less you shorten stems one season, the earlier the blossoms appear the following season.

Also, because members of this group vary in their vigor, they likewise vary in the amount of pruning they need to control their size. *C. montana* and *C. Armandii*, for example, are extremely vigorous, while little wood needs to be removed from weak growers such as *C. alpina* and *C. macropetala*. You may even have to pinch and shorten shoots of vigorous growers in summer to keep growth in check.

The following species and varieties are included in this group:

C. afoliata
C. alpina
C. alpina sibirica
C. Armandii
C. australis
C. chrysocoma
C. cirrhosa
C. cirrhosa var. balearica
C. columbiana
C. foetida
C. Forsteri
C. gentianoides
C. hexasepala
C. hookeriana
C. indivisa
C. × jeuneana
C. macropetala
C. marata
C. marmoraria
C. Meyeniana
C. montana
C. nepalensis
C. ochotensis
C. parviflora
C. petriei
C. phlebantha
C. quinquefoliata

Bud on 'Crimson Star', a Group 2 clematis.

C. Spooneri
C. uncinata
C. × vedrariensis
C. verticillaris

'Alexander'
'Apple Blossom'
'Blue Bird'
'Burford White'
'Candy'
'Columbine'
'Continuity'
'Crimson Star'
'Elizabeth'
'Francis Rivis'
'Frankie'
'Grandiflora'
'Highdown'
'Jacqueline du Pré'
'Louise'
'Madeleine'
'Maidwell Hall'
'Markham's Pink'

'Pamela Jackman'
'Peveril'
'Picton's Variety'
'Rosy O'Grady '
'Rosy Pagoda'
'Rubens'
'Ruby'
'Snowbird'
'Snowdrift'
'Tetrarose'
'White Columbine'
'White Moth'
'Willy'
'Wilsonii'
'Wisley'

GROUP 3

Clematis in this group flower more or less throughout the season on both new shoots and older stems, with the bulk of the flowers usually appearing during the summer. Some of these plants bear a profusion of early flowers on short shoots, and then another crop of flowers later in the season. Those plants with large flowers typically bear them on the ends of longer shoots.

Pruning this group is a little trickier than pruning the other groups. If you cut a plant back sharply before growth begins, you miss the earliest flowers. But if you prune severely after the first flush of blooms, you miss the later ones. No wonder that the recommendation is often made not to prune at all. But then the plant becomes a tangled mess.

In fact, Group 3 clematis can be contained by pruning without undue sacrifice of flowers. One option is to cut back the whole plant drastically every few years just before growth begins, with little or no pruning in the intervening time; in this case you give up only the earliest blossoms of one season. Or divide the plant in half, and severely prune each half in alternate years. The most refined approach is to thin out lightly and disentangle stems before growth begins, then go over the plants again after the earliest flowers fade, severely shortening the stems that have borne those flowers.

The following plants are included in this group:

C. florida
C. fusca
C. × Jackmanii
C. japonica
C. × phlebantha
C. Potaninii

'Alba (C. × Jackmanii)'
'Alba Plena'
'Alice Fisk'
'Andrew'
'Annabel'
'Asao'
'Barbara Dibley'
'Barbara Jackman'
'Bees Jubilee'
'Belle Nantaise'
'Belle of Woking'
'Blue Diamond'
'Bracebridge Star'
'Capitaine Thuilleaux'
'Carnaby'
'Cassiopeia'
'Chalcedony'
'Charissima'
'Corona'
'Countess of Lovelace'
'Crimson King'

'C. W. Dowman'
'Daniel Deronda'
'Dawn'
'Dr. Ruppel'
'Duchess of Edinburgh'
'Edith'
'Edouard Desfossé'
'Elizabeth Foster'
'Elsa Späth'
'Empress of India'
'Étoile de Malicorne'
'Étoile de Paris'
'Fair Rosamond'
'Fairy Queen'
'Fireworks'
'Four Star'
'General Sikorski'
'Gillian Blades'
'Gladys Picard'
'Gokonosho '
'Guiding Star'
'Haku Ookan'
'Henryi'
'Herbert Johnson'
'H.F. Young'
'Hidcote Purple'
'Horn of Plenty'
'Imperial'
'Ishobel'
'James Mason'
'Jim Hollis'
'Joan Picton'
'Joan Wilcox'
'John Paul II'
'Kacper'
'Karin'
'Kathleen Dunford'
'Kathleen Wheeler'
'Keith Richardson'
'Ken Donson'
'King Edward VII'
'Kiri Te Kanawa'
'Lady Londesborough'
'Lasurstern'
'Lawsonia'
'Lincoln Star'
'Lord Nevill'
'Louise Rowe'
'Mammut'
'Marcel Moser'
'Miriam Markham'
'Miss Bateman'
'Miss Crawshay'
'Moonlight'
'Mrs. Bush'

'Mrs. George
  Jackman'
'Mrs. James Mason'
'Mrs. N. Thompson'
'Mrs. Oud'
'Mrs. P.B. Truax'
'Mrs. Spencer Castle'
'Myojo'
'Nelly Moser'
'Pennell's Purity'
'Percy Lake'
'Percy Picton'
'Peveril Pearl'
'Phoenix'
'Prince of Wales'
'Prins Hendrik'
'Proteus'
'Rouge Cardinal'
'Royalty'
'Rubra (C. ×
  Jackmanii)'
'Saturn'
'Scartho Gem'
'Sealand Gem'
'Sir Garnet Wolseley'
'Snow Queen'
'Superba'
'Susan Allsop'
'Syliva Denny'
'The President'
'Titania'
'Veronica's Choice'
'Violet Elizabeth'
'Vyvyan Pennell'
'Wada's Primrose'
'Walter Pennell'
'Wilhemina Tull'
'Will Goodwin'
'William Kennett'

GROUP 4

Uh oh, another group? Clematis do not fall as neatly as one would hope into the three flowering groups, and a few varieties choose to straddle the fence between Groups 1 and 3.

Prune these plants heavily before growth begins, and you get a profusion of blossoms late in the season. Just prune lightly and you get larger blossoms that are borne early and then repeat occasionally through the summer — but the plants also keep growing larger and larger. The dilemma is similar to that faced with Group 3, except more so. So prune Group 4 clematis severely every other year, or else divide the plant in half and severely prune each half in alternate years, in each case, just before growth begins.

The following plants are included in this group:

C. fargesii var. *souliei*

'Beauty of Richmond'
'Beauty of Worcester'
'Blue Gem'
'Corona'
'Daniel Deronda'

'Duchess of
  Sutherland'
Ernest Markham'
'Hagley Hybrid'
'John Warren'
'Lady Caroline Nevill'
'Lady Northcliffe'
'Marie Boisselot'
'Maureen'
'Mrs. Cholmondeley'
'Mrs. Hope'
'Niobe'
'Richard Pennell'
'Serenata'
'Sieboldii'
'Silver Moon'
'Venus Victrix'
'Ville de Lyon'
'Violet Charm'
'W.E. Gladstone'

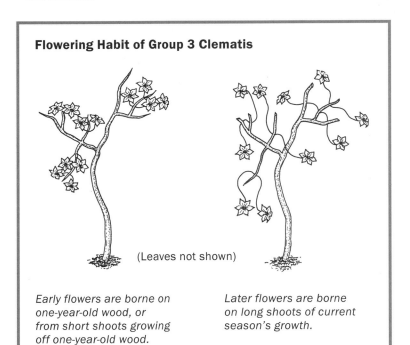

Flowering Habit of Group 3 Clematis

(Leaves not shown)

Early flowers are borne on one-year-old wood, or from short shoots growing off one-year-old wood.

Later flowers are borne on long shoots of current season's growth.

CHAPTER EIGHT

EDIBLE FRUITS AND NUTS

This luscious bounty is the result of regular— and correct—pruning.

Most fruit and nut plants require regular pruning. Even those plants that bear reasonable crops without such care will usually bear more or better fruits if pruned. (Nuts are fruits, so I will herewith dispense with repeating "and nuts" every time I write "fruits.")

Think of the sweetness of a perfectly ripe pear or strawberry: That sweetness comes from sugar, a carbohydrate, the fuel that energizes cells in plants. Producing luscious fruits demands lots of energy from a plant, so your aim in pruning fruits is first to ensure that the plant has enough energy to make the fruits, and then to direct a good portion of that energy to the fruits themselves.

Since sunlight is the ultimate source of energy, allowing the plant to combine carbon dioxide and water to make stored energy, or carbohydrates, you will use your pruning tools to help the plant— tree, bush, or vine—drink in as much sunshine as possible. Left to their own devices, most fruit plants eventually shade themselves to the point of bearing relatively few fruits for the size of the plant, and poor-quality fruits at that.

Keeping the canopy of branches open has two other benefits specific to fruit plants. An open canopy allows sprays to penetrate those plants that require spraying. And good air circulation and sunlight speed the drying of leaves and fruits, decreasing the incidence of disease.

You are also going to use pruning to apportion energy within your fruit plant, balancing the amount of leaf and shoot growth with the amount of fruits ripened. Leaves are needed to capture the sun's energy and shoots are needed on which to hang fruits. But beyond what is needed for these purposes, what we demand of these plants is fruit! (I am getting a little carried away here—fruit plants do gratify also with their beauty, and some make great climbing trees.)

Have you ever noticed a wild apple tree, blueberry bush, or grape vine, never pruned (except by wind, ice, and pests) yet apparently loaded with fruit? Look more closely next time—for the amount of space the plant occupies, is it really bearing a large crop? Probably not. And look at the fruit, and taste it. It is small and not especially sweet. Cultivated fruits are—or should be—large and luscious, and they get that way by breeding or selecting the best from wild plants, by being well fed and watered, and by being pruned to balance growth among leaves, shoots, and fruits.

Tree fruits

A good crop of large fruits puts a heavy weight on branches, so special attention must be paid to training a fruit tree to a sturdy framework. This may even mean pruning back part of a branch just to keep it from breaking under a potentially heavy load of fruit—what sweet work!

Pruning the young fruit tree

The first years a fruit tree is in the ground are important to its future performance—in terms of luscious fruits and even its beauty as a plant. These are the years that the tree lays down what will be, for better or for worse, its permanent framework of branches. Your goal is to help that tree develop branches that are strong enough to support their load of fruit, and to do so without shading each other. (Strength is not a consideration if the branches of your fruit tree are going to be physically supported for their whole life, as is the case for trellised or espaliered plants.) You also want the tree to grow rapidly, to fill the space you have allotted it. And, of course, you want to pick your first fruits

THE BARE BONES

TREES, BUSHES, AND VINES THAT PRODUCE EDIBLE FRUIT

WITH FEW EXCEPTIONS, prune fruit plants while they are dormant.

WITH A YOUNG FRUIT TREE, choose as scaffold limbs branches that are 6 in. apart and leaving the trunk at wide angles. If the tree is initially a single stem, cut back that stem at planting to 2 ft. to 3 ft. above ground level, then select side branches as the plant grows. If the tree already has branches, save those that are wide angled and in good position, and remove all others. Shorten those that you save to a few inches. Do no more pruning on a young tree than is absolutely necessary or you will delay fruiting.

MATURE FRUIT TREES need annual pruning. The amount of wood to remove to reduce the fruit load and to stimulate new shoot growth depends on the size of the particular fruit and the bearing habit of the particular tree.

PRUNE FRUIT BUSHES little or not at all when young, then annually remove the oldest wood and thin out the youngest wood. The younger the wood on which most fruits are borne and the more new shoots that grow each year from ground level, the more severe the annual pruning that is needed.

AT PLANTING, CUT VINES back to a few buds to channel energy into growth of a single (sometimes two) stems. From then on, training depends on the fruit and the kind of trellis or arbor you provide. For details about specific fruits, see the Plant List, which begins on p. 141. Renewal wood is provided by cutting back growth to within few buds of permanent cordons or the trunk.

as soon as possible. Whatever you do to your young tree, keep in mind these goals: good form, rapid growth, and early fruiting.

Your pruning shears is only one of the tools you'll employ to train your tree. You will also use your fingernails to pinch growing points, perhaps a knife to notch or ring bark, and strings or weights to bend branches downward. You will not need a saw during the training period; if you do, you have neglected your tree too long.

A fruit tree, as you receive it from a nursery, is either a whip, which is just a single stem, or a feathered tree, which is a young tree that already has side branches. The feathered tree, being more developed, is more desirable and more expensive. Fruit trees usually are dug from the nursery field while they are dormant, to be sold bare root. Occasionally, the trees are dug with a ball of soil and sold balled and burlapped, with their roots more or less intact, or are grown and sold in pots, in which case their roots are not disturbed at all.

Take a look at the roots of your plant before you set it in the ground—after all, this is the last look you should ever get at them! With a potted plant, tease out the roots around the outside of the root ball to encourage them to grow into the surrounding soil. Use a stick or a fork, and if some of the roots have circled around inside the pot so tightly that you cannot tease them outward, make some vertical slits in the root ball with a knife. (Circling roots are "pot bound" from spending too much time in the pot. Avoid purchasing a tree that is excessively pot bound, because it will eventually strangle itself.)

Treat the roots of a balled and burlapped tree the same as those of a potted tree. If any long roots were

Slitting the Root Ball of a Potted Tree

wrapped around the root ball when the tree was packed up, spread them out or, if you do not want to dig a hole big enough to accommodate them, cut them back. Do not fold them into the planting hole.

Look closely at all the roots of a bare-root tree. Cut back any that are too long to fit into the planting hole, or dig a larger hole. Also cut back into healthy tissue any roots that are dead or diseased. Some roots may have had their ends frayed as the plant was lifted out of the soil. Trim these roots back cleanly so that, with less surface area to the wound, healing will occur more rapidly.

Now plant the tree.

Next, turn your attention to the top of the young plant. Keep in mind the shape that you want for your tree when it grows up. In contrast to many ornamental trees, which are "high-headed," you probably want the first side branch on a fruit tree to originate fairly low, because then you have more fruit within reach, or more fruit, plain and simple, especially if the tree is a dwarf that will never grow higher than 7 ft. anyway. On the other hand, you do not want that first limb to be so low that it droops to the ground under its weight of fruit, or makes it difficult for you to mow, mulch, or cultivate beneath the tree.

Although many different tree forms have been spawned over centuries of training and pruning fruit trees, three forms predominate: the central leader, the open center, and the modified central leader. The leader referred to here is the main stem of the tree, a continuation of the trunk. The central-leader tree has a single, dominant leader off which grow branches of decreasing length as you move up the tree. (A compact central-leader tree is sometimes called a "dwarf pyramid.") These branches will become the scaffold limbs, or main branches, of the tree. The open-center tree has a vase shape, with three or four leaders growing off the trunk in an outward and upward direction. Branches grow off these leaders. The modified central-leader tree is a hybrid of the first two systems. The tree starts out as a central leader, and at a height of about 7 ft., growth of the leader is stopped as it is bent over or headed back to a weak side branch. The ideal form for a particular tree will depend not only on your whims, but also on the plant's natural growth habit.

For any of the three basic tree forms, branch selection begins the first season. In the case of the open-center tree, once you have selected three or four side branches, cut the central stem off just above the topmost side branch. The tree then continues upward and outward growth along these side branches, now officially leaders (but not central leaders). In the case of the central-leader or young modified central-leader tree, select side branches growing off the central leader.

Side-branch selection determines the future shape and strength of the tree, so

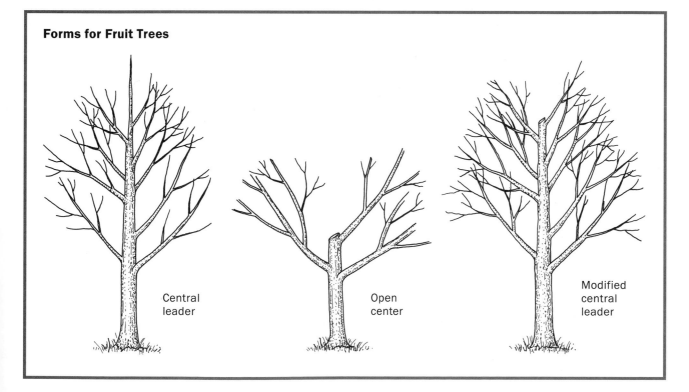

Forms for Fruit Trees

Central leader

Open center

Modified central leader

select with care. Each side branch needs adequate space in which to develop. Start with the first branch about 2 ft. from the ground, then space subsequent ones about 6 in. to 18 in. apart as you move up the trunk, the spacing depending on the eventual size of the tree (larger tree, larger spacing). Ideally, branches should originate in a spiral arrangement up the trunk so that each branch has space to spread and does not rob minerals and water coming up from the roots from another branch that is close and directly above.

As you select new side branches during the first few years of growth, your tree will look admittedly sparse. But do not be tempted to space branches closer together or closer to the ground. Throughout the life of the tree, the location of those branches will never change. In fact, they will crowd somewhat closer with age as they thicken.

Selecting Side Branches on a Young Fruit Tree

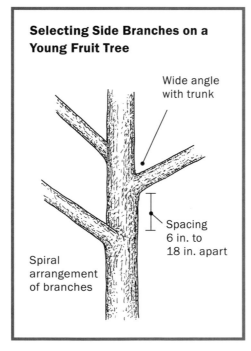

Wide angle with trunk

Spacing 6 in. to 18 in. apart

Spiral arrangement of branches

Besides adequate spacing, each side branch needs to be firmly anchored to the leader, or, in the case of the open-center tree, leaders. A strong union is possible only when a leader envelops the base of the attached branch, and this is possible only when a branch is thinner than the leader off which it grows. Such a side branch typically grows out at a wide angle to the leader, and this also makes for a strong union. A branch emerging at a narrow angle tends to accumulate dead bark, which weakens the union, in the crotch between the branch and the leader.

Do not neglect the development of the central leader on a tree trained either as a central-leader tree or modified central-leader form. This leader should be truly a central leader, at all times the most dominant and upright stem of the tree— the horticultural top dog. If the leader branches to make two equally vigorous leaders, remove one completely and immediately. Do not let premature fruiting of the developing central leader rob it of strength or cause it to bend over.

So there's the ideal: a strong, central leader with well-spaced, firmly anchored branches; or, in the case of the open-center tree, a short trunk capped by three of four strong and firmly anchored leaders off which grow side branches. Trees rarely conform to this ideal if allowed to grow naturally. (If toying with natural growth makes you uneasy, take comfort in the fact that no wild peach tree ever bore a 3-in. diameter fruit practically bursting with ambrosial juice.)

How do we coax a newly planted tree into having good form? First, the easy stuff… prune dead or diseased wood

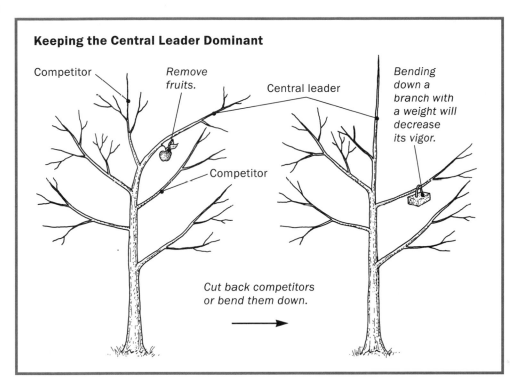

Keeping the Central Leader Dominant

Competitor

Remove fruits.

Central leader

Bending down a branch with a weight will decrease its vigor.

Competitor

Cut back competitors or bend them down.

back into healthy tissue, and also prune back broken stems. If your new tree is a whip, head it back to promote low branching. How low you head the whip will determine the height of the lowest branches as well as their vigor. Commercial growers generally head whips back to 2 ft. or 3 ft. above ground level. Lower heading results in fewer, but longer, branches; higher heading, the opposite (see the drawing on p. 128). Expect a more vigorous response from a more vigorous (thicker) whip. Prune for lower branching if the site is windy.

A feathered tree already has side branches, so save those worth saving, and remove the others. Whether or not you shorten a well-placed branch that you save depends on how you are growing the tree. If the tree is a dwarf, perhaps trellised, and you want the earliest possible fruiting, do not shorten any branches except those that are drooping. If you are growing a large, freestanding

tree, shorten branches to stubs to stimulate vigorous regrowth and delay fruiting so that energy is channeled into shoot growth. In this latter case, shorten most severely those branches that are spindly. If the tree is to have a central leader and the leader on your feathered tree continues, unbranched, far above the bottom tier of branches, also head back the leader to promote the next tier of branching.

Only two other conditions necessitate further pruning of the tops immediately following planting. The first is with a bare-root tree that may suffer from lack of water its first season in the ground. Traditional reasoning has held that the tops of bare-root trees need pruning in order to balance the inevitable loss of roots that occurred when the tree was dug from the nursery. In fact, such pruning is needed only when water is short, to avoid water loss through leaves. Moreover, if a plant receives good care

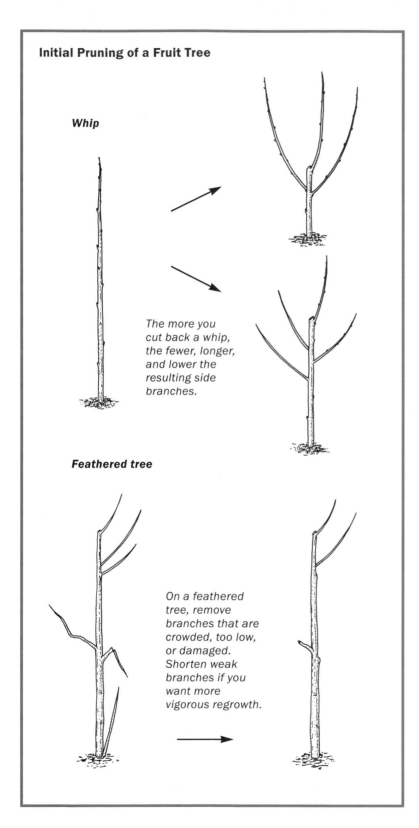

Initial Pruning of a Fruit Tree

Whip

The more you cut back a whip, the fewer, longer, and lower the resulting side branches.

Feathered tree

On a feathered tree, remove branches that are crowded, too low, or damaged. Shorten weak branches if you want more vigorous regrowth.

once in the ground, natural hormones produced in the buds, especially terminal buds, stimulate root growth. Why not water instead?

The other condition possibly requiring top pruning in the first season is if the tree is heavily branched and the site is windy. In that case, thin out branches to keep the tree from sailing in the wind. Or stake the tree—trees on certain rootstocks need staking anyway, when young or throughout their life.

As the central leader grows, induce it to keep sending out side branches by heading it back from time to time. As a general rule of thumb, each year cut off about one-third of the previous season's growth while the plant is dormant. Alternatively, cut back the leader by a few inches during the growing season each time it grows a few inches above the point where you want a side branch. The uppermost bud that remains after heading the leader usually sends out a vertical shoot that becomes a continuation of the leader, and lower buds push out side branches. If the top few buds push out vigorous upright shoots, cut away all but the top one. Select new side branches that are well spaced along the leader and firmly anchored to it.

Branches generally need little additional pruning. Usually they branch further and stay subordinate to the leader. (Leaders need coaxing to make side branches because upright growth promotes apical dominance, the result of a hormone produced in the topmost bud suppressing growth of buds farther down the stem.) If a side branch is not branching or is threatening the leader with overly exuberant growth, shorten it or, better still, bend it to a more horizontal position with weights or string. Also shorten any side branch that is too lanky back to where it turns downward if it is drooping. The largest side branches should be those lowest along the central leader, so that the tree is wider at the bottom than at the top.

With the open-center tree, head back the three or four leaders so that each is well furnished with branches. But make sure no branches originate so low that they interfere with each other. The aim is for growth that is upward and outward, like a vase. What needs to be pruned to achieve this goal depends on the plant's natural growth habit. More upright trees need more vertical shoots removed, and naturally drooping trees need more "hangers" removed.

A few neat tricks can help your tree along in its development. Suppose a sprout is emerging in a perfect position to become a scaffold limb, except that it makes a narrow angle with a leader. Widen the angle by inserting a clothespin or toothpick between it and the leader (see the photo on p. 130). Another way to get wide-angled branches is to head back a whip when it is dormant, then cut back the central stem again when the new

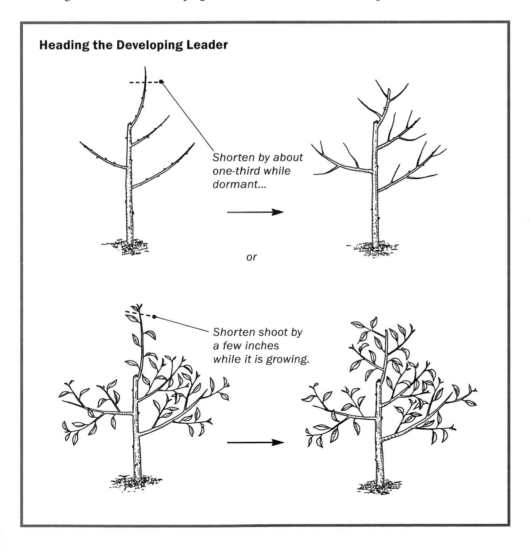

Heading the Developing Leader

Shorten by about one-third while dormant...

or

Shorten shoot by a few inches while it is growing.

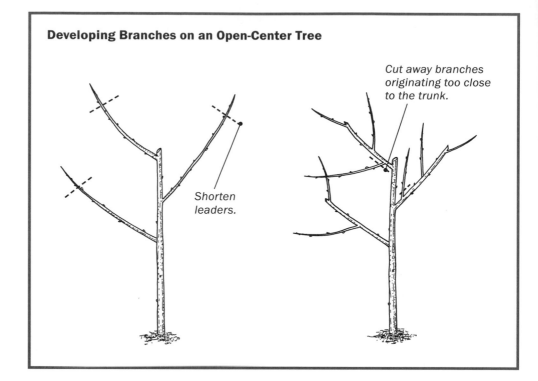

Developing Branches on an Open-Center Tree

Shorten leaders.

Cut away branches originating too close to the trunk.

A toothpick is a convenient tool for spreading young stems.

topmost shoot is about 6 in. long, removing all the upper upright shoots. What remains will be wide-angled, new shoots, perfect for three or four leaders of an open-center tree. And what if no side branch is growing where you want it to? Sometimes—only sometimes—cutting a notch into the bark above a bud will induce that bud to grow out into a shoot. Removing a leaf on an actively growing shoot also can cause the bud where the leaf was attached to send out a shoot. What if the leader made only feeble growth for the season? Head it back severely to stimulate vigorous regrowth.

A few more pruning cuts complete those necessary to train your young fruit tree. Perhaps hardest (psychologically, not physically) to remove are flowers or fruits. Your young tree should be channeling its energy into growth, not fruit, so be judicious about when to start allowing fruits, and how many to allow. Otherwise, your plant may never become more than a mere runt. And do not forget to keep fruits off a developing central leader, because they not only sap the leader's strength, but also can weigh it down, pulling it over so that it loses apical dominance.

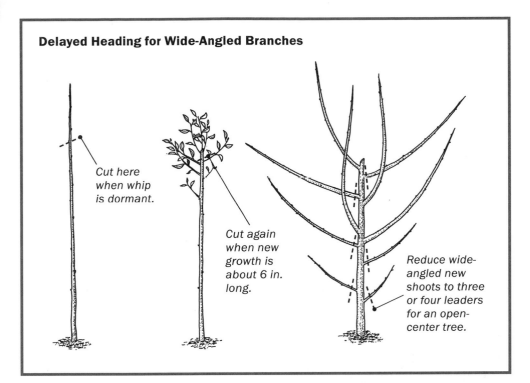

Delayed Heading for Wide-Angled Branches

Cut here when whip is dormant.

Cut again when new growth is about 6 in. long.

Reduce wide-angled new shoots to three or four leaders for an open-center tree.

Your tree likely will grow more branches than those you are going to retain as scaffold limbs. Smaller secondary branches may even crowd too closely on larger branches. In hot, sunny climates, save a few temporary branches on the trunk to avoid sunburn of young bark. Otherwise, remove excess branches on your tree.

Also keep on the lookout for very vigorous vertical shoots—called watersprouts or suckers—arising from the tops of branches or from down near the ground. Those high in the tree ruin its form and create excessive shade. Those arising near ground level may be growing from the rootstock of a grafted tree, and so would grow on to produce useless fruit. Remove any watersprout or sucker

Notching the bark above a bud will sometimes cause that bud to form a shoot, creating a side branch just where you want it.

The quickest and most effective way to get rid of a watersprout is just to grab it and snap it off while it is still succulent.

right at its base as soon as you notice it. Ripping it off with a quick jerk of your hand rather than cutting it reduces the chances of new sprouts growing from the same point.

Finally, remember the third goal in training a tree: minimum delay before the plant begins fruiting. A young fruit tree needs some pruning, but excessive pruning stimulates too much vigorous shoot growth, and most young trees already have plenty of that. Despite all that has been said here, minimize delay in reaping your edible rewards by pruning no more than is absolutely necessary!

Pruning the mature fruit tree

Don't stop pruning any tree bearing good crops. The tree still needs annual pruning, just as it did when it was young, although for different reasons. Prune the mature tree to keep it healthy, to keep it within its allotted space, and to keep it bearing regular crops of the best fruit possible. True, some tree fruits seem to bear well with little pruning, but these are mostly uncommon fruits that have yet to be studied in rigorous detail. They too may turn out to do better with annual pruning.

Pruning keeps a tree healthy by ridding it of diseased and dead wood, and by creating conditions unfriendly to disease-causing microorganisms. Whenever you see a diseased stem on a tree, cut it off back into healthy, lighter-colored wood. Under certain conditions, such as when pruning fire-blighted stems from a pear tree in summer, you could spread disease on your pruning shears, so sterilize the tool between cuts with a dip in alcohol or 10% bleach solution. (Winter pruning does not present this hazard, so no sterilization is necessary.) Also cut away dead wood in such a way as to promote

most rapid and thorough healing (for details, see pp. 30-33).

Most fungi and bacteria that cause disease thrive in dark, dank conditions. If you prune to keep the tree canopy open to light and air, then leaves, twigs, and fruits dry quickly. Stems bathed in light also are able to grow more vigorously and better resist diseases. Generally, do such pruning while a plant is dormant, though in some cases, you might do it during the growing season to allow better air circulation around ripening fruits. Keeping an open canopy also reduces branch rubbing, another possible entryway for disease.

The greatest skill involved in pruning fruit trees is striking a good balance between some naturally opposing tendencies of these plants. You want to balance shoot growth throughout the plant, counteracting the natural tendency of a tree to pump most of its energy into shoots at the top of the canopy. On a top-heavy tree, the lower branches are shaded and the fruit is mostly high up, out of reach. Avoid this situation by making mostly thinning cuts on upper branches and heading cuts on lower ones.

You also want to balance shoot growth and fruiting. Shoot growth is needed for leaves, to make sugars, and for branches on which to hang fruits; yet the fruits are what we are really after. You want to balance high yields with high quality. The more fruits a tree bears, the less energy doled out to each fruit, so the fruits are smaller and less tasty. This is of little consequence with a naturally small fruit like a sweet cherry, but can spell the difference between a drippy "wow" and a mealy "ho-hum" for a naturally large fruit like a peach.

Finally, you want to balance this year's crop with next year's. Developing fruits produce hormones that suppress flower-bud initiation, so a large crop one year results in a light crop the next. Dormant pruning of stems to remove potential flowers, and pinching or knocking off excess flowers or fruitlets, can avoid cycles of feast and famine.

How much pruning is needed to balance all these opposing forces depends on where the particular plant bears its flowers, and on how big its fruits are. The peach tree bears fruit only on stems that grew the previous season, so it needs fairly severe annual pruning to stimulate an annual flush of vigorous new shoots for the following year's crop. An apple tree, which bears fruits on short, knobby branches as aged as ten years old, needs little such stimulus. Both fruits are large, so the trees do need pruning of branches, flowers, or fruits to reduce the current crop, increasing its quality and ensuring a good return bloom the following season.

Even after dormant branch-pruning has removed potential fruits, you may have to go over the trees to thin individual fruitlets by hand. The sooner after fruits initially form that you do this, the greater the effect on fruit quality and next year's crop. However, delay spring fruit thinning until the risk of frost, which will damage fruitlets, has safely past. A few weeks after bloom, most fruit trees suddenly shed weaker or damaged fruitlets—the so-called "June drop." You may want to hand thin in two installments, the first right after bloom and the second after June drop.

Whenever you thin, selectively remove smaller fruitlets and any damaged ones, just as the tree naturally does. Generally, leave space between fruitlets equal to two or three times the mature size of the fruit. Pinch off fruitlets one by one or, if you have many trees, knock them off in quantity with a blast of water or by batting them with a piece of hose attached to the end of a broom handle.

(Commercially, apples and some other fruits are thinned with chemicals.)

Except where you need a replacement shoot, always remove, right at its base, any watersprout or root sucker, just as you did when training the tree. These vigorous shoots create shade and upset the form of the plant.

Although fruit trees are generally pruned while they are dormant, there also is a place for for pruning them during the summer. Response to summer pruning depends on when during the growing season you prune, what you cut, the particular variety of fruit, and the weather. No wonder generalizations are hard to make about summer pruning! Summer pruning can promote the formation of fruit buds, at its best smothering branches with flowers and then fruits, exactly the type of growth sought after on an espalier. And "Espalier" (pp. 212-225) is the chapter in which the details of summer pruning are covered. At the very least, summer pruning can open up the canopy as fruits are ripening, limiting diseases and, for those fruits that need direct light to color up (not all do), increasing fruit color. Do

Thinning fruits increases the quality of those that remain.

such pruning around midsummer, when there is less chance of regrowth because lateral buds have probably already become dormant for the season.

Ideally, no fruit tree would ever grow larger than you want it to. Either you have enough space to accommodate its natural size, or else you choose a specific rootstock that keeps the plant small. In the real world (a suburban yard, for example), a dwarfing rootstock does not exist for most fruits and space may not be available for a fruit or nut tree 30 ft. high and wide. And who wants to climb a high ladder to bring in the harvest? Fortunately, you can limit the size of any fruit tree with judicious pruning; the sidebar on the facing page tells how.

Renovating a neglected fruit tree

A neglected large and craggy fruit tree may have a certain rustic charm, but that tree is a sorry tree indeed, in terms of producing tasty fruits. How sorry depends on the fruit and the environment—some nut trees get along well despite neglect, and I have known a nearly neglected, old cherry tree to bear plenty of fruit of good quality.

But an old fruit tree usually has plenty of problems: The fruits may be too high, too few, and too small; pests are likely rampant; and the shaded interior of the tree will probably consist of nothing but wood (which still must be fed by the plant), not fruit or leaves.

Renovating a tree can bring it back to its former glory, but before you even pick up your pruning tools, ask yourself whether your efforts will be justified. Is the tree of a particularly good variety? Do you really want a tree where that tree is? Some trees do not live long enough to justify drastic renovation, which should be spread over two or three years; and then another two years might be required

before the tree is bearing a full crop. Peach trees, for instance, are not long-lived and recover poorly from wounds, especially the large wounds needed for renovation. Some young trees could already be cropping in that time, so before beginning renovative pruning, consider "pruning" the tree with a saw— at ground level.

If you do decide to renovate the old tree, start while your tree is dormant. First make some large cuts low in the crown to thin it out and, if you want, to lower it and limit its spread. Cut one or two major limbs back to their origin or to sturdy side branches. If more major limbs need cutting back, wait a year, and if still more must go, hold off for yet another year. If you cut too much in one year, there is risk of sunburn on once-shaded bark.

New sprouts may grow near some of your pruning cuts. Some of these sprouts, especially those of moderate vigor, might be in good positions to make permanent new limbs. Save those, and cut away the others, especially when many are clustered near a pruning cut.

With major cuts out of the way for now, progress to more detailed pruning, using a small pruning saw and lopper. Look over the stems and cut back to sound wood any that are diseased, dead, or broken. Also remove stems that are overcrowded or weak. Cut back any drooping stem to a branch near the place where the stem starts drooping. As always, take into account the kind of tree you are working with—American persimmon, for example, has a naturally drooping growth habit.

Finally, stand back and admire your work. Cleaned up, an old fruit tree looks even more charming than it did when it was neglected and overgrown. Now give your tree a hug.

CONTROLLING THE SIZE OF FRUIT TREES

Pruning to keep any tree within bounds should consist mostly of thinning cuts. Remove an offending stem by cutting it back to its origin, to a sturdy side branch within the canopy, or to a weak side branch farther out. Less regrowth is likely to occur from such cuts than from merely heading back smaller stems that are too high or too wide around the periphery of the crown. Making fewer large cuts lower in the tree also is less work than making many small cuts high in the tree. Start pruning your tree to limit its size before it becomes full size. For example, top the leader, or bend it over, before it grows as high as you want your tree to grow. Prune to limit tree size while a tree is dormant or while it is actively growing.

Root pruning also can dwarf a fruit tree. Root prune by pushing a shovel into the ground in a ring around the plant, 2 ft. to 4 ft. from the trunk, sometime between late fall and early spring. (Mechanical cutter bars pulled by tractor have been designed for this job in orchards.)

Fruiting itself can slow down shoot growth, and if your tree is reluctant to start fruiting, you can coerce it into puberty by bark ringing. This technique involves making a cut around the trunk, or two cuts, ¼ in. to ½ in. apart, with the bark between the cuts removed. By the end of the season the ring will have healed. You can even ring individual branches, rather than the trunk.

Good judgment is needed for root pruning or bark ringing. Either technique, done too severely or too frequently, done on a weakened tree, or done just before a summer of drought, could kill the tree. Both techniques have been applied mostly to apple trees, so be cautious about applying them to other fruits. Never ring stone fruits (*Prunus* species) because wounded bark heals poorly and is especially attractive to pests. At their best, though, either technique decreases shoot growth and, in the case of ringing, increases fruiting.

Judiciously applied, bark ringing may encourage a tree to start fruiting. Make parallel cuts a short distance apart, then remove the bark between the cuts.

PRUNING A NEGLECTED FRUIT TREE

1. This apple tree has not been pruned for years.

2. Cutting away some vertical limbs quickly lowers the tree and lets more light in.

3. Drooping branches, which bear poor fruit, are lopped off.

4. Renovation is finished for this year, but must be continued over a period of a few years.

Bush fruits

It is in the nature of a bush that its stems are short-lived, as they are always being replaced by new ones thrown up from ground level. (What did you think made a bush bushy?) So pruning the young fruit bush is important only in terms of its survival and health, and so that you get to pick your first crop as soon as possible. No sturdy framework of permanent stems is necessary.

Pruning the young fruit bush

A bush that has been grown in a pot, or that has been dug from a nursery field with its roots more or less intact, then balled and burlapped, needs little or no pruning when it is planted. Knock the potted plant out of its pot, then use a stick or a fork to tease out the roots at the outside of the root ball. If the plant has started to become pot bound, with roots circling around the outside edge of the root ball, loosen the roots from the root ball so that they radiate outward when you set the ball in its planting hole. Slicing a little way into the root ball from top to bottom with a knife deals with congestion within the root ball. A balled and burlapped bush needs nothing done to its roots, except the cutting back of any lanky roots that might have been tucked in around the root ball when the plant was packed up.

With the bare-root bush, inspect the roots carefully before you plant. Cut off any dead roots, and cut roots that are diseased or have frayed ends back to healthy, light-colored tissue.

With just a few exceptions, the stems of your new bush do not need pruning right after you set the plant in the ground. Of course, you should check for stems that are dead, diseased, or broken, and remove them. Also, if the site is very windy, thin out stems to prevent wind from rocking the plant or yanking it out of the ground before the roots have grabbed hold of the soil. The tops do not need pruning just because it was bare root ("to balance the inevitable root loss that occurred during transplanting" said the old books) so long as you provide the plant with sufficient moisture throughout its first season. Minimizing pruning and using mostly thinning cuts helps get your bush off to a good start because shoot buds, especially terminal buds, produce hormones that promote root growth.

A few fruit bushes (noted in the Plant List on pp. 141-176) benefit from being cut clear to the ground right after they are planted. The benefits are threefold: First, removing all wood eliminates possibly diseased stems that could spread infection to new shoots. Second, with all stems removed, the young plant can put its initial efforts into growing shoots and roots rather than bearing any fruits on older stems. And third, the decapitated plant will send up many vigorous, young shoots near ground level, which—in the

Pruning is part of the prescription for an abundant harvest—in this case, of blueberries.

cases of plants that bear on one-year-old wood—will bear a respectable crop the next season.

After any initial pruning, the frequency and degree of subsequent pruning needed by a young fruit bush depends on the particular fruit. Bushes mature quickly, so this quickly moves us into the realm of maintenance pruning.

Maintenance pruning

Most fruit bushes demand annual pruning for sustained, high-quality harvests. This keeps a bush open to air and light, limiting diseases by promoting quick drying of the stems, leaves, and fruits. And abundant light improves quality of the fruit.

Annual pruning also renews the plant, as you cut away the old stems to stimulate growth of young stems and make room for them. How long before you cut away an old stem from a bush depends on the particular fruit. Bush fruits that bear *only* on vigorous stems of the previous season must have all of these stems cleared out after they finish fruiting. Other bushes produce stems that can bear for a few years before they peter out and need replacement. In any case, lop the old stem back to ground level, or back to a young, vigorous side branch originating low in the plant.

Most maintenance pruning for fruit bushes takes place while the plant is dormant, preferably in late winter. Timing is less critical for plants that are cold hardy, because pruning wounds on these plants are less likely to be damaged by cold, and there are few or no cold-damaged stems to prune from these plants at winter's end. In addition to pruning to keep a bush open and replace old stems, also cut away dead, diseased, and damaged stems, and shorten any that droop to the ground.

A few months after you finish your annual dormant pruning on a fruit bush, you will discover a pleasant by-product of your efforts: The fruit is now wonderfully easy to harvest! No more squirming through a tangle of stems—with some plants a thorny tangle—to reach the fruits, or jumping up in the air grasp at a cluster out of reach. The fruits are just splayed out before you, within easy reach.

Renovating a fruit bush

Neglected, a fruit bush may grow too high and too wide, and probably too dense. Because bushes so readily send up new shoots at or near ground level, an easy way to renovate is merely to lop the whole works down to the ground when the plant is dormant. Following this drastic pruning, the plant will put out many vigorous sprouts. Thin them out so that they are not crowded, and the bush is up and running again. The one problem with lopping the whole plant to the ground is that you sacrifice at least one year of fruit.

There is a less drastic approach to renovation, one that is more trouble but keeps the plant bearing fruit without an intermission. This involves gradually renewing the bush over a period of two or three years. Cut away only a portion of the oldest stems at or near ground level each year, when the plant is dormant. At the same time, thin out some of the youngest stems. After a few years, all the old, decrepit stems will be gone, and the bush will consist of various ages of healthy, bearing stems. How many new stems to leave after each year's thinning as well as how long to leave an older stem before cutting it away depends, of course on the particular plant's bearing habit, which is detailed in the Plant List (which begins on p. 141) for each fruit.

Vine fruits

A fruiting vine generally consists of a permanent trunk, perhaps some cordons (which are permanent branches or, if only one, a continuation of the trunk), and non-permanent fruiting arms. With the young plant, your goal is to induce development of the trunk, and, if planned, one or more cordons as quickly as possible. Achieve this goal by providing good growing conditions and by pruning.

Pruning the young fruiting vine

Most fruiting vines are sold bare root. Inspect the roots before you put the plant in the ground, and cut off any that are diseased or dead. To promote healing, cut back to healthy tissue damaged roots or roots with frayed ends. Also cut back any roots that are too long to fit in the hole that you have provided for the plant—or make the hole bigger.

A potted vine, or one that is balled and burlapped, requires little or no pruning of its roots. Just tease out the roots from the outside of the root ball to encourage their growth into the surrounding soil. And if roots are circling the outside of the root ball of the potted vine, pull them loose or slit the root ball. This prevents the roots from continuing to grow around and around, eventually strangling the plant.

Now for the top of the plant. Cut it back to within 1 ft. of the ground to stimulate vigorous growth of a single shoot. If the plant has more than one stem, cut back the sturdiest of them and remove all the others.

In some cases, fruiting vines are deliberately trained to develop more than one permanent trunk. If that is your plan, cut off any spindly stems, then leave two or three sturdy ones and head them back to about 1 ft. Don't worry if a plant destined to have a multiple trunk starts with a single stem. Even after you head back that single stem, buds near ground level will push out other shoots.

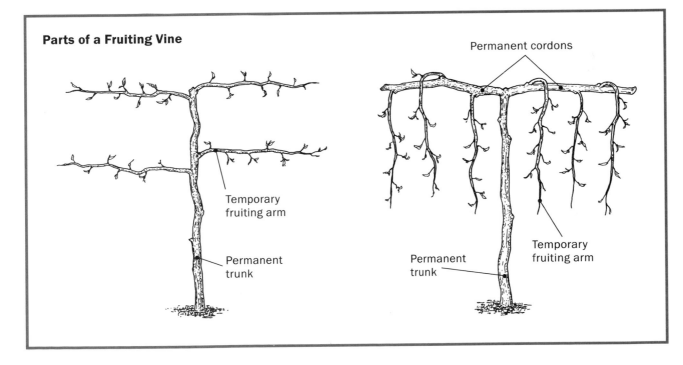

Parts of a Fruiting Vine

Permanent cordons

Temporary fruiting arm

Permanent trunk

Temporary fruiting arm

Permanent trunk

Help your vine get up off the ground during its first season by tying the trunk-to-be to a stake or, in the case of twiners, by twisting the shoot around the stake. This lending hand does more than just make a tidy plant. Keeping the growing shoot vertically oriented invigorates it by stimulating production of a hormone in the shoot tip that keeps the tip growing and suppresses the growth of side shoots. Side shoots would steal energy from the growing trunk and are superfluous, anyway. Throughout the growing season, rub out any young, green side shoots that do try to grow. If you are remiss about this task, cut them away when the plant is dormant. Keep an eye out for sprouts growing near the ground also.

Suppose your young vine does not act as planned its first season, and grows just a few spindly shoots? In that case, begin again, with drastic heading back of the dormant plant. (Also try to pinpoint and correct any deficiencies in growing conditions.)

Maintenance pruning

You have only to look at a wild grape vine to recognize the need for regular pruning of any fruiting vine. Wild grapes clamber high into trees, putting their fruits well out of reach. And the grapes that you can get to are hardly of the highest quality (genetics is admittedly also a factor here), because the vine's primary aim is to make as many seeds as possible, not luscious fruits. Wild vines also use up energy that could go to the fruits in feeding all that wood that carries the plant high into the trees. And a free-growing vine tangles around itself, creating dark and dank conditions with many dead and diseased branches.

Convinced that your fruiting vine needs pruning? Fruiting vines vary in their bearing habits as well as the quantity of fruit they can ripen to highest quality, so maintenance pruning for each plant is detailed in the Plant List. The one common thread is that they all do need annual pruning in order to bear good yields of savory fruits, to remain healthy, and to keep the fruit easily accessible.

Renovating a fruiting vine

Fruiting vines are easy to renovate. The simplest way to do it is to lop the whole plant, while it is dormant, down to the ground. (With evergreen vines, lop in winter, when the plant is resting.) Treat new growth just as you would on a young plant—a very vigorous "young" plant, with that grown-up root system now fueling fewer buds.

Because you miss out on a year or more of fruit when you lop the whole plant to the ground, you might opt for a less drastic method of renovation. In this case, peer among the stems and select a new trunk, then side arms or cordons, whatever is needed. Cut away everything else. As with the more drastic renovation, prune while the plant is dormant, both for its sake and because if the vine is deciduous, you can more easily see its stems when they are leafless.

Even with the latter renovation, you will be surprised at how much wood you remove from the plant. Renovating a vine will seem ruthless, but don't worry—the plants recover well and quickly.

Plant List

Acerola cherry *(Malpighia glabra):* Prune this evergreen shrub only as needed to shape it.

Almond *(Prunus dulcis* var. *dulcis):* Train the young tree to an open-center form. Once you have selected your tree's main branches and eliminated others, only a minimum amount of pruning is needed. Nuts are borne mostly on spurs on older wood, although some varieties also bear laterally on one-year-old wood. As your tree ages, prune to keep the interior of the crown open and to stimulate some growth for new fruiting wood. Pruning, fertilization, and watering should result in 6 in. to 10 in. of new growth each year. Rather than pruning every year, you can instead make larger cuts and prune every two or three years.

Apple *(Malus sylvestris):* Which of the three common methods of training—central leader, modified central leader, or open center—is most suitable for a particular tree will depend on the variety. Train an upright grower such as 'Red Delicious' or 'Jonathan', especially if grown on a vigorous rootstock, as a central leader, because that is its natural inclination. 'Golden Delicious' has a naturally spreading habit, so can be trained to an open-center form.

Keep pruning to a minimum during the formative period, or you will unduly delay fruiting. The "dwarf pyramid," as promoted in many British publications, is a small, central-leader tree whose scaffold limbs are repeatedly headed in order to develop a dense pyramid—unfortunately at the expense of early fruiting. Nonetheless, your tree may need an occasional heading cut to invigorate a stem or to promote branching, especially if the plant is a weak grower such as 'Empire' or a so-called "spur-type" variety. A weak tree on a dwarfing rootstock needs rather severe heading to prevent its becoming a runt bearing too many fruits too early in its life. On a tree that is growing moderately or vigorously, bend stems toward a horizontal position when you want to promote

branching. This technique will also slow growth and promote early fruiting.

Apples have been grown so extensively and for so long (even the Latin word for "apple," *pomum,* also meant "fruit") that many training systems have been developed. Apples are ideal for the centuries-old practice of espalier, a method of growing treated in a separate section of this book (pp. 219-222). In the last few decades, a number of training systems have been developed to capitalize on the ability of dwarf trees to yield prodigious quantities of fruit (for the amount of space they occupy), and to do so early in their life. I'll discuss one of these systems, the slender spindle, a few paragraphs hence, on p. 142.

Once an apple tree matures, it requires only moderate pruning. Most varieties bear their fruits on spurs, which are stubby branches elongating only about ½ in. per year. (If a branch on an apple tree mutates to become especially spurry and new trees are propagated from this branch, then you have a "spur-type" variety, such as 'Macspur' and 'Sturdeespur Delicious'.) Because spurs grow off wood that is more than two years old, an apple tree needs little new growth to keep fruitful. Some varieties—'Gala' is one example—also flower on one-year-old wood, but fruit set is poor and fruits are small from such flowers.

(continued on page 142)

Apple spurs, on which fruits are borne, eventually need to be thinned to prevent overcrowding and to make way for new growth.

Prune your mature tree mostly when it is dormant. Completely cut away overly vigorous stems, most common high in the tree, as well as weak twigs, which often hang from the undersides of limbs. Shorten stems that become too droopy, especially those low in the tree. After about ten years, those fruiting spurs become overcrowded and decrepit, so thin out and shorten them to invigorate them and give them more room. When a whole limb of fruiting spurs declines with age, cut it back to make room for a younger replacement.

Slender spindle is a productive way to grow apple trees.

A few apple varieties—'Cortland' and 'Idared', for example—do not bear fruits on spurs, but at the ends of willowy stems about 6 in. long. Train these so-called tip bearers to open-center or modified-central-leader form. Avoid shortening too many stems on mature trees or you will end up cutting off too much of your potential crop. Leave stems of moderate length, and encourage compactness and branching by shortening very long stems instead.

Pruning apple trees in summer can have some benefits. In some cases, summer-pruning promotes fruit-bud formation. This approach is used mostly with apples grown as espaliers, so is dealt with in that section of the book (pp. 219-222). Summer pruning also can enhance the red color of red apples. Cutting away some shoots just before the fruits begin to ripen lets them bathe in light, which is needed to make them rosy red.

The slender spindle system is a relatively new way to train and prune an apple tree, bringing with it the advantages of high yields and early fruiting—usually in the tree's second season! The essence of this system is to begin with a branched young tree, if possible, then do an absolute minimum of pruning and keep bending branches towards the horizontal. Dwarf rootstocks are a must, and the tree must be supported by a sturdy post throughout its life.

Begin training your slender spindle its first season. As soon as you plant, cut off any branches within 1 ft. of the ground, and head back the leader 10 in. above the highest branch. Also cut off any upright branches on the upper portion of the tree, any that are more than half as thick as the leader, and any that are crowding. If your tree is merely a whip, head it back to 2½ ft. to 3 ft. above ground level. Varieties that make many spurs are shy to branch, so head these varieties more severely. As the season progresses, branches will grow. About midsummer, bend them almost to a horizontal position with weights or with strings tied to stakes in the ground. To maintain a moderate amount of vigor in spur-type varieties, do not bend their branches too low.

Continue the following seasons as you did the first season. Head the leader, select new branches, and bend the branches. To dampen the increasing vigor of branches higher up in the tree, bend them increasingly lower. If any branches grow too long, shorten them early

(continued on page 144)

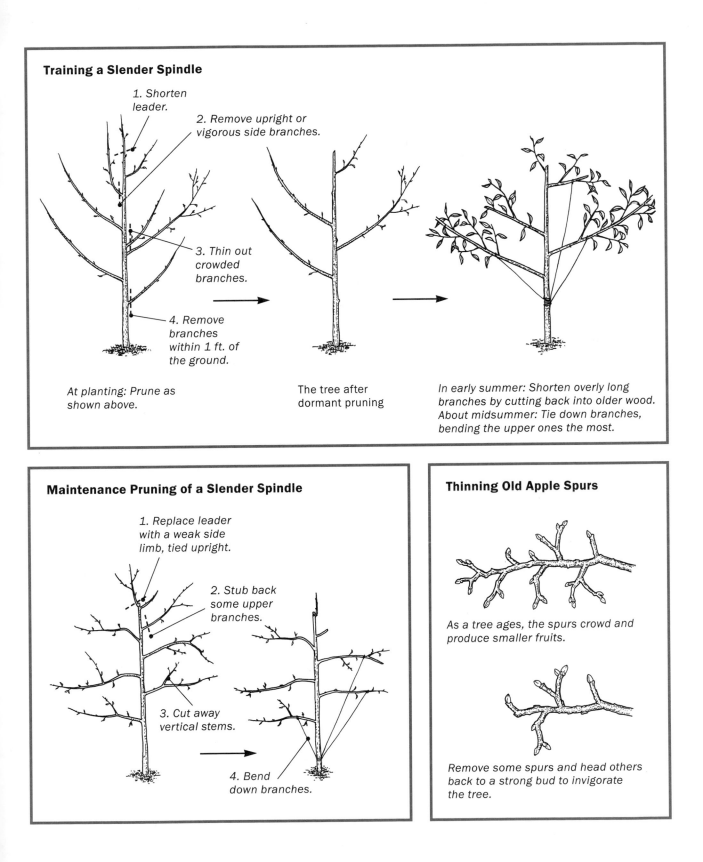

Training a Slender Spindle

1. Shorten leader.

2. Remove upright or vigorous side branches.

3. Thin out crowded branches.

4. Remove branches within 1 ft. of the ground.

At planting: Prune as shown above.

The tree after dormant pruning

In early summer: Shorten overly long branches by cutting back into older wood. About midsummer: Tie down branches, bending the upper ones the most.

Maintenance Pruning of a Slender Spindle

1. Replace leader with a weak side limb, tied upright.

2. Stub back some upper branches.

3. Cut away vertical stems.

4. Bend down branches.

Thinning Old Apple Spurs

As a tree ages, the spurs crowd and produce smaller fruits.

Remove some spurs and head others back to a strong bud to invigorate the tree.

in the season, when new growth is a few inches long, back into older wood. Do not shorten branches the same year that you bend them; wait a year or two. Prune and regulate growth so that branches make your tree taper out from top to bottom.

Maintenance pruning of a slender spindle begins when the tree reaches a height of 6 ft. or 7 ft. Each year, cut back the leader, while it is dormant, to a weak lateral, then tie the lateral in an upright position to the pole—that's your tree's "safety valve," to take up excess vigor. Periodically cut old branches high in the tree back to stubs, from which will grow renewal branches, or to fruit buds. Remove excess vertical shoots and bend down those you retain. If the lower limbs grow too wide, cut them back into older wood (see the drawing at top right on p. 143).

No matter what training and pruning system you use for apple trees, if you do it correctly, you will eventually be rewarded with a snowball of bloom in spring. That leaves you one more pruning job: fruit thinning. Apples respond thankfully to a 5-in. spacing, with no more that one fruit per flower cluster. Don't worry, only about 5% fruit set constitutes a full crop following a snowball bloom. (And each fruit needs the work of 40 leaves for nourishment.)

Apricot *(Prunus Armeniaca):* Apricot is susceptible to a number of diseases that infect the wood, so prune just before growth begins in spring. Where springs are wet, summers are dry, and there is ample time for wood to harden off before cold weather, you can even wait until summer to prune.

Train the young tree to an open-center or modified-central-leader form. Trained against a wall as a fan-shaped espalier, the blossoms, which open very early in spring, can be easily protected from frost. (See p. 222 for information on training and pruning an apricot espalier.)

Because an apricot tree bears fruit on wood from one to three years old, prune enough to stimulate a moderate amount of new growth each year. Using a combination of heading and thinning cuts, strive for new-shoot growth of 12 in. to 18 in. and plenty of light bathing all the branches. Cut away older wood, as well as diseased or dead wood. More severe pruning will reduce your crop, but the fruits will be larger. Fruit thinning is unnecessary unless the crop is very heavy, in which case thin the fruits so that they are about 2 in. apart.

Avocado *(Persea americana):* Prune avocado after the particular variety's normal harvest season. The time varies: June for the variety 'Fuerte', autumn for 'Haas', and so forth.

Although avocado wood is weak, the branches are firmly anchored, so that little pruning is needed in developing a tree's framework. Just make sure that the trunk is sturdy enough to hold up the tree. At a windy site, slow upward growth of a young tree to give the trunk a chance to thicken. With an upright variety such as 'Zutano', pinch terminals as the tree grows to promote low branching. Otherwise, you will have to climb high in a ladder to pick most of the fruit when the tree is mature.

Even the mature avocado tree needs little pruning beyond the removal of diseased, dead, or misplaced wood. You can use pruning to control the tree's size. Severe pruning does not stop this tree from flowering with abandon (although fruit set is reduced), but watch for sunburn on once-shaded bark. If your pruning does suddenly expose the bark, paint it with diluted white latex paint. Rather than pruning to keep a tree small, consider planting a naturally dwarf variety such as 'Gwenn' or 'Whitsell'.

Banana *(Musa acuminata):* Although a banana plant might grow to a height of 20 ft. or more, the true stem of the plant is the rhizome, the thickened, underground stem at the base of the plant. The above-ground portion of the plant is herbaceous, a tightly wound sheath of leaves—a pseudostem—with new leaves, and, finally, a cluster of fruits, pushing up from below. After fruiting, a particular pseudostem dies (but not the whole rhizome), at which point you should cut it down.

A single rhizome produces more than one pseudostem, and your other pruning task is to reduce the number of pseudostems to prevent excessive shading and competition for water and nutrients. As a general rule, allow three pseudostems per plant: one fruiting, one ready to follow, and one just peeking up from below. Pseudostems that you save should be spaced out around the rhizome. If you have a choice, remove pseudostems originating high on the rhizome, because they are poorly anchored and apt to topple from wind. Also remove short pseudostems having very broad leaves, which indicate some problems during emergence. Remove a pseudostem by forcing a machete downward between the pseudostem and the rhizome.

A bulbous male flower precedes the female flowers, which become the bananas you eat. The females do not need to be fertilized to make fruits, so you can cut off the male flower, possibly diverting more energy into the developing fruits—whether or not it does, you can eat the male flower.

Blackberry *(Rubus* spp.): Cultivated blackberries may be erect, semi-erect, or trailing. All types have perennial roots but biennial stems—called "canes"—which fruit their second season, then die. Annual pruning is a must.

Plants are usually sold bare root and dormant, and if this is the case with your plants, cut all canes to ground level right after you plant. This prevents disease carryover on old canes as well as premature fruiting, and stimulates the growth of buds below ground. To keep fruit off the ground and make harvesting easier, train plants to a trellis, which can be as simple as two wires—one at 3 ft. and the other at 5 ft. above ground level—strung between sturdy posts. Trellising is not absolutely necessary with erect blackberries.

After this banana pseudostem bears fruit, it will be replaced by a younger pseudostem.

Prune erect and semi-erect blackberries twice each year (see the top drawing on p. 146). In summer, pinch out the tips of new canes just as they reach a height of 3 ft. Pinching induces the growth of lateral branches, which will bear fruit the following season. All canes do not reach this height simultaneously, so go over the planting a few times during the summer. Prune again while the plants are dormant, first removing, at ground level, all canes that fruited the previous season. (You could, instead, have cut them away during the summer, right after harvest.) Also remove any young canes that are crowded, spindly, or diseased. Finally, shorten the fruiting laterals to a length of 12 in. to 18 in., allowing more growth on the sturdier laterals because they can bear more fruit.

Prune trailing blackberries by first cutting away any canes that have fruited. Do this right after harvest or when the plants are dormant. While the plants are dormant, also thin out new canes to the most vigorous eight to ten per plant. Shorten overly long canes to 7 ft. and laterals to between 12 in. and 18 in.

(continued on page 147)

Pruning Erect and Semi-Erect Blackberries

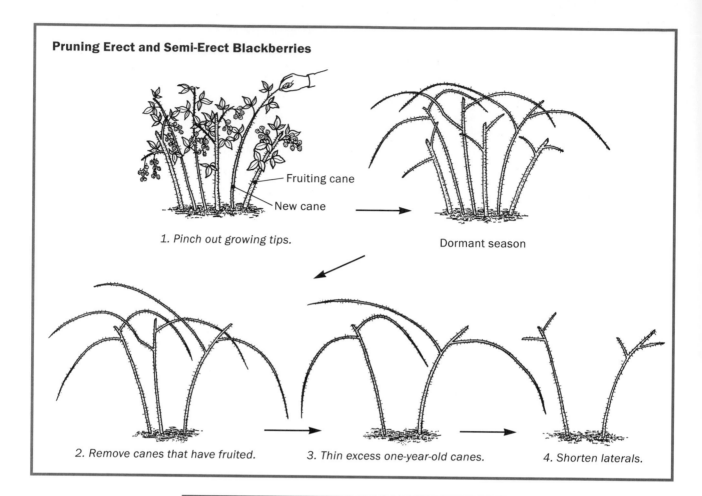

Fruiting cane

New cane

1. Pinch out growing tips.

Dormant season

2. Remove canes that have fruited.

3. Thin excess one-year-old canes.

4. Shorten laterals.

Pruning Trailing Blackberries (Dormant Season)

1. Cut away canes that have fruited.

2. Thin new canes to about 10 per plant.

3. Shorten new canes to about 7 ft.

4. Shorten laterals to 12 in. to 18 in.

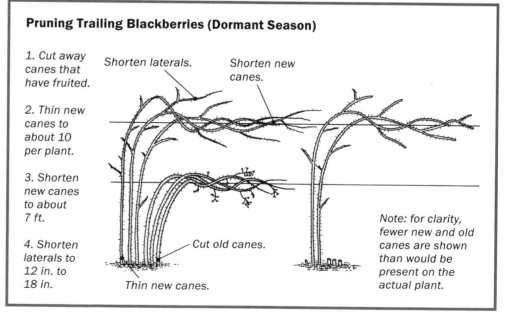

Shorten laterals.

Shorten new canes.

Cut old canes.

Thin new canes.

Note: for clarity, fewer new and old canes are shown than would be present on the actual plant.

After you dormant-prune trailing black-berries, weave or tie the canes up to the trellis. You can just let each season's new canes trail along the ground, where they will be out of the way of the fruiting canes. Or train new canes on one wire or in one direction along the trellis, and fruiting canes along the other wire or in the other direction.

Blueberry *(Vaccinium spp.)*: The three species of cultivated blueberries—highbush (*V. corymbosum*), rabbiteye *(V. asheii)*, and lowbush *(V. angustifolium)*—bear fruits on one-year-old wood, but their pruning needs vary because of their widely differing growth habits. They are all bushy, with lowbush plants growing only about 1 ft. high, highbush plants growing about 6 ft. high, and rabbiteye plants soaring to 15 ft. or more. The only pruning these species need the first three years is removal of dead and diseased stems. If you can bring yourself to do it, remove flowers the first few years to divert energy into shoot growth rather than fruits.

A highbush blueberry stem typically remains productive for about four years, so the first step in annual dormant pruning of these plants is to cut away, near ground level, stems more than four years old. After that, head back young, weak stems less than ¼ in. thick to strong branches or buds, and remove older twiggy growth. Thin out stems in the center of the bush if they are crowded and shorten or remove stems that droop to the ground. Certain varieties, such as 'Cabot' and 'Pioneer', produce an excessive number of fruit buds on fruitful shoots. With such varieties, shorten each fruiting stem so that it has only three to five fruit buds. These are plump as compared to the pointy vegetative buds.

Prune rabbiteye blueberries in a manner similar to highbush blueberries, but less heavily because of the rabbiteye's inherent vigor. Be careful not to prune so much that you stimulate excessive shoot growth at the expense of fruiting, but prune enough to keep the interior of the bush from becoming too shaded, and to keep the plants from growing too tall. Prune a mature bush mostly by selectively cutting the oldest and largest stems to the ground.

Lowbush blueberries spread beneath the ground with underground stems, called rhizomes, and new shoots originate directly from these rhizomes as well as from buds on stems above ground. The best fruits are borne on the youngest stems, especially those that grow directly from the rhizomes. Therefore, prune lowbush blueberries severely, cutting the plants completely to the ground every second or third winter. The plants do not bear at all the season following pruning, so if you do not want to miss a year of fruit, divide the planting into halves and prune an alternate half of the bed each year. Or divide the planting into thirds and prune a different third each year—the reduced production of second-year stems will be offset by the increased proportion of the bed bearing fruit each year.

Buffalo berry *(Shepherdia spp.)*: Buffalo berry bushes require little or no pruning.

Butternut *(Juglans cinerea)*: Male flowers appear on one-year-old wood and female flowers appear on growing shoots. Despite the young growth needed for flowers, butternut requires little pruning beyond that needed to train it to a sturdy framework when young, and to remove diseased, broken, or misplaced wood as the tree ages.

Carambola *(Averrhoa Carambola)*: See Starfruit

Cashew *(Anacardium occidentale)*: Cashew is a sprawling tree that never gets tall and bears plenty of new flowers at the ends of new shoots. The plant needs little pruning.

Cherimoya *(Annona Cherimola)*: Prune cherimoya during the brief period just before growth begins, when the plant is leafless. Because the wood is brittle, train the tree to a sturdy framework. Cherimoya has several buds at each leaf, and if a scaffold branch is growing out at too narrow an angle, you can stub it back and a new branch will grow—at

(continued on page 148)

Shortening a blueberry stem leaves fewer plump fruit buds, but the berries will be larger.

a wider angle—from one of the other buds. A cherimoya tree grows rapidly in its youth, then slows down and never becomes very large. Keep the tree even smaller than its natural size if you plan to hand-pollinate, which is often necessary in dry climates.

Fruit is borne mostly on growing shoots, with some fruit also produced at old leaf scars on older wood. Severe pruning reduces flowering on young shoots, as well as fruit set; on the other hand, the trees bear fairly well without any pruning. Nonetheless, moderate pruning is the best course to follow for good fruit size and to minimize breakage of limbs weighed down with fruits at their ends.

Cherry *(Prunus* spp.): A sweet cherry tree *(P. avium)* can grow quite large, and if you want to let it grow to full height, train it as a central leader. To limit height, lop the leader back to a weak branch for a modified central-leader form. Sweet cherry trees have a natural tendency to develop bare stems, devoid of branches. Counteract this tendency by heading the developing leader about 12 in. above the point where you want each tier of scaffold limbs, and similarly head scaffold limbs for secondary branching. Once mature, the tree requires little pruning, because fruits form both on young wood and on spurs on older wood, and because the potential crop does not respond to fruit thinning. Prune just as growth begins in spring.

In contrast to the sweet cherry tree, the tart cherry tree *(P. Cerasus)* is naturally small and spreading. Train tart cherry trees to either open-center or modified central-leader form. Like sweet cherries, tart cherry fruits are borne on young wood and on spurs on older wood. Beyond basic annual pruning, prune tart cherry trees a moderate amount to keep them invigorated. Prune more severely where winters are bitterly cold. Severe pruning will stimulate more vigorous, but less fruitful, young stems, so that most of the fruiting is taken up by flowers on spurs. Flowers on spurs are more cold hardy than those growing laterally on young stems.

Duke cherries *(P. × effusus)* are thought to be natural hybrids of sweet and tart cherries. The fruits, growth habits, and pruning needs of duke cherries lie intermediate between those of the sweets and the tarts.

Nanking cherry *(Prunus tomentosa)* and sand cherry *(P. Besseyi)* are two bush species occasionally grown for their fruits and as ornamentals. Both species fruit well with little or no pruning. During the dormant season, occasionally cut away old stems at ground level, thin out the center of a bush for light and air, and cut away dead or diseased wood.

Cherry-of-the-Rio-Grande *(Eugenia aggregata)*: Prune this evergreen shrub only as needed to shape it. Fruits are borne at the bases of new shoots.

Chestnut *(Castanea* spp.): Chestnut needs minimal pruning. Train the young tree to a sturdy framework with a single trunk. Prune the mature tree, which bears flowers on growing shoots (the male catkins toward the ends and bisexual catkins lower down), only to remove crossing, dead, or diseased wood.

Citrus *(Citrus* spp.): Citrus grow as bushy evergreen trees that need little or no pruning—just as well, given the capricious response of citrus to pruning cuts. Do most of what little pruning is necessary just before the spring flush of growth where winters are cold, or anytime in perpetually hot climates. With 'Valencia' oranges or other citrus having some fruit on the branches year round, prune when there is the least fruit on the tree (late summer with 'Valencia').

On the young tree, prune mostly to space branches and to remove suckers growing below the graft. The plant is naturally so bushy that little specific training is needed, or possible. Because it is often hard to force stems into the roles you select for them, wait until a plant is a few years old, and older stems have calmed down in growth, before selecting scaffold limbs. Or just leave the plant to its own whims.

148 CHAPTER EIGHT

Prune a mature tree just enough to keep it from growing too large and to thin out the interior if it becomes too shaded. Flowers form on older wood as well as in the leaf axils of growing shoots, with the best fruit set on the latter flowers. The bark is susceptible to sunscald, so paint bark with a 50:50 mixture of white latex paint and water whenever your pruning suddenly exposes the bark to the sun. Where brown rot is a problem, prune back low hanging stems so that spores from the soil cannot reach the fruits. Even where brown rot is not a problem, the lower "skirt" of a citrus tree eventually becomes dense with old wood that is not only unproductive, but also interferes with getting at the tree. Fight your way under such a tree, and lop off some of those branches from below to let in light and air.

Lemon trees have a particularly gawky growth habit, naturally making long stems that are easily broken under their weight of fruit. Stems also interlace to make harvesting difficult. Prune a lemon tree frequently and lightly, thinning and shortening stems.

Because citrus wood has many dormant buds, older trees that are healthy but not fruiting satisfactorily can be rejuvenated with drastic pruning. "Skeletonize" a tree by removing all wood thicker than 1 in. to 1½ in. in diameter. "Buckhorning" is a more drastic way of rejuvenating a tree by dramatically lowering it (but also delaying fruiting). Saw all major limbs to 1-ft. long stubs, then remove any remaining twiggy growth. Thin out some of the vigorous shoots that follow buckhorning. With any drastic pruning, remember to paint all newly exposed bark white to prevent sunscald.

In spite of their capricious nature with regard to pruning, citrus can be sheared as hedges or trained as espaliers.

Cranberry (*Vaccinium macrocarpon*): Cranberries are low evergreens whose lanky stems sprawl along the ground. Along the length of the trailing stems grow short, upright fruiting stems. And wherever a trailing stem touches moist earth, roots develop. With time, the fruiting stems become overcrowded, and the sprawling stems begin to pile high. Prune cranberries in winter by thinning out fruiting uprights and cutting away some of the sprawling stems.

Above: A buckhorned citrus will soon resprout, then become productive again.

Left: This Eureka lemon hedge screens a steep yard from the street.

(continued on page 151)

Pruning Red Currant as a Stool (Dormant Season)

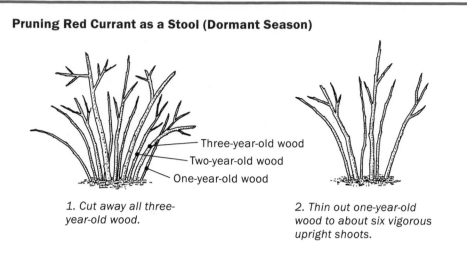

— Three-year-old wood
— Two-year-old wood
— One-year-old wood

1. Cut away all three-year-old wood.

2. Thin out one-year-old wood to about six vigorous upright shoots.

Note: for clarity, three rather than six of each age of shoot are shown.

Pruning Red Currant to a Leg

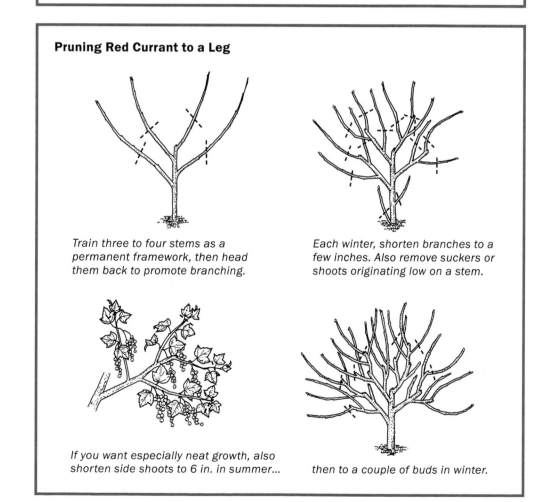

Train three to four stems as a permanent framework, then head them back to promote branching.

Each winter, shorten branches to a few inches. Also remove suckers or shoots originating low on a stem.

If you want especially neat growth, also shorten side shoots to 6 in. in summer...

then to a couple of buds in winter.

Currant *(Ribes* spp.): Red and white currants (various combinations of *R. rubrum, R. sativum,* and *R. petraeum)* are essentially all the same fruit, differing only in color. They bear mostly on two-year-old and three-year old wood, and a little toward the bases of vigorous, year-old shoots. Prune while the plants are dormant. Currants can be pruned as a bush, or "stool," or to a more upright form, or "leg."

To grow a bush as a stool, with new stems originating at or below ground level, prune any shoot right down to the ground after its third season. To prevent overcrowding, also thin out one-year-old stems by cutting to the ground all except a half-dozen of those that are the sturdiest and the most upright.

Especially in Great Britain, red and white currants are sometimes grown with a permanent framework of branches on a "leg," which is a trunk only a few inches long. Train the young bush so that three or four stems grow outward and upward, without crowding, from the leg. Build up a more or less permanent framework of branches by heading these stems to promote branching. Each winter, shorten new stems that grew off the permanent framework branches to a few inches in length. For tighter growth, such as when you espalier a red currant, prune back side shoots in summer to about 6 in. just as the fruit starts to color, then go over those shoots again in winter, shortening them to no more than a couple of buds.

Black currants *(R. nigrum)* bear their best fruits on stems that grew previous season. Each year, while the plants are dormant, cut either to the ground or to a low, vigorous branch any wood that has borne fruit. As an alternative, prune black currants at harvest time, cutting off the fruiting stems (which can then be stripped of their fruits). In either case, go back over the plants while they are dormant, thinning out crowded young stems and removing stems drooping to the ground.

(continued on page 152)

PRUNING BLACK CURRANT

1. 'Consort' black currant, before pruning, has two-year-old stems and one-year-old stems. Black currants bear fruit on one-year-old stems.

2. Prune away, or to vigorous side shoots, all two-year-old stems.

3. After pruning, only the one-year-old fruit-bearing stems remain.

Clove currant *(R. odoratum,* although sometimes called Missouri currant or buffalo currant, and sometimes confused with *R. aureum)* fruits in the same way as red and white currants. With stems arching to the ground, and new suckers popping up even a few feet from the mother plant, clove currant is naturally unkempt. Besides removing old stems and thinning young stems, tidy up the plant by shortening stems arching to the ground. Remove a sucker by grabbing it and jerking upward. Then trace the attached underground stem back to the mother plant, where you can cut it off.

Date *(Phoenix dactylifera):* Like other palms, the date palm has a single growing point at the top of its trunk. At its base, the plant produces offshoots, which can be used for making new plants. To propagate from an offshoot, dig soil away from it, taking care not to injure the roots. Then sever the offshoot from the main plant with a wide chisel or sharp shovel. To reduce water loss, cut off all but a dozen leaves from the offshoot, then keep the leaves wrapped in burlap, with only their tips exposed, for a year after transplanting.

Although more leaves generally mean more and better fruits from a bearing palm tree, there are circumstances that warrant pruning off some leaves. You may have to remove some foliage to make room for positioning bags, if you use them to protect the fruit clusters from rain. Leaf removal also decreases the humidity around the fruits, reducing the incidence of fruit checking and blacknose. Therefore, cut off enough leaves so that the lower ends of the fruit bunches are exposed. Do this in early summer. When this pruning results in the loss of many leaves, as happens with varieties such as 'Halawy' and 'Khadrawy', which have short fruit clusters, you also have to reduce the crop in proportion to the leaf loss.

As your plant ages, remove old and dying leaves. The leaves die after three to seven years, but do not fall off naturally. It is easier to cut the leaves off before their bases become hard and dry. If healthy leaves are damaged by cold, do not cut them off; a good part of each leaf may still be functioning.

Thinning the fruits results in more consistent harvests of higher-quality dates, even when no healthy leaves need to be pruned off. Remove half to three-quarters of the flowers within each bunch by cutting off the ends of all fruit strands, and then completely removing some individual strands. Where strands are numerous and short, as with 'Halawy' and 'Khadrawy', mostly remove whole strands, rather than shorten them. For high-quality, large dates such as 'Medjool', you can reduce the number of fruits by selectively removing flowers on a strand.

Reducing the number of bunches is yet another way to thin the crop. Remove all bunches the first three years that an offset is in the ground, then gradually increase the fruit load each year. A mature 'Deglet Noi', for example, can mature about a dozen bunches, each weighing about 20 lb. Do not overthin date fruits, though, or puffiness, blistering, and blacknose can result. The bearing capacity of a particular date palm depends on growing conditions, plant age, plant vigor, and variety.

Elderberry *(Sambucus canadensis):* Elderberry is a suckering shrub that fruits reasonably well even when neglected. Annual pruning will, however, bring out the best from the plant in terms of beauty and fruit production. Prune when the plant is dormant, thinning out new suckers where they crowd or spread too far, and cutting away wood older than three years old. When you thin suckers, remove first those that are diseased, broken, or most spindly.

Feijoa *(Feijoa Sellowiana):* See Guava

Fig *(Ficus carica):* The fig is an adaptable plant that you can train either as a bush or as a tree. The bush form is preferable where figs are marginally cold hardy; a cold winter might kill back a single trunk of a fig tree, but perhaps not all stems of a fig bush. If you grow fig as a tree, train it to an open-center form or, where sunlight is intense, to a modified open-center form (not a modified central leader!), with stems eventually filling in the center to prevent sunburn. With most varieties, branching is usually sufficient so that few or no heading cuts are needed during training. A notable exception is 'Calimyrna' ('Smyrna'). Training the plant to a sturdy framework is especially important with 'Mission', because of the tendency for this variety's limbs to split under the weight of the crop. With any variety trained as a tree, remove suckers growing near the ground.

A fig plant is capable of bearing fruits laterally toward the end of last year's wood—this early crop is called the "breba" crop—as well as on the current season's growth. Many varieties set fruit without pollination, but some require the assistance of a special wasp (*Blastophaga psenes*) and a nonedible fig (caprifig) to set fruit. With varieties that set both breba and main crops, the breba fruit can be different from the main crop fruit. 'Mission' brebas, for example, are few and small, while the main crop fruits are large, round, and abundant. The variety 'King' needs pollination for the main crop, but not for the breba crop.

How a variety bears its fruit influences pruning technique. 'Beall', 'Flanders', 'King', 'Mission', 'Pasquale', 'Tena', 'Ventura', and 'Verte' produce good breba crops, so the dormant plants should not be pruned heavily or you will cut off the previous year's wood, which will bear that crop. Prune 'Adriatic' ('Grosse Verte'), 'Alma', 'Blanche', 'Brown Turkey', 'Calimyrna', 'Celeste', 'DiRedo', 'Everbearing', 'Excel', 'Magnolia', and 'Osborne' more heavily, because they yield only light breba crops. Prune 'Kadota' ('Dottato') and 'Panachee' most heavily, for the late crop only. Stems on these last two varieties are commonly stubbed to 3 in. to 4 in., stimulating vigorous new growth that will be loaded all along its length with an especially uniform crop of fruit.

Allowing for varietal differences, prune mature fig plants enough to stimulate new growth (about 1 ft.) each year and to prevent overcrowding of branches. Even varieties grown for their breba crop need pruning to stimulate enough new growth for the next year's crop. Thin out crowded wood and head back long stems, but try to avoid making too many heading cuts, especially on varieties yielding good breba crops. 'Mission' tends to develop large drooping stems from scaffold limbs; cut these off. 'Calimyrna' and 'Kadota' tend to grow long, unbranched stems that eventually bend over and sunburn; shorten or remove them before they age. You can promote an earlier and heavier breba crop on 'Brown Turkey' by cutting off the very tips of the stems just before growth begins for the season.

Because the fruit is such a delicacy and the plants do not mind having their roots confined, figs have long been grown in greenhouses and in pots where the climate is too cold for outdoor figs. (The minimum temperature tolerated depends to a large extent on the variety, but the stems of figs are generally cold hardy to about 15°F.) Root restriction and root pruning of potted figs help check rampant growth and keep the plants fruitful. Summer pruning, by pinching out the growing tip after every foot or so of growth early in the season, is frequently employed to promote profuse branching for a heavier breba crop.

In cold climates, you also could bend the stems to the ground and cover them with soil, dirt, leaves, or other insulating material for protection from cold. To maintain a supply of flexible, fruiting wood, prune such a plant by a renewal system. In autumn, cut to the ground any wood that is two years old (or older, if the plants have not previously been pruned like this), then reduce the number of one-year-old stems. Bend the stems that remain down to the ground slowly, so that they do not break (see the drawing on p. 154). Forcing a spade into the ground to cut the roots on one side of the plant makes it easier to bend the whole top to the ground in the opposite direction. Wait until the weather is sufficiently cold before covering the plant, or else the buried wood will rot. In spring, uncover the plant and pull it upright before growth begins.

(continued on page 154)

Do not prune a fig variety that bears on one-year-old wood too heavily or you will remove the crop.

Filbert *(Corylus* spp.): Filbert grows as a small tree or a large shrub. If you choose to grow the plant as a tree, train it to an open-center form. Prune the mature plant moderately every year, enough to stimulate new growth on which the following year's nuts will be borne, and to reduce the tendency to alternate years of heavy and light cropping. The more one-year-old stems you see when you dormant prune, the greater the present year's potential crop and the more severely you should prune. The combined effects of pruning, fertilization, and water should result in new shoots that grow 6 in. to 10 in. in a season in order to give you consistent crops of large nuts.

Commercial filbert orchards are sometimes pruned by cutting three-quarters of all the wood out of every fifth tree on every fifth year. Pruned trees yield no crop the season following pruning, but very good yields of large nuts for the next couple of years.

British gardeners employ a kind of summer pruning called "brutting" to subdue overly vigorous growth on a filbert tree. To brut, you grab a vigorous stem when it is about 12 in. long, then bend it over enough to break it but leave it hanging on the plant. Brutting allegedly also helps ripen nuts and induce shoots to carry female flowers.

Gooseberry *(Ribes* spp.): A gooseberry bush bears some of its fruits laterally on one-year-old wood, but most fruit is borne on spurs on wood that is two and three years old. Annual pruning improves fruit quality, and makes it easier to reach within the thorny bushes to pluck the berries.

Usually the plant is grown as a "stool," which, after pruning, consists of a half-dozen shoots each of one-, two-, and three-year-old wood, all originating at ground level. Prune a stooled plant when it is dormant, by cutting to the ground some of the one-year-old stems and all those that are more than three years

(continued on page 156)

Overwintering a Fig

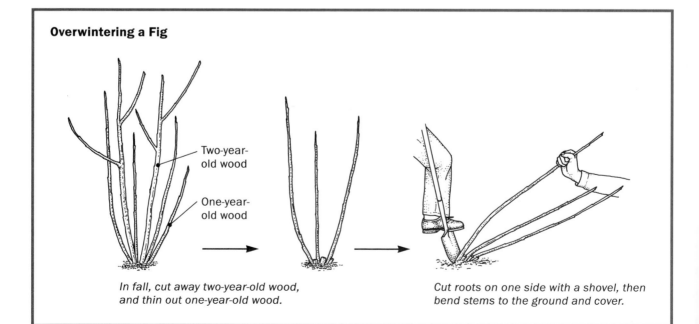

Two-year-old wood

One-year-old wood

In fall, cut away two-year-old wood, and thin out one-year-old wood.

Cut roots on one side with a shovel, then bend stems to the ground and cover.

PRUNING GOOSEBERRIES

1. This 'Welcome' gooseberry bush is awaiting its annual pruning.

2. After cutting to the ground stems that are more than three years old, thin out the youngest stems.

3. Shorten lanky stems because they would lie on the ground once laden with fruit.

4. Thinning some of the remaining stems lets air circulate and makes harvesting easier.

5. Here is 'Welcome' ready for another season.

Pruning a Gooseberry 'Tree'

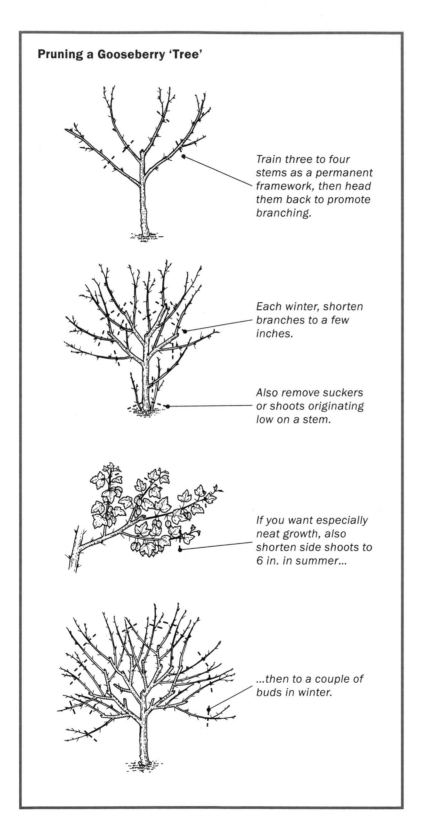

Train three to four stems as a permanent framework, then head them back to promote branching.

Each winter, shorten branches to a few inches.

Also remove suckers or shoots originating low on a stem.

If you want especially neat growth, also shorten side shoots to 6 in. in summer...

...then to a couple of buds in winter.

old. Darkening and peeling bark on older stems helps you distinguish them from younger stems. Also shorten lanky stems that otherwise would droop to the ground under their load of fruit.

Another way to grow gooseberry is as a small tree, on a "leg," with a trunk only a few inches long, or grafted atop a longer trunk of *R. odoratum*, *R. aureum*, *R. divaricatum*, *R. nidigrolaria*, or *R. sanguineum*. For tree forms, train the head of a young plant to a permanent framework of three or four branches pointing upward and outward. Shorten these stems each winter for a couple of years to induce further branching and create a permanent framework.

Side shoots will grow off the permanent framework. Prune these side shoots according to how neat you like your plants and how large you like your gooseberries. More severe pruning gives a neater bush with fewer, yet larger, fruits. At the very least, each winter cut away any side shoots that are crossing, drooping, or otherwise

Bearing Habit of Grape

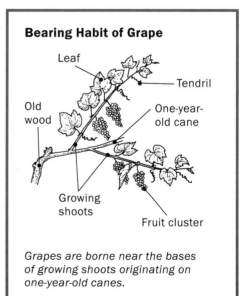

Leaf

Tendril

Old wood

One-year-old cane

Growing shoots

Fruit cluster

Grapes are borne near the bases of growing shoots originating on one-year-old canes.

misplaced. Very vigorous side shoots can be left to fruit if they are not overcrowding the bush, or they can be cut away entirely.

If your goal is really tidy plants and really large gooseberries, shorten all side shoots in early July to about 5 in. Then, during the winter, cut them back again, to about 2 in. Summer pruning also has the benefit of incidentally removing tips of stems infected with powdery mildew, and this may help limit the spread of disease.

Grape *(Vitis* spp.): Grapes are borne, of course, on vines, and these vines are capable of prodigious growth. The three types of grapes cultivated for their fruit are the European wine grape *(V. vinifera,* also known as the vinifera grape), the American grape (mostly *V. labrusca,* also known as the fox grape), and the muscadine grape *(V. rotundifolia).* Annual dormant pruning is necessary for any grape vine to remain healthy and bear the best-tasting fruits, with all those fruits conveniently within reach. Be ready to prune off quite a bit from your vine—over three-quarters of the previous year's growth!

Grapes bear fruits mostly near the bases of shoots growing from canes, which are one-year-old stems. You can easily distinguish a cane from older wood because the bark on a cane is smooth and tan, whereas that on older wood is dark and peeling. Not all canes are equally fruitful. Those that are most fruitful are moderately vigorous, about pencil thick, with 6 in. to 12 in. of space from node to node. Generally, it is the first few buds on a vinifera or a muscadine cane that give rise to fruitful shoots; therefore, these varieties are "spur pruned," with their fruitful canes shortened drastically. On American grapes, those fruitful shoots arise from buds farther out along the canes, so these varieties are "cane pruned," leaving fewer but longer canes; see the sidebar on p. 158 for one cane-pruned system. (The so-called French-American hybrids bear similarly to American grapes, as do the following vinifera varieties: 'Thompson Seedless', 'Chardonnay', 'Sauvignon Blanc', 'White Riesling', 'Barbera',

'Cabernet Sauvignon', 'Grenache', and 'Salvador'. Cane-prune all of these.)

With a spur-pruned vine, all of the previous season's growth is cut back to one to four buds—these shortened canes are now "fruiting spurs." (Do not count the cluster of buds at the very base of a cane.)

Below: This grape vine consists of a trunk topped by two horizontal cordons off which are growing last year's fruiting canes.

Left: The vine has been spur pruned by shortening all canes back to about two buds and thinning some out where overcrowded.

The fatter canes, which are capable of bearing more fruit, can be left longest. Adjust the total number of buds that you leave on the plant according to its vigor, allowing more buds when the previous season's growth was more vigorous. When you finish pruning, the spur-pruned vine will look like a small tree, with a 6-ft. trunk capped by a cluster of fruiting spurs and, soon, growing shoots.

(continued on page 159)

The Kniffin System for Training Grape Vines

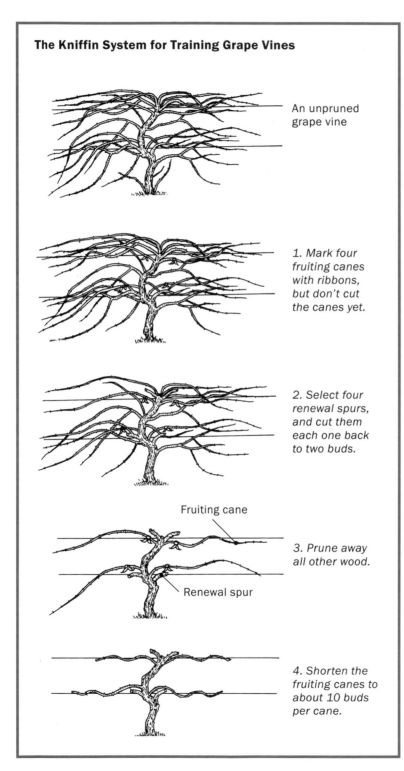

An unpruned
grape vine

1. Mark four
fruiting canes
with ribbons,
but don't cut
the canes yet.

2. Select four
renewal spurs,
and cut them
each one back
to two buds.

Fruiting cane

3. Prune away
all other wood.

Renewal spur

4. Shorten the
fruiting canes to
about 10 buds
per cane.

The Four-arm Kniffin System is a common method of growing a cane-pruned vine, using, for support, a two-wire trellis, with one wire 6 ft. and the other wire 3 ft. above ground. The mature plant consists of a trunk with four canes growing from it, two trained in opposite directions along the upper wire and two similarly trained along the lower wire. Prune while the vine is dormant, beginning by selecting four canes to carry the season's fruits. These canes should be moderately vigorous and originate close to the trunk and near the wires. You are going to save these canes, so mark them with ribbons so that you do not accidentally cut them off. With this year's fruiting canes selected, plan for the following season's crop by forcing new shoots (which will become fruiting canes in a year) to grow from well-placed short branches, called renewal spurs. Select four branches, two near the upper wire and two near the lower wire, that have plump buds near their bases. The age of the wood to be saved for renewal spurs is unimportant, just as long as the wood has healthy buds near its base. Form the renewal spurs by cutting each of these well-placed branches back to two to four buds. Next, cut away all growth except for the renewal spurs and the canes you saved. Finally, shorten each of the canes to about 6 ft. in length, leaving about 10 buds per cane. The more vigorously the cane grew the last season, the less you need to shorten it.

Spur-pruned or cane-pruned vines can also be grown as cordons. A cordon is a permanent arm from which grow fruiting canes and renewal spurs, or, in the case of a spur-pruned vine, only fruiting spurs. A cordon is ideal for covering an arbor. With a cane-pruned variety, select canes and renewal spurs that are well spaced along the cordon, then cut away all other wood. With a spur-pruned variety, just stub all growth to within a few buds of the cordon. In either case, prune enough so that there is about 1 ft. of space between canes or fruiting spurs along the cordon. Because muscadine grapes can support such large crops, the plants are commonly grown as large single or multiple cordons.

As might be expected of a plant that has been cultivated for thousands of years, many ways have been devised for training grapes.

Different methods of training influence the amount of heat, air, and sunlight the growing vine is exposed to, all of which can influence fruit quality and ripening. In very cold climates, consider training a vine to multiple trunks—in case of winter damage to one—or to a low trunk that grows from ground level at an angle so that canes can be laid on the ground and mulched for winter protection. With the latter method, tie the canes along a low wire just before growth begins. Then, as the growing season progresses, tie fruiting shoots growing from these canes to an upper wire, to bathe in sunlight and air. Old trunks are most susceptible to winter cold damage, so periodically replace an old trunk with a young one, not even sacrificing one season's harvest if you trained your vine to multiple trunks.

(continued on page 160)

Pruning Cordon-Trained Grapes

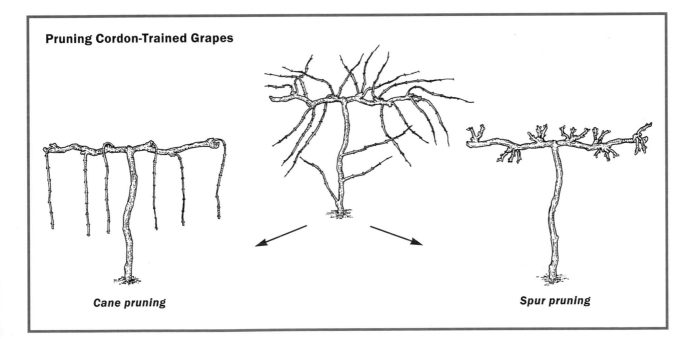

Cane pruning

Spur pruning

Special techniques have evolved to increase fruit quality. Removing some clusters or berries within clusters increases the size and quality of fruits that remain. Thin fruits early in the season, and when thinning excess clusters, selectively remove those toward the end of a shoot. On spur-pruned varieties, generally allow only one cluster per shoot. In cold climates, fruit thinning also hastens ripening and leaves the vine more hardy going into winter. Clipping off leaves around a cluster can increase air circulation and decrease diseases. And girdling the bark of a healthy vine as fruits are setting can increase berry size, while girdling as ripening begins can hasten ripening.

Thinning grapes within a cluster decreases disease and makes the remaining berries tastier and larger.

For centuries, vinifera grapes have been grown in greenhouses—and some of those vines are centuries old! Because of limited space, the size of the vine must be restricted by a combination of winter and summer pruning. Where space permits, grapes can be trellised and grown the same as outdoor grapes, always balancing the number of fruits left with the amount of light available and the amount of foliage that space allows.

The traditional method for growing greenhouse grapes is to train a single shoot from the outside wall up along the ridge to the peak of the house. (Where climate permits, the roots can be planted just outside the greenhouse and the vine threaded in through a hole low in the wall. This practice has been used to force grapes out of season or to make possible growing them where summers are not warm enough.) As the single shoot is trained up to the peak, any laterals that appear are pinched as soon as they have four leaves; sublaterals are completely removed. In winter, shorten the single shoot and cut off the laterals.

That single shoot becomes the permanent cordon of the established vine. Once the vine is fruiting, each winter shorten all laterals to single bud spurs. Two flowering shoots typically grow from each spur, and once flowers show, remove the weaker of the two shoots. Tie the remaining shoot to a crosswire support and pinch out its growing tip, three leaves past the last bunch to show. Remove lateral shoots as they appear and when flowers open, remove all but one flowering cluster per flowering shoot. Mmmmmmm.

Grumichama *(Eugenia brasiliensis):* Prune this evergreen shrub only as needed to shape it.

Guava *(Psidium* spp. and *Feijoa Sellowiana):* Guavas are represented by two botanical genera, both of which are in the Myrtle family. The plants are similar in that they both become medium-sized shrubs or small trees, depending on how you want to train them. Both also are ornamental and can be grown as informal bushes, or, with some sacrifice of fruit, can be sheared for a formal effect.

The common guava *(P. Guajava)* and the strawberry guava *(P. littorale* var. *longipes)* bear their fruits in leaf axils of growing shoots. For best fruiting, prune heavily to stimulate new fruiting shoots and to prevent limb breakage by fruits borne far out on the periphery of the plant.

Feijoa, sometimes called pineapple guava *(Feijoa Sellowiana)*, bears fruit towards the base of the previous season's wood. So that you can enjoy both the flowers and the taste of the fruits, do what little pruning is necessary after flowers fade in spring. The fleshy petals, purple tinged white, are as tasty as they are pretty.

Hazelnut *(Corylus* spp.): See Filbert

Jaboticaba *(Myrciaria cauliflora):* Jaboticaba is a slow-growing, evergreen tree with the unusual habit of bearing single fruits or clusters of fruit right on the bark and large limbs and on out to the tips of small branches. No pruning is needed.

Jackfruit *(Artocarpus heterophyllus):* This odd tree bears fruits right on the trunk and larger limbs—and a good thing, too, because each fruit can weight 40 lb. or more! The tree itself can grow large, so prune it when you want to control its size.

Jostaberry *(Ribes nidigrolaria):* Jostaberry is a relatively new fruit, a hybrid of gooseberry, European black currant, and Worcesterberry. Fruits develop laterally on one-year-old wood as well as on spurs of older wood. This robust bush needs annual dormant pruning to keep it from growing too large and to thin the fruits. Each year cut away at ground level one or two of the oldest stems, and thin out any overcrowded young stems.

Jujube *(Ziziphus Jujuba):* Jujube is a small to medium-sized tree that requires little or no regular pruning by you. One reason is that many of the branches that grow at each node are deciduous, falling from the plant at the end of the growing season. The roots tend to sucker, often sending up shoots many feet from the mother plant, and an appropriate tool for removing the suckers is a lawnmower. In China, where jujubes are very popular, fruit yield on mature trees is increased by girdling right after the blossoms fade. But before you go at your tree with your girdling knife, be aware that the crop is increased at some sacrifice of sweetness.

Juneberry *(Amelanchier* spp.): Both tree and bush species of juneberries are grown for their fruits. The tree species require little pruning, and even at that, not every year. The bush species most commonly grown for its fruit is the saskatoon *(A. alnifolia)*. On this plant, stems that are between one and four years old bear the best fruit. Older stems bear fruits that tend to be small and dryish. Therefore, cut to the ground any stems more than four years old and thin out, again at ground level, stems that grew the previous season, leaving only a half-dozen of the most vigorous ones.

Kiwifruit *(Actinidia* spp.): Besides the fuzzy kiwifruit *(A. deliciosa)*, other *Actinidia* species are cultivated for their equally delicious fruit. Most notable among these are the so-called "hardy kiwifruits," *A. arguta* and *A. Kolomikta*. All the plants are rampant vines that need to be pruned twice a year.

Although they can casually and decoratively clothe arbors and pergolas, train kiwi plants to a trellis if you want the maximum amount of fruit and if you want that fruit to be easy to pick. A single wire strung between posts could have a cordon trained along it with fruiting arms drooping down. Better, though, is a trellis consisting of T-shaped supports, 6 ft. high with 6-ft. crossarms, and three to five 12-gauge wires strung between crossarms (see the drawing at left on p. 162).

No matter what kind of support you provide, initially restrict the vine to a single shoot and get it up off the ground by tying it, as it grows, to a post. Pinch off any other shoots that attempt to grow off the primary shoot or from the ground. When the trunk-to-be reaches the height of the middle wire of the T-trellis (or the wire of the single-wire trellis), pinch out the tip to make two new shoots, which you can train as permanent cordons along the wire in either direction.

Lateral shoots, which will be the fruiting arms, will grow off this cordon and either drape over the outside wires or directly down. Stimulate the growth of these fruiting arms by shortening the developing cordon every year, during the dormant season, to within 2 ft. of where it began growth the previous season. If the tip of the cordon ever stops growing or makes tight, thin curls around the wire, cut it back to a strong bud to jump-start

(continued on page 162)

Jackfruit is enormous and odd-looking, but delectable.

vigorous growth again. Thin out fruiting arms so that they are 1 ft. apart along the cordon, then tie the arms to the outside wire of the T-trellis so that wind cannot whip them around.

Once each cordon is about 7 ft. long, your plant has filled its trellis. After that, annual dormant pruning is as follows: First, shorten each cordon to the point where it began growth the previous season. Next, stimulate shoot growth for next year's fruit, because fruits are borne toward the bases of currently growing shoots arising from wood that grew the previous season. The fruiting arms give rise to laterals that fruit at their bases, and during each dormant season, shorten each lateral so that it is 18 in. long. Buds on these laterals will likewise grow into shoots that fruit at their bases in the subsequent season. In winter, shorten these sublaterals to 18 in., and remove those that are crossing or spindly. Following winter pruning, retain only a

single strong fruiting cane, either the original arm or one of its laterals or sublaterals. When a fruiting arm with its lateral, sublateral, and subsublateral is two or three years old, cut it away to make the room for a new fruiting arm.

Did you notice how similar the fruiting habit of kiwifruit is to grape? As expected, you also could treat them in a similar fashion, each year cutting back fruiting arms to replacement arms near their point of origin.

Kiwifruit vines are strong growers that also need summer pruning to keep them in bounds. Keep the main trunk clear of shoots by cutting them away any time you notice them. Shorten excessively rampant shoots growing from the cordons to short stubs, leaving buds for future replacement arms. Cut away tangled shoots before the vine starts to strangle itself. And finally, shorten fruiting arms and their laterals if they get too long.

Training a Kiwifruit Vine

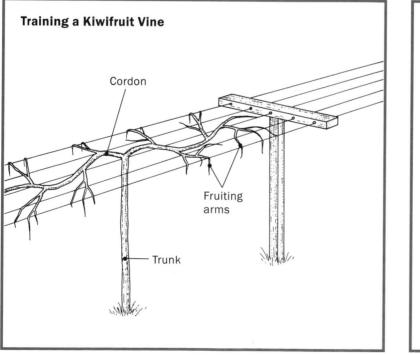

Cordon

Fruiting arms

Trunk

Fruiting Habit of Kiwifruit

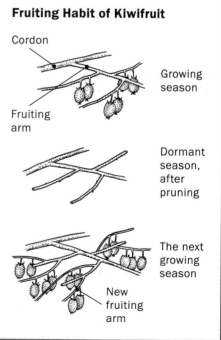

Cordon

Fruiting arm

Growing season

Dormant season, after pruning

The next growing season

New fruiting arm

Because male plants are needed only for their bloom, prune them severely right after they bloom, removing about 70% of the previous year's growth. Cut back any flowering shoot to a new shoot, which will flower the following year. Male vines do not need to put any energy into fruit production, so they generally are more vigorous than female vines.

Litchi *(Litchi chinensis):* Litchi grows to be a round-topped evergreen tree that is ornamental in its own right, and made more so when loaded with the red fruits that form at the ends of stems. The tree can be reluctant to flower (making it only a handsome ornamental) because flowering requires just enough cold (or drought) to induce dormancy, but not so much as to damage this somewhat cold-tender tree. Careful management is thus required to keep a tree fruitful wherever the climate is less than ideal. Litchi is a native of China, where the traditional advice is that you should "keep the tree calm" for fruitfulness. Prune when the fruit is ripe, cutting off the last foot or so of stems as you harvest clumps of fruit. In summer, pinch new growth. To control tree size, cut away upright stems. In climates where winters are too warm or wet to induce the natural dormancy needed for flowering, try girdling selected stems in autumn.

Fruit set is usually good when a plant does flower. Although rarely practiced, fruit thinning can increase fruit size.

Longan *(Euphoria Longan):* Longan requires regular pruning so that the plant has good form and produces regular crops of good-sized fruits. Large panicles of flowers form at the ends of stems, and if fruit set is good, the resulting fruits will be undersized and next year's crop will be reduced. Avoid this by thinning the fruits, cutting back whole stems that terminate in fruiting panicles. Longan stems also have a natural tendency to be bare except toward their ends. Head these stems back to stimulate the growth of laterals.

Loquat *(Eriobotrya japonica):* Loquat is a small evergreen tree growing in flushes through the year, with the largest flush in spring. Prune the young tree so that its stems are well spaced. On the mature tree, flowers form at the ends of some shoots as they cease elongating. Even though only a dozen or fewer flowers are likely to set fruit from clusters of 50 or more, further fruit thinning is often necessary. Clip off whole clusters or individual fruitlets at any time through winter until early spring. The tree needs little other pruning beyond occasional shortening of stems (which incidentally thins fruit) to let light within the canopy. Remove wood infected with fire blight.

Loquat flowers form at the end of shoots.

Macadamia *(Macadamia integrifolia, M. tetraphylla):* Train young trees to a central leader. Leaves form in whorls, with three buds above each leaf. The uppermost bud gives rise to an upright shoot, which is fine for extending the leader of a young tree, but makes a weak scaffold limb. Strive to space branches about 1 ft. apart along the leader, heading the leader if no branches are growing where you want them. If one of the upper of the three buds starts growing to become an upright scaffold limb, cut it back and a lower bud will grow into a wide-angled scaffold limb. Reduce the number of branches where they crowd on a scaffold limb.

Macadamia bears racemes consisting of up to 100 flowers in the axils where leaves are or were attached, but usually sets only about a dozen nuts on each raceme. With heavy flowering and natural thinning, the mature trees need little pruning.

(continued on page 164)

Mango *(Mangifera indica):* Train the young mango tree to a sturdy framework, heading back gangly shoots that sometimes develop in order to induce branching. These evergreen trees grow in flushes through the season, with extension growth initially from terminal buds. Hundreds or even thousands of flowers form in panicles at the ends of some stems, and when this happens, further extension is from branches on those stems. If a flower panicle is damaged or does not set any fruit, a new panicle may form laterally on the stem.

Mature mango trees require little pruning, mostly to get rid of dead and crowded wood and to keep the trees from growing too large. Shortening a stem in late summer or fall brings fruit production back within the crown on lateral flower panicles lower on the stem. Control tree height by selectively removing vigorous upright stems. (Commercial growers sometimes hedge mangos—nonselectively cutting all stems growing beyond a certain point—to keep the trees in bounds.) The trees tend to alternate heavy and light crops, and pruning, by removing stems with flower clusters, might help even out yields. Bark girdling in late summer, following harvest, can also help improve yields and decrease vigor, but should be done with caution. One method is to ring individual branches that would be pruned off anyway after harvest.

Mangosteen *(Garcinia Mangostana):* Mangosteen is a small evergreen tree bearing fruits at the ends of shoots. Little pruning is needed beyond the thinning of inner stems.

Medlar *(Mespilus germanica):* A medlar tree needs training in its early years to build up an attractive and sturdy framework. Beyond that, what little pruning is needed is confined to the removal of dead and crossing stems and the thinning out of spindly stems to admit light and air into the canopy. Blossoms are borne singly on the ends of short shoots that grow from lateral buds on one-year-old wood and from spurs on older wood. Be careful not to prune off the extremities of too many branches, for this is where many of the

flowering shoots arise. Where winter cold damages the plant, the year-old stems bear more of the fruits than the less hardy spurs. Prune accordingly.

Mulberry *(Morus* spp.): Once you have trained your mulberry tree to a sturdy framework, no special pruning techniques are required. Fruits are abundant, appearing from axillary buds of growing shoots and on spurs on older wood. Prune only as needed to remove dead, exhausted, and overcrowded wood. To train a mulberry to a tidy form, develop a set of main limbs, then prune branches growing off these limbs to six leaves in July in order to make short, fruiting spurs.

Natal Plum *(Carissa grandiflora):* Prune this evergreen shrub only as needed to shape it.

Nectarine *(Prunus Persica* var. *nucipersica):* The nectarine is nothing but a fuzzless peach, differing from the peach only in the gene that makes fuzz. Refer to "Peach" (p. 166) for specific pruning guidelines.

Olive *(Olea europaea):* Olive can grow to be an ancient tree, with strong yet limber wood. Unpruned, the plant grows dense with twigs and sends up many basal sprouts, making it more of a shrub than a tree in its youth. Train the young plant to an open-center form with three scaffold limbs, thinning out overcrowded wood and watersprouts, and heading back drooping wood. Rub off buds near ground level that threaten to become suckers; once a sucker takes hold, pull it off rather than cut it back, to reduce the possibility of resprouting. To hasten fruiting, keep your pruning to the absolute minimum. Wait until the tree has been in the ground for three to five years and is bearing fruit before pruning to develop good secondary branching. Even then, avoid making severe cuts.

Prune the mature tree mostly to keep it from growing too large, to let light bathe all branches, and to encourage a continual supply of new fruiting wood. Fruits form in leaf axils along, but not to the end, of the previous year's stems (and sometimes from dormant buds in one- or two-year-old wood). Many flowers make up each panicle but only three to five fruits per foot is sufficient for a full crop. When fruit set is heavy, fruit thinning will increase fruit size and oil content, hasten fruit maturity, and allow a good crop the following year. The most effective way to thin fruits is by hand, in late spring or early summer. Thinning fruits by pruning stems is effective only with stems bearing heavy loads of fruit, or else too many leaves are proportionately removed. In years of heavy crops, cut some of these stems right after fruit set.

When pruning stems, avoid severe cuts. Where summers are dry and little or no irrigation is available, prune the stems in summer to reduce the number of leaves competing with the fruit for water. If olive knot disease is a threat, prune in summer or, if you prune in winter, sterilize your pruning tools between cuts. Cut away galls produced by this disease. If frost has damaged your tree, wait until early summer to prune.

To rejuvenate an old olive tree, cut back some large limbs, whitewash the newly exposed trunk to prevent sunburn, and thin out new shoots that develop.

Papaya *(Carica Papaya, C. pubescens):* The papaya is hardly a tree, with its short life and weak, hollow stem (except at the leaf nodes). Plants are usually grown from seed, and start fruiting within a year or two of sowing. Male, female, or hermaphroditic flowers form in leaf axils. (Sprouts on what was a male tree sometimes start to bear female flowers, but not reliably.) Usually the plant grows as a single stem, unless the growing point is damaged naturally or by pruning. But no pruning at all is necessary.

After about three years, a papaya plant begins to bear fewer and smaller fruits. The increasingly tall plant also becomes more liable to topple. You could rejuvenate it by cutting it down to within 18 in. of the ground, making the cut at a slant and just slightly above a node so that water does not collect in the stump. The stump would send out new sprouts, which might fruit sooner than if you started a new seedling. On the other hand, sprouts from an old stump may

not yield well, and older trees commonly become infected with a virus. Given the speed with which seedlings bear fruits and the potential drawbacks of old plants, the best pruning option is to cut your papaya all the way to the ground—i.e., kill it—and sow some new seeds.

Passionfruit *(Passiflora spp.):* Tasty passionfruits follow beautiful passionflowers. The flowers form in the leaf axils of growing shoots. Annual pruning is not a necessity, but does keep the vine—which clings to everything, including itself, with strong tendrils—from becoming too tangled. Pruning also keeps the fruit within easy reach, although you can simply let ripe fruits just drop to the ground. As a minimum, thin out tangled growth and shorten stems in mid-winter. For more tidiness and productivity, train the vine up to a trellis consisting of T-shaped end posts with three wires strung between them. Form a permanent cordon along the middle wire and let branches drape over the outside wires. Each winter, cut every branch to a stub just a few inches long, or at least thin the branches out and shorten them. Go over the vines in summer to thin tangled growth, but leave some shade in hot climates or the fruit will sunburn.

Easiest of all to prune is the temperate species, *P. incarnata*, commonly known as maypop. Maypop dies to the ground each year, but then resprouts each spring with vigor, also sending up suckers from its rapidly spreading roots. Just jerk excess suckers out of the ground with a little tug, or grow the plant in a bed surrounded by grass and let your lawnmower do the pruning. No stem pruning is needed.

Pawpaw *(Asimina triloba):* Pawpaw grows to become a small tree that needs little pruning beyond the training stage. The roots sucker, throwing up shoots at some distance from the trunk, so remove these shoots or else you will end up with a pawpaw thicket such as forms in the wild. (If your tree is grafted, its root suckers will bear fruit that is different from those on the mother tree.) Fruits are produced on stems that grew the previous

(continued on page 166)

season, so prune occasionally while the plant is dormant to stimulate growth for the following year's fruit. Not much stimulation is needed, though. Each flower contains several separate ovaries, so can give rise to a cluster of fruits.

Peach *(Prunus Persica):* The ideal time to prune either the young or the mature tree is during blossoming. Peach is very susceptible to bark diseases, and wounds heal quickest as growth is beginning. This delayed dormant pruning also makes it easy for you to recognize and selectively remove winterkilled wood.

Peach is a naturally spreading tree, so has been traditionally trained to an open-center form. (For greater productivity, commercial growers now also train peaches to central-leaders or even trellised V's.) Most important with the young tree is to use the minimum number of cuts in training, in order to minimize the delay before you taste your first fruits. If possible, train the tree with the lowest limb pointing southwest so that it shades the trunk and lessens the chance of sunburn. (White latex paint on the trunk also helps.) As you train your young tree, take into account its natural growth habit. Dwarf varieties such as 'Compact Redhaven' naturally form more side branches than do full-size varieties, so require fewer heading cuts. For an espalier, train your peach to a fan, whose pruning is covered in more detail on pp. 224-225.

A young tree typically grows very vigorously, shading the interior of the canopy even after careful dormant pruning. To keep the interior of the tree fruitful, prevent shading by thinning some of the very vigorous upright shoots early in the growing season. As the tree matures, it will produce fewer and fewer such sprouts.

Although the young peach tree should be pruned as little as possible, the mature tree needs more severe pruning than most other fruit trees. Having large fruits, the peach responds well to fruit thinning—one result of pruning. Another reason for severe pruning is

that fruits are borne only on one-year-old stems. Use mostly thinning cuts because these serve to keep the canopy open for maximum fruit yield and color. Remove vigorous upright growth, thin remaining stems, and occasionally cut back into two- or three-year-old wood. Cut back drooping stems as well as any very short stems—both types typically produce small fruits for lack of sufficient leaves. More heading cuts, in contrast, increase fruit size, but at the expense of yield and color. Strive for 18 in. to 24 in. of new growth each year in response to pruning (in combination with watering and feeding). When you are finished pruning a peach tree, the branches should be open enough to let a bird fly right through the crown.

Make adjustments in your pruning for differences in growing conditions. Where summers are dry and trees are not irrigated, make severe heading cuts to stimulate rapid growth early in the season, before good growing conditions cease. Where water and nutrients are available throughout the growing season, thinning cuts are sufficient.

When fruit set is good, branch pruning alone does not remove a sufficient number of fruits. Hand thin the fruits. If you are pressed for time, you can thin with a forceful stream of water or by banging off excess fruitlets with a piece of hose attached to the end of a stick. The sooner that you thin the fruits, or even the blossoms, the greater the effect on fruit size, the earlier the fruits ripen, and the greater the benefit to next year's crop. Of course, with early thinning you also run the risk of too few fruits; a late frost or an insect such as the plum curculio might provide an unfortunate supplement to your thinning. The best course to follow is to do a light early thinning, then to go over the trees again about six weeks later, after the natural period of shedding fruitlets ("June drop") is over. Final fruit spacing should be about 8 in., unless fruits are concentrated only on some stems, in which case fruits can be closer. (About 35 leaves are needed to nourish each fruit. Do you want to count?)

Pear (*Pyrus* spp.): Pears are naturally upright trees that bear most of their fruits on long-lived spurs, stubby branches that grow only a fraction of an inch each year. The young trees grow vigorous shoots that sometimes are tardy in settling down to fruit. Old trees go to the other extreme, often becoming overburdened with too many fruiting spurs and insufficient new growth. Counteract these tendencies with minimal pruning of the young tree, and more aggressive pruning of the old tree.

Train the young pear tree as a central leader or as modified central leader. Use any of the techniques described in the general section on training fruit trees (pp. 123-132) to create wide-angled scaffold limbs. With their long-lived spurs, pears also make very neat espaliers (see pp. 219-222 for more information on pruning a pear espalier).

As the tree matures, the weight of the fruit will keep branches down, and then you can begin pruning for fruit rather than for limb positioning. Thin out stems where growth is too dense, mostly high in the tree. Pull off watersprouts as soon as you notice them. Also cut away weak wood, such as spindly stems hanging from the undersides of limbs.

Such stems are not very fruitful and the fruits they do bear are poor quality. If a long limb is drooping downward, cut it back to a strong side branch or to a point where it is not drooping. When fruiting spurs become too old and crowded to bear well, head and thin them to give them room and to stimulate new growth.

Vigorous shoots are particularly susceptible to fire blight disease, so avoid severe pruning, which stimulates such growth. If you do see evidence of fire blight, prune it out. Throughout the growing season, prune stems whose leaves have been blackened by this disease at least 6 in. back into healthy wood. (Don't confuse fire blight with sooty mold, which also blackens leaves. Sooty mold is superficial and can be rubbed off the surface of leaves. In addition to blackened leaves, a fire-blighted stem curls around at its tip in a characteristic shepherd's crook.) Sterilize your pruning tools between cuts to avoid spreading the disease to healthy stems. In winter, again prune back blighted stems and also cut out dark, sunken cankers in major limbs. You don't have to sterilize the pruning tools between cuts made in winter.

(continued on page 168)

As the name implies, fire blight blackens a pear branch as if it had been singed by fire.

As pear spurs age, they need to be thinned out to stimulate and make room for growth of younger spurs.

Thinning Old Pear Spurs

On old trees, crowded spurs produce smaller fruits.

Remove some spurs and head others back to a strong bud to invigorate the tree.

Pineapple Side Shoots

Slip (along fruit stalk)

Sucker (along stem)

Ground sucker (from ground)

Pruning pear stems also thins the fruit—but not enough. Go over the tree after fruit set and hand thin so that fruits are spaced 5 in. apart. Because the beginnings of next year's flower buds don't form until some 60 days after the current year's blossoms appear, there is no need to rush fruit thinning for good return bloom in the year following a bumper crop.

Pecan *(Carya illinoinensis):* Male flowers appear on one-year-old wood, and female flowers appear on growing shoots. Nonetheless, pecan requires little pruning beyond that needed to train it to a sturdy framework when young and to remove diseased, broken, or out-of-place wood as the tree ages.

Persimmon *(Diospyros* spp.): Persimmons grow to become large trees with drooping branches. That drooping habit is sometimes expressed in young trees by their long, willowy shoots. While training a tree, shorten such shoots or support them with stakes. Only a few terminal buds normally extend the growth of a stem, so head or bend any stem where you want it to branch lower down. Create an open-center or modified-central-leader form for the plant. Avoid the open-center form in hot, dry climates or else the bark and fruit might sunburn. No matter what the form, a strong framework is important since persimmon wood is brittle.

Persimmon fruits are formed in the leaf axils of new shoots that grow from last year's wood, especially those shoots growing near the end of one-year-old wood. Some pruning is thus needed to stimulate new growth each year. Prune during the dormant season, heading back some one-year-old stems to decrease fruit load the upcoming season, and to keep bearing wood near the main branches. Be careful not to cut off the ends of too many one-year-old stems or you will harvest too few fruits. The American persimmon *(D. virginiana)* needs little pruning, because it naturally drops some stems that have borne fruits.

Except where fruit set is low, hand thin Oriental persimmon *(D. Kaki)* fruits if you want them to grow large. The presence of a male tree is likely to cause overbearing on Oriental persimmon varieties capable of setting fruit without pollination. American persimmons are naturally small, so don't expect them to get bigger as the result of hand thinning.

Pineapple *(Ananas comosus):* A pineapple plant is a compressed stem, a whorl of leaves whose growing point eventually becomes a stalk capped by the pineapple fruit. Side shoots grow from this compressed stem. Those arising at ground level are called ground suckers and those along the stem are simply called suckers. Side shoots that originate on the fruit stalk are called slips, while those that originate where the plant stem and the fruit stalk meet are called hapas.

Unpruned, a pineapple plant sprawls along the ground as side shoots jut out and the plant bows under its own weight. Pruning keeps the plant neater and gives better fruits. Prune a month or two after you harvest the fruit, cutting off slips and hapas. Ground suckers ripen quickest but also give the smallest fruits, so you may want to remove them. If, after removing slips, hapas, and ground suckers, the number of remaining suckers still seems excessive, thin them out.

Pistachio *(Pistacia vera):* Pistachio is a naturally bushy tree, rarely growing higher than 20 ft. Whether grown with multiple trunks or as a modified central leader, training is very important for the first four or five years. Terminal buds are vegetative with strong apical dominance that suppresses the growth of buds farther down the stem. As a result, stems grow mostly from their tips, eventually becoming so long that they arch down to the ground and sunburn. Make as many heading cuts as are necessary into old or young stems in order to get branching every 30 in., then head branches to induce further branching.

Most of the lateral buds on one-year-old wood of pistachio are flower buds only. (On many other fruits, buds are mixed vegetative and flower buds.) This flowering habit makes for a lot of flowers, but, again, few branches. On the mature tree, even heading cuts may not induce branching, which is why training the young tree is so important. The properly brought-up mature tree probably needs only light annual pruning consisting of many heading cuts into both young and old wood. Why "probably?" Because the pruning needs of pistachio have not yet been clearly established.

Pitanga *(Eugenia uniflora):* This evergreen can be grown as a shrub or small tree. Flowers are borne at the juncture of new and old growth. Prune to encourage some new growth as well as to thin out wood that is crowded or decrepit.

Pitomba *(Eugenia Luschnathiana):* Prune this evergreen shrub only as needed to shape it.

Plum *(Prunus spp.):* Plums represent several species, differing dramatically in fruit size, color, and flavor, and less so in growth and fruiting habit. Plants range from bushes to trees, the latter of which are trained to open-center or modified central-leader form. European plums *(P. domestica)* include varieties such as 'Lombard' and 'Yellow Egg', as well as prune plums such as 'Italian' and 'Stanley', and gages such as 'Reine Claude' and 'Jefferson'. Japanese plums *(P. salicina)* are represented by such varieties as 'Abundance', 'Burbank', and 'Satsuma', and American plums *(P. americana* and other species) by the varieties 'De Soto' and 'Hawkeye'. Broadening the palette (and your palate)—and further confusing the nomenclature—are the many hybrids between plum species: For example, 'Ember' and 'Monitor' are hybrids of American and Japanese plums, and 'Kaga' and 'Hanska' are hybrids of American and another oriental species *(P. Simonii).* Plums also have been hybridized with sand cherries and with apricots, the latter cross producing "plumcots," "pluots," and "apriums."

Pruning plums is easier than categorizing them. Beyond training, which is unnecessary for many of the bushy hybrids, plums require little pruning. The plants fruit abundantly on spurs and, in the case of the Japanese plums, on one-year-old stems as well. Prune mostly to let light into the center of the tree, and for a moderate amount of new growth for next year's fruit. Occasionally remove the oldest wood at ground level from bushy plants of the American species. Generally, there is no need to thin plum fruits. Go ahead and prune more heavily if you want to keep the plant smaller—a plum tree can tolerate it. And you will have to prune even more if you grow a plum as an espalier (see p. 225).

Japanese plums are large fruits, and the crop can be heavy enough to break limbs. Prune these plums more severely than the others so that the tree does not have long, breakable branches of fruit, and because you need to stimulate abundant new growth for next year's fruit. If fruit set is heavy, hand thin the fruits to 5 in. apart.

There is one more type of plum, the Damson plum *(P. insititia),* usually used for jam and pastry filling, but pretty good eaten fresh. This wildish tree needs the bare minimum of pruning.

Pomegranate *(Punica Granatum):* Train the young pomegranate to either a single trunk or to five or six trunks. In areas where pomegranate is not reliably cold hardy, multiple trunks provide insurance that the whole plant does not die to the ground in winter. Flowers are borne on spurs of two- and three-year-old wood, so the mature plant plant requires only light annual pruning, just enough to stimulate some new growth each year and to thin out excess fruits. Also cut suckers to the ground, unless any are needed to replace a damaged trunk.

Prickly Pear *(Opuntia spp.):* These mostly thornless cacti require no pruning.

(continued on page 170)

Quince can be trained as a handsome small tree, shown here, or as a bush.

Quince *(Cydonia oblonga):* Quince is a small tree or large bush that flowers at the ends of short shoots growing from one-year-old wood. Train your quince as a bush, or as a tree with one or a few trunks. The mature plant needs little pruning. Use a combination of heading and thinning cuts to keep the plant open to air and light, and to stimulate a foot or two of new growth each season. Do not confuse this quince with the pink-flowered flowering quince *(Chaenomeles* spp.), whose fruits may be edible, but are unpalatable.

Raspberry *(Rubus* spp.): Raspberries may be red or yellow (both *R. idaeus* or *R. idaeus* var. *strigosus),* purple *(R.* × *neglectus),* or black *(R. occidentalis)*—and some black raspberries, also called blackcaps, produce nearly white fruit. Red and yellow raspberries spread as new canes grow up from wandering roots, while black and purple raspberries hopscotch along as the tips of their canes arch to the ground to root and form new plants. No matter what their color, all raspberries

have perennial roots but biennial canes. Summerbearing red and yellow raspberries canes just grow their first year, then begin to die after they have fruited in their second season. Everbearing, sometimes called fallbearing, red and yellow raspberries begin to fruit at the ends of first-year canes in late summer and autumn, then fruit lower down on those same canes the next summer before those canes die. Black raspberries and purple raspberries fruit just like summerbearing red and yellow raspberries, except that fruits form on laterals of second-year canes. The one constant in pruning all these raspberries is to cut all old canes completely to the ground right after you plant, if the plant is dormant.

Prune summerbearing red and yellow raspberries in three steps. First, cut to the ground any canes that have fruited. Do this anytime from immediately after harvest until just before growth begins the following spring. Second, while the plants are dormant, thin out canes that grew the previous season

(continued on page 173)

Fruiting Habit of Raspberries

Summerbearing red and yellow raspberries

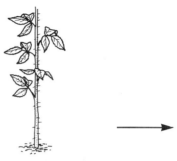
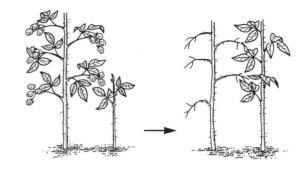

First season:
Plant produces only stems and leaves.

Second season:
Last year's canes bear fruit, then die; new canes will fruit the following year.

Everbearing red and yellow raspberries

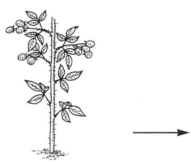
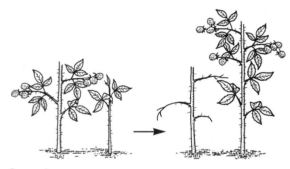

First season:
Fruits are borne at tops of new shoots in late summer and fall.

Second season:
Early-summer fruits are borne lower down on last year's canes, which then die; new canes bear in late summer and fall.

Black and purple raspberries

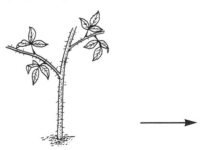
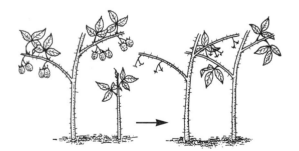

First season:
Plant produces only stems and leaves.

Second season:
Last year's canes bear fruit, then die; new canes will fruit the following year.

Pruning Summerbearing Red and Yellow Raspberries

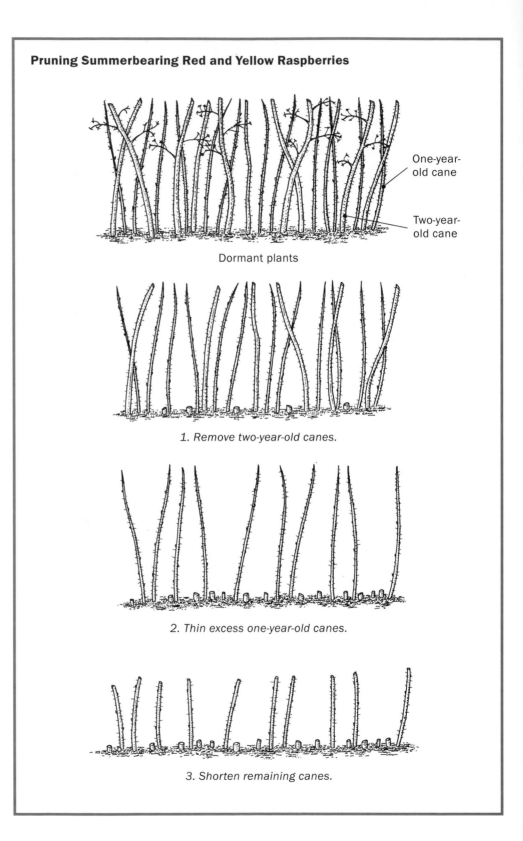

One-year-old cane

Two-year-old cane

Dormant plants

1. Remove two-year-old canes.

2. Thin excess one-year-old canes.

3. Shorten remaining canes.

so that the row is no wider than 12 in., with 6 in. or more between canes. You could have done some of this pruning while the canes were first growing, and this would cause less weakening and crowding of plants, and leave you less to thin during the dormant season. No matter when you do your thinning, selectively remove those canes that are thinnest, diseased, or broken.

The third step in pruning summerbearing red and yellow raspberries is to shorten the remaining canes. How much to shorten them depends on how you trellis your raspberries, because the only reason to shorten them is for convenience and to prevent the canes from flopping around in the wind. The longer the canes, the more fruit you will harvest. If you tie the canes to two wires, one 2 ft. and one 5 ft. off the ground, shorten the canes to about 6 ft. With this same trellis, you can leave the canes nearly full length if you bend them along and weave them around the upper wire.

Prune everbearing red and yellow raspberries the same way as the summerbearers, with one slight difference. The canes you save, pruned in the third step, will have started fruiting at their ends late the previous season, and will "finish" fruiting lower down. Therefore, shorten those canes to just below where they stopped fruiting the previous season. The old fruit stalks still hanging on the canes will tell you where to cut.

A simpler way to prune everbearing red and yellow raspberries is just to mow the whole planting down each autumn. Do this and you do not need a trellis or have to worry about cold damage or deer browsing in the winter. Diseases are less of a problem because they cannot be harbored on old canes over winter. By following this system, however, you only

(continued on page 175)

PRUNING RED RASPBERRIES

1. Unpruned red raspberry canes are unkempt and crowded.

2. Old canes must be cut away, then young ones thinned out.

3. Long canes can be kept neat by weaving them into the upper wire.

4. Pruning complete, these neatly trellised raspberries will yield a good crop, easily picked.

Pruning Black and Purple Raspberries

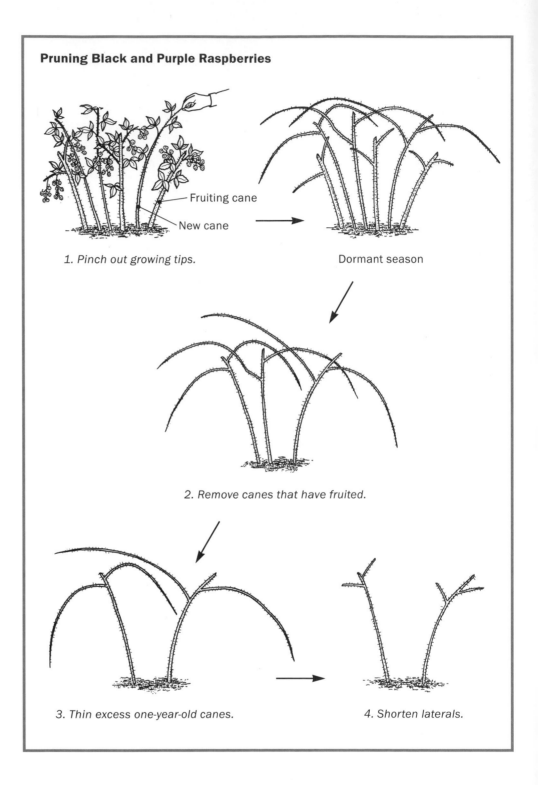

Fruiting cane

New cane

1. Pinch out growing tips.

Dormant season

2. Remove canes that have fruited.

3. Thin excess one-year-old canes.

4. Shorten laterals.

get to harvest berries borne on new shoots at the end of the season, so you sacrifice the summer crop.

Prune black raspberries and purple raspberries in four easy steps. The first step is to prune away any canes that have fruited, anytime from right after harvest until growth begins the following spring. The next step, in summer, is to prune off the top 2 in. of each growing cane as it reaches a height of 18 in. This summer topping stimulates the growth of branches, which will fruit the following growing season. If you are willing to trellis your plants, either by tying all canes to a pole at each hill or to a single wire strung between posts, your bramble patch will be neater; you will also harvest more berries because you can wait to top each cane until it is 3 ft. high. Whether you top at 18 in. or at 3 ft., go over the plants a few times during the summer, as often as new canes reach pruning height.

Do the last two steps in pruning while the plants are dormant, preferably just before growth begins in spring. Cut any diseased, damaged or spindly canes to the ground. And finally, shorten branches that resulted from your summer pruning so that they are 4 in. to 18 in. long, leaving those that are fattest the longest.

Rose Apple *(Syzygium Jambos):* Prune this evergreen shrub only as needed to shape it.

Salal *(Gaultheria Shallon):* Prune only as needed to shape the plant.

Sapodilla *(Manilkara Zapota):* This compact evergreen bears fruits in leaf axils toward the ends of small, young stems. Little pruning is needed beyond the removal of vigorous uprights.

Starfruit *(Averrhoa Carambola):* Starfruit, also called carambola, is a medium-sized evergreen tree that bears its star-shaped fruit on old wood. It needs little pruning beyond removal of vigorous uprights to prevent shading and crowding.

Strawberry *(Fragaria* spp.): Most pruning of strawberry plants is of runners, the long stems that that grow out from the crown to crawl atop the ground, producing new plants at nodes. Left alone, the mother, daughter, and granddaughter plants strew about, creating shade that results in fewer fruits and more diseases.

‘Earliglow’ strawberry, awaiting harvest.

For best health and fruiting, each strawberry plant needs about 1 square foot of space all to itself. Plants grown in the "hill" system are originally planted 1 ft. apart, so must have all their runners removed. Plants grown as a "matted row" are planted a few feet apart, with runners allowed to fill in between mother plants. With "spaced row" plants, an intermediate training system, you allow just some of the runners to form, usually four per plant.

A net keeps birds away from the ripening fruit.

All newly planted strawberries need their flower buds pinched off until the plants are established. Do this for about two months after planting.

Renovation of a June-bearing strawberry bed is an annual affair that forestalls the bed's eventual decline. (Not forever, though. After

(continued on page 176)

five or ten years, replant a new bed elsewhere.) The time to renovate is right after harvest. Begin by cutting off all the leaves with hand shears or with a mower set high, then raking them away. Next, dig out excess plants where they are crowded, selectively removing those that are oldest. Fertilize, then water, and the plants, after their short rest, will send out new leaves. (Replant, rather than renovate, a bed of everbearing or day-neutral strawberries when it declines.)

As with other herbaceous perennials, the crown of a strawberry plant does branch and become decrepit with age, at which time it can be divided. This method of revitalizing a plant is used only with strawberries that make few or no runners, such as alpine strawberries. To divide the crown, dig up the plant, then cut off young branch crowns—with attached roots—from the outer edge of the crown and plant them. But alpine strawberries reproduce reliably from seed, which is just as easy as dividing crowns and avoids the risk of propagating a disease-infected plant.

Surinam Cherry *(Eugenia uniflora):* See Pitanga

Tree Tomato *(Cyphomandra betacea):* Encourage branching of the developing tree by pinching out the growing point of the trunk at between 3 ft. and 8 ft., depending on how high you want the head. The mature tree flowers on growing shoots. Prune stems back to within the crown each year to encourage new growth and to prevent fruit from being borne only at the periphery of the crown, subjecting limbs to breakage. There is no need to thin the fruits.

Walnut *(Juglans* spp.): Both English walnuts *(J. regia,* and sometimes called Persian walnuts) and black walnuts *(J. nigra)* are grown for their nuts. Male flowers form in catkins that grow off year-old wood and female flowers form on the current season's shoots.

Train English walnut to open-center, central-leader, or modified central-leader form, but if you expect the tree to grow large, the latter two forms make sturdier trees. If a shoot destined to become a scaffold limb is too upright, rub it off and a new one, with a wider crotch angle, will grow from a secondary bud. Also, varieties differ in their natural growth habit. For example, 'Placentia' and 'Payne' are naturally spreading, and 'Eureka' and 'Franquette' are naturally upright.

Prune mature English walnut trees annually to keep them invigorated and to prevent the interior of the crown from becoming shaded. On older varieties, such as 'Franquette' and 'Hartley', only terminal buds and those just below where nuts were borne the previous season grow out to become new flowering shoots. More modern varieties grow flowering shoots from many lateral buds when the plants are young. These fecund varieties need more severe pruning in order to prevent overbearing, especially on young trees which would otherwise never become more than runts. Head back young stems on these trees by one-quarter to one-half, and regularly thin fruiting branches to let light into the canopy.

For nut production, black walnut rarely needs pruning once the tree has been trained to a sturdy, central-leader framework. Modify your pruning, though, if your eventual goal is also to harvest the trees for their beautiful wood. In this case, you want a straight, knot-free trunk, which you get by removing branches before they grow too large. As soon as the base of the first branch is 1 in. in diameter, remove all branches from the trunk halfway up the tree. As the tree grows, continue to remove branches until you have at least 9 ft. of clear trunk.

White Sapote *(Casimiroa edulis):* The tree tends to grow long, unbranched stems, so head the leader when it is 3 ft. high and head the branches when they have grown 1 ft. to 2 ft. Prune the mature tree to control its size.

CHAPTER NINE

HOUSEPLANTS

Houseplants are either herbaceous plants or merely diminutive versions of woody trees, shrubs, or vines that grow outdoors. The woody houseplants generally are tropical or subtropical evergreens—after all, who would want a deciduous houseplant?

For instruction on how to prune any houseplant, just look up the plant in its category—conifer, palm, broadleaf evergreen, vine, etc.—elsewhere in this book. Then prune the houseplant version just as you would the full-size version, pruning more heavily to keep it smaller, and taking into consideration the fact that the plant will never experience cool or cold weather.

The only special pruning a plant needs when grown as a houseplant is root pruning. Once a plant has grown as large as you want it to, the soil must be periodically renewed around its roots. The only way to accomplish this without increasing the size of the pot is to cut off some roots.

Depending on the vigor of the plant, root pruning may be needed once a year or every few years. The best way to tell when root pruning is needed is to knock

Houseplants need occasional pruning. Leave the ladder outside.

This potted plant is rootbound.

a plant out of its pot and look at the roots. If they are going around and around in a thick mat at the surface of the root ball, root pruning is needed. Or the plant might call out by itself for root pruning, with a mass of roots sneaking out of the drainage hole in the bottom of a pot, futilely searching for new soil.

When you root-prune, either tease long roots out of the root ball and shorten them with your pruning shears, or else slice pieces of soil and roots off the edge of the root ball with a sharp knife. (Don't expect the knife to be sharp when you're done!) Then tease out the remaining roots at the outside of the root ball. Return the plant to its pot and pack fresh soil in around the root ball.

Once the plant is back in its pot, the stems also will need some pruning in order to keep the top of the plant in proportion to the size of the container while retaining a pleasing shape. The goal here is beauty, not growth. After all, you're not seeking maximum growth from a houseplant that already is full size—full size for your house, that is.

Every technique recommended for full-size plants can be applied to houseplants. Head stems and pinch shoots for bushiness, and thin out wood to prevent regrowth. To lower an indoor tree, shorten major limbs to side branches within the crown, just as you would on an outdoor tree. The difference between working on the dwarf and the full-size tree is that with the dwarf the work is more intimate—and your feet are on the ground!

PRUNING A HOUSEPLANT

1. To keep it from growing larger, this potted kumquat needs annual root and shoot pruning.

2. Slice off the outside layer of roots and soil.

3. Teasing roots at the outside of the root ball will get them growing quickly out into the new soil.

4. Just cut back occasional larger roots.

5. Pack new soil in around the old root ball.

6. After shoot pruning to keep the top of the plant in bounds, the potted kumquat is ready to grow.

CHAPTER TEN

HERBACEOUS PLANTS

Even herbaceous perennials benefit from judicious pinching, snipping, and dividing.

Herbaceous plants are the ephemerals of the garden, vanishing with hardly a trace at the end of each season. To get them on with their show as quickly as possible, allow most herbaceous plants just to grow like all getout, unrestrained. Remember, any leaves that you remove slow a plant down, in growth and in flowering. Nonetheless, for form, flowers, or fruits, herbaceous plants are sometimes pruned—and that is the subject of this chapter.

Note that many plants grown as herbaceous annuals in temperate gardens are woody perennials in warm-winter climates. For instructions on pruning them as woody perennials, see the appropriate section elsewhere in this book.

Pinching to promote bushiness

Pinching out the tip of the stem of an herbaceous plant stops that stem's growth and causes the lower buds, in the leaf axils, to grow out into shoots. As a result, the plant becomes bushier. Therefore, while not absolutely necessary, pinching the tips of plants such as lavatera, marigold, and zinnia makes them fuller.

Early in the growing season, when any and every flower is still to be cherished, you may find that the top bud on, for example, a marigold seedling is a flower bud, or even an already opened flower! Grit your teeth and pinch it off. Not only will doing so make the plant bushier, but it will also channel energy destined for that flower into the growth of new shoots. Allowing a small seedling to flower prematurely saps its strength, so the plant is likely to remain a runt. Defer your pleasure. (As consolation, read the tongue-in-cheek words that Charles Dudley Warner wrote in 1888 in *My Summer in a Garden:* "The principal value of a private garden is…to teach patience and philosophy, and the higher virtues—hope deferred, and expectations blighted, leading directly to resignation, and sometimes to alienation. The garden thus becomes a moral agent, a test of character, as it was in the beginning.")

But do not carry pinching to excess—it does delay flowering. And, not that large flowers are always better than small flowers, but the more flowering shoots on a plant, the more flowers but the smaller the size of each flower. A single pinch is usually sufficient for marigolds and other naturally bushy flowers. Certain chrysanthemums look best with repeated pinching (but see the Plant List, which begins on p. 185). With snapdragon and some other spiky flowers, you have a choice: Do you want a single large spike, or several smaller ones?

Pruning for extra-large flowers or fruits

Just as pinching the tips of stems makes bushier plants with more, but smaller, flowers, limiting the number of shoots or flowers has the opposite effect. This is how you grow a "football" 'mum, a "dinnerplate" dahlia, or a giant tomato. (Again, see the Plant List for special information on pruning 'mums, dahlias, and tomatoes.)

Channel any plant's energy into fewer growing points by pinching off side shoots, pinching off lateral flower buds, or limiting the number of stems growing from the crown of a perennial plant. Remove a side shoot or lateral flower bud while either is still young enough to be succulent and pinched off. At that stage, removing the side shoot hardly affects overall plant growth because the side shoot is not yet contributing to the energies of the plant. And a young flower bud has not yet drawn too much energy from the plant. *Aster novi-belgii*,

Pinching for Bushiness

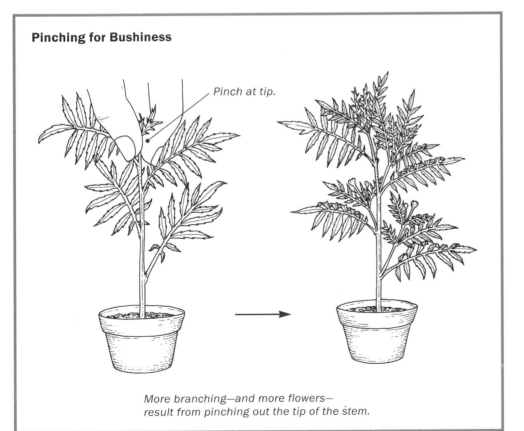

Pinch at tip.

More branching—and more flowers—result from pinching out the tip of the stem.

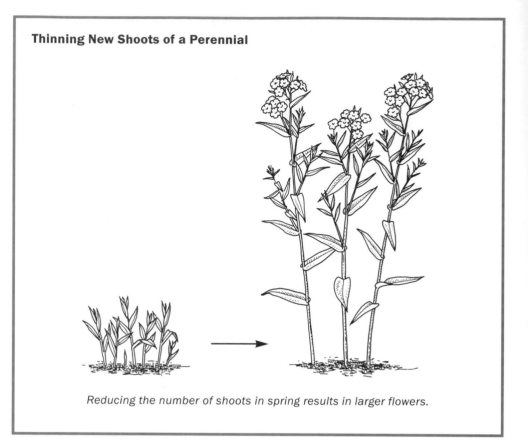

Thinning New Shoots of a Perennial

Reducing the number of shoots in spring results in larger flowers.

perennial phlox *(Phlox paniculata)*, and thick-leaf phlox *(P. carolina)* are examples of perennial flowers that perform better if you reduce the number of shoots they send up from ground level. When shoots are 2 in. high, remove all but three per plant.

Deadheading for neatness and continued bloom

Removing spent flowers from an herbaceous plant—called deadheading—keeps things tidy and allows the plant to channel its energy into more flowers rather than producing seeds. The raison d'être for annual plants, from their perspective, is to make seeds. Once that occurs, they are apt to slacken their efforts at making more flowers. Deadheading keeps annuals energetic.

Even some perennial flowers, such as delphinium *(Delphinium* hybrids) and Canterbury-bells *(Campanula Medium)*, put on a second show later in the season if their spent flowers are cut back after their first show of the season.

You would have quite a time trying to cut off individual flower stalks of a plant such as sweet alyssum *(Lobularia maritima)*, which forms a low-growing mound completely showered with blossoms. Deadhead this plant by shearing the whole mound back with either grass or hedge shears after a flush of bloom. This plant sprawls out of bounds, and shearing also puts the plant back in place. Other annuals that benefit from this treatment (it's really not the plant, but we gardeners who benefit) include nasturtium *(Tropaeolum* spp.)

and petunia *(Petunia × hybrida)*, although in some sites, any of these trailing plants look best completely unrestrained. Perennials that benefit from shearing include basket-of-gold *(Aurinia saxatilis)*, cottage pink *(Dianthus plumarius)*, sea pink *(Armeria maritima)*, edging candytuft *(Iberis sempervirens)*, spike speedwell *(Veronica spicata)*, and horned viola *(Viola cornuta)*. Sheared plants appear stunned for a couple of days after the operation, but good growing conditions soon have them happily lumbering along the ground and, in some cases, flowering again that same season.

Deadheading also keeps a planting tidy by preventing unwanted self-seeding. Especially fecund plants include feverfew *(Chrysanthemum Parthenium)*, perennial phlox *(Phlox paniculata)*, thick-leaf phlox *(P. carolina)*, and, with a common and botanical name to scare any fastidious gardener, giant hogweed *(Heracleum Mantegazzianum)*.

Crown division to rejuvenate a perennial

Although an attraction of perennial flowers is their perennial nature, "perennial" does not mean that the plants never need any care. With time, these plants suffer from age as their clumps spread outward, the old centers dying out, or inch upward and then weaken from exposure. Crown division keeps a plant young.

As soon as you see the first green shoots of an aged perennial poking through the ground in the spring, run to the garage, grab a shovel, and lift the clump out of the earth. Shake some soil from the roots so that you can see what you are doing, then start cutting apart the crown. Depending on how the crown grows and its age, use your bare hands, a shovel, a sharp knife, or hand pruning shears.

The pieces that you want to save for replanting are the youngest ones, typically those at the outer edge of the

Periodically shearing alyssum after each flush of blossoms sets the stage for repeat shows.

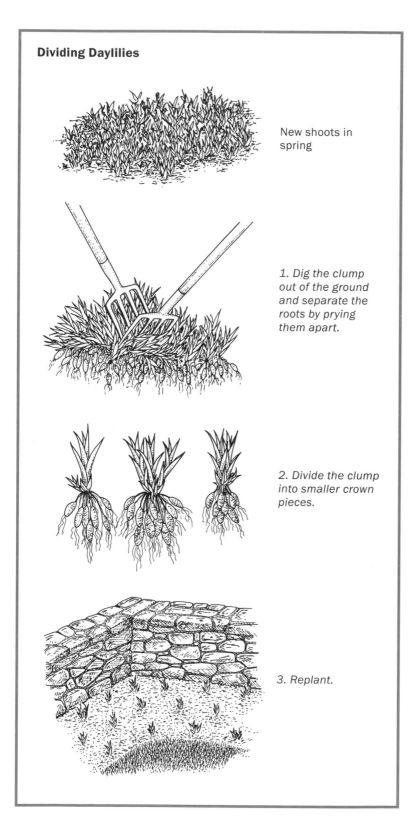

Dividing Daylilies

New shoots in spring

1. Dig the clump out of the ground and separate the roots by prying them apart.

2. Divide the clump into smaller crown pieces.

3. Replant.

crown and having some roots attached. Replant only the most vigorous young crown pieces, first enriching the soil, if necessary, with humus, fertilizers, and other amendments.

Perennials vary in the frequency with which they need division. To look their best, asters and hardy chrysanthemums require division every year. The same goes for bee balm (*Monarda didyma*), tansy (*Tanacetum vulgare*), goldenrod (*Solidago* spp.), and artemisia (*Artemisia* spp.), not for the sake of appearances, but to keep them from spreading. Division every three or four years is sufficient for sea pink (*Armeria maritima*), phlox (*Phlox* spp.), coralbells (*Heuchera sanguinea*), Canterbury-bells (*Campanula Medium*), snow-in-summer (*Cerastium tomentosum*), Siberian and Japanese irises (*Iris siberica* and *I. kaempferi*), veronica (*Veronica* spp.), yarrow (*Achillea Millefolium*), and Shasta daisies (*Chrysanthemum × superbum*).

Don't be too eager to divide certain perennials. Bridle your spring-induced enthusiasm and wait until after blossoms fade to divide Oriental poppies (*Papaver orientale*), bleeding heart (*Dicentra spectabilis*), bearded iris (*Iris* spp.), and Virginia cowslip (*Mertensia virginica*), all of which go dormant by midsummer. And think twice before dividing hellebore (*Helleborus* spp.), peony (*Paeonia lactiflora*), monkshood (*Aconitum Napellus*), butterfly weed (*Asclepias tuberosa*), lupine (*Lupinus* spp.), and baby's-breath (*Gypsophila* spp.). Once a decade is probably enough for these perennials, and even then, they show their initial resentment by not blooming for a year or so afterwards.

Plant List

Carnation (*Dianthus* spp.): For ordinary growing out in the garden, carnations do not demand pruning. Even so, a planting of cottage pinks (*D. plumarius*) looks neater and has a more concentrated period of repeat flowering if the plants are sheared right after blooming. And for larger blossoms on clove pink (*D. Caryophyllus*), pinch off lateral flower buds as they appear.

In the greenhouse, prune clove pink to schedule the flowers as well as to regulate the number of stems and bloom size. Young plants are commonly pinched so that they develop a few flowering stems. After those first blooms, there is a lull before blossoms again appear. The duration of the lull is influenced by available light. To spread out the production of flowers, sacrificing somewhat their total number and slowing the time to peak bloom, pinch again a month after the initial pinching. This time, pinch the tips of half the number of stems that sprouted as a result of the first going-over. Carnations also require cool temperatures for best bloom, so cut back plants from winter to early spring, or pinch them back from early spring to early summer, to delay flowering until the end of summer. As with outdoor clove pinks, remove lateral flower buds whenever you want larger flowers.

Chrysanthemum (formerly *Chrysanthemum* spp., but now also includes *Dendrathema grandiflora, Nipponanthemum nipponicum* and others): 'Mums run the gamut, from plants that are bushy mounds to those that are stately, upright, and capped by one or a few corpulent blooms. The colors and forms of flowers are equally variable. For ordinary garden culture, buy either a bushy variety or an upright, large-flowered variety, whichever you want, and just let the plant grow unfettered—pruning is not absolutely necessary. However, pruning will improve the form of either type, and is a necessity for show-quality and commercial flowers.

An important point to keep in mind, no matter how you prune, is that 'mums wait until days grow short and temperatures cool before forming flower buds. The number of shorter days needed to induce flower buds ranges from seven to fourteen weeks, depending on the variety. Low cushion 'mums need the least amount of time, while some of the large 'mums need the most. (And those of the latter that do flower very late must therefore be grown in a greenhouse or in pots that can be brought indoors in autumn.) At any rate, once a plant changes gears and enters the flowering mode, it responds differently to pruning than when it was vegetative.

To "pinch" out the growing point of a 'mum means removing only ½ in. or so at the tip of the stem. Regrowth and healing are less satisfactory when you remove any more of the shoot than that. Apply the same philosophy when taking off side shoots— rub them off while they are young.

Now, onto the details of pruning…

Out in the garden, a naturally bushy 'mum might look better if it was even more bushy. Promote bushiness by pinching out growing points when shoots are 6 in. tall. Repeat this pinching whenever new shoots grow to 6 in. Cease pinching no later that 90 days before

Pinch the growing points of chrysanthemums in spring and early summer for dense blooms in fall.

(continued on page 187)

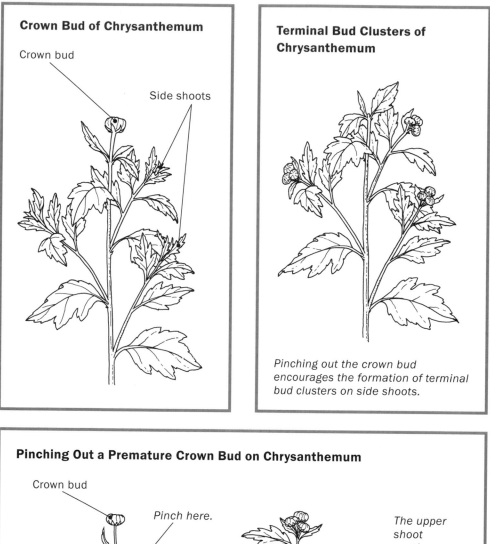

Crown Bud of Chrysanthemum

Crown bud

Side shoots

Terminal Bud Clusters of Chrysanthemum

Pinching out the crown bud encourages the formation of terminal bud clusters on side shoots.

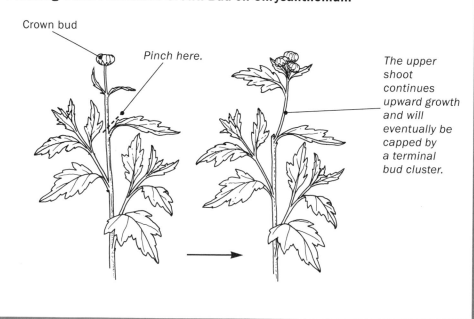

Pinching Out a Premature Crown Bud on Chrysanthemum

Crown bud

Pinch here.

The upper shoot continues upward growth and will eventually be capped by a terminal bud cluster.

the normal bloom date (by July, in any case); that's when plants start to develop flower buds, and you don't want to remove them.

Growing 'mums for extra-large blossoms is another matter, and can be an exacting science. First choose an appropriate variety—some will not make extra-large blossoms even when the number of flower buds is reduced. Then deliberately remove all but from one to three shoots on each plant, and do not allow any branches to grow on them. Stake each shoot separately to keep it rigidly upright.

The change from vegetative to flowering phase is gradual. If you do not pinch the tip of a stem at all as days shorten, the top bud may become a "crown bud," which is a single flower bud with narrow, strappy leaves farther down the stalk, and still-vegetative shoots pushing out just below. These vegetative shoots also will be eventually capped by flowers.

If you pinch out stem tips so that crown buds do not form, nonflowering side shoots—usually three—continue upward growth. Depending on how many and how large you want your blossoms, retain one or all of these shoots. Eventually, the plant enters a full flowering phase, with the end of a shoot capped by a "terminal bud cluster," which is a cluster of flower buds. ("Terminal" in this case refers to the plant's last-ditch effort at flowering for the season.) The flowers are on long stems having normal 'mum foliage—all of which is important for a show chrysanthemum. For a large blossom from a terminal bud cluster, pinch out all but the top flower bud.

As long as a crown bud does not develop while a plant is small, either a crown bud or a terminal bud can give rise to an equally large flower. If a crown bud forms on a small plant, merely pinch it out and select one of the vegetative shoots to become an extension of the main shoot. Only a terminal bud, however, can make a "spray," which is a large flower surrounded by smaller flowers, all blooming together.

The timing of the last pinch, as well as the number of stems and flowers to allow each plant, has been carefully calculated for the best show from a number of varieties. The reason for this is the exacting requirements for time and appearance of bloom that are demanded from commercial and competition 'mum growers.

One more way to grow 'mums is as a cascading floral display. For this, you need wires or canes on which to train two stems.

(continued on page 188)

A cascade of sunny yellow 'mums.

Training Greenhouse Cucumbers

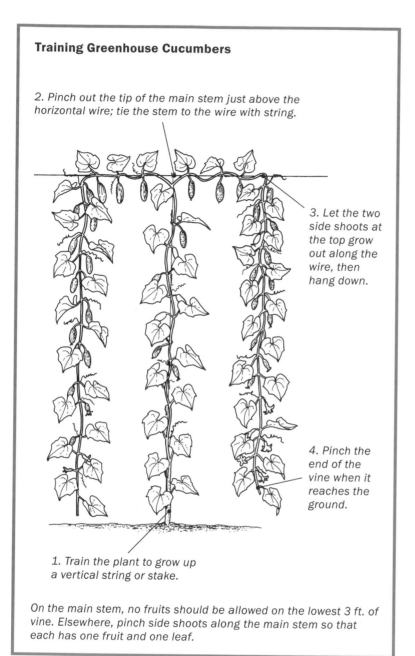

2. Pinch out the tip of the main stem just above the horizontal wire; tie the stem to the wire with string.

3. Let the two side shoots at the top grow out along the wire, then hang down.

4. Pinch the end of the vine when it reaches the ground.

1. Train the plant to grow up a vertical string or stake.

On the main stem, no fruits should be allowed on the lowest 3 ft. of vine. Elsewhere, pinch side shoots along the main stem so that each has one fruit and one leaf.

To keep growth vigorous, initially train shoots upward at a 45° angle. Pinch side shoots completely off, or pinch out their tips when they have made three leaves. As the frame fills, gradually pull wires or canes down to a horizontal position, then further, to create a cascading effect.

Dahlia *(Dahlia* spp.): Dahlias do not demand pruning, but pruning can increase either the size or the number of flowers. On plants with naturally large blossoms, side shoots typically do not grow until the shoot tip forms a flower bud. To promote the development of side shoots, pinch out the tip of a shoot in early summer. Remove the top pair of side shoots that develops in order to spread vigor among the side shoots down along the stem. At the other extreme, you could channel energy into a single "dinnerplate" dahlia by pinching out all side shoots or lateral flower buds that form. Or, for a combination of the above treatments, pinch plants in early summer to promote branching, then disbud the resulting stems so that each develops just one flower.

Greenhouse Cucumbers *(Cucumis sativus):* If you have seen how cucumbers can sprawl in the garden, you can understand why pruning is needed to check and organize their growth in the confines of a greenhouse. To make the best use of space, always a precious commodity "under glass," train the plants upward on strings or thin stakes, then out along horizontal wires. With good growing conditions, as well as careful training and pruning, one highly productive plant can be grown in an area of about 6 square feet.

After making its first few leaves, a new plant will start producing a tendril along with each leaf. You cannot rely on the tendrils to pull the plant up, so twist the stem around the string or stake as it grows. Pinch out the tip of the main stem when it grows one leaf beyond the horizontal wire, then tie a piece of string around the stem and the wire to keep the plant from slipping downward. Pinch all side shoots that grow off the main stem back to a leaf, except for the two side shoots at the top, one of which you will guide in each direction along the top wire. After they travel along the wire for a bit, allow the ends of each of the top laterals to hang downward, then pinch their ends when they reach the ground.

Besides a tendril, you also could find a fruit at each node along the stems, especially with modern greenhouse cucumbers bearing all female flowers rather than the mix of male and female flowers borne on older varieties. Do not let any fruits form on the lower 3 ft. of the main stem. At all the remaining nodes on the plant (wherever there is a leaf), allow only a single fruit and that single leaf to remain. Pinch back any laterals or sublaterals that try to grow.

Fruits form only in new leaf axils, so the pruned plant could ultimately become bare of fruit and leaves. Before this happens, renew the plant by letting a healthy young shoot replace the main stem. Train the young shoot just as you did the old main stem, which you then cut away.

Throughout the life of the plant, adjust growth so that all the leaves are bathed in light, and balance the number of fruits with the growing conditions and the variety. For example, prune less severely if you grow an old-type cucumber with male and female flowers, because then a fruit cannot form at each node. When natural light ebbs in late autumn and winter, allow more space between the main stem and drooping laterals. You might even let two leaves grow on each lateral from the main stem and sublateral from each of the two top laterals. But pinch off any fruit that forms at the second leaf to increase the ratio of leaves to fruits.

Through this all, keep in mind that pruning is also needed to keep a plant healthy. Cut away any dead or injured growth as soon as you notice it. And while you want the maximum number of leaves to intercept whatever light is available, you also need good air circulation around those leaves to

avoid diseases. This might call for occasionally snipping off a large leaf.

Go over your plants at least once a week. For plant health and ease of training and pruning, you do not want a confusion of stems—not for cucumbers in a greenhouse, at least.

Tomato side shoots form at the junction of a leaf stalk and the main stem.

Tomato *(Lycopersicon Lycopersicum):* Tomatoes are pruned when grown on stakes, and those varieties suitable for staking and pruning are so-called "indeterminate" types. These varieties form fruit clusters at intervals along their ever elongating stems, which are *indeterminately* long. "Determinate" varieties, in contrast, have stems that do not keep getting longer, because their terminal buds become flowers, then fruits (see the drawing on p. 190). Determinate varieties are not pruned because the result would be nothing more than a single short stem capped by a single cluster of fruits. Seed catalogs and packets usually specify whether a variety is indeterminate or determinate.

Growing upward rather than outward, staked indeterminate plants can be set as close as 18 in. apart to give the greatest yield of tomatoes from a given area of ground. Air

(continued on page 190)

Bearing Habit of Tomato

Indeterminate varieties
Flowers and fruits are borne along stems. The plant increases in size as any or all stems elongate.

Determinate varieties
Flowers and fruits are borne at the end of shoots. The plant increases in size by growth of the side shoots.

Axillary flowers

Terminal flowers

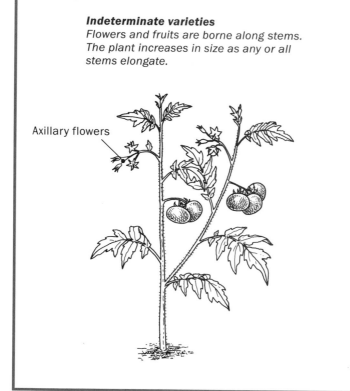

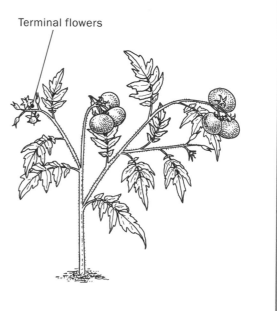

circulating around the leaves and fruits of these upright plants reduces disease problems, and fruits held high above the ground are free from dirt, slugs, turtles, and other potential soil-level calamities. The fruits ripen earlier and are larger (though fewer) than fruits of the same variety on sprawling plants.

To avoid root damage later on, "plant" a stake next to each tomato plant when you set the plant in the ground. You will have to tie the plant to the stake, because a tomato vine lacks tendrils, holdfasts, or other means to hold itself up. Material for ties should be strong enough to hold plants up for the whole season, and bulky enough so as not to cut

into plants' stems. Torn pieces of rag or lengths of twine work well.

On indeterminate varieties, maintain a single stem by removing all side shoots right after you plant, and continuing to do so as the plant grows. Side shoots originate from buds in the leaf axils, which is where a leaf joins the stem. Tomatoes have compound leaves, so do not mistake the junction of a leaflet and a leafstalk for a leaf axil. Snap off each side shoot with your fingers, thereby avoiding the danger of transmitting diseases between plants with the blades of knives or pruning shears. Ideally, remove any shoot before it is more than 1 in. long. As you prune, occasionally step back and refocus your eyes

Left: Staked tomatoes yield cleaner and earlier fruits—and more of them, from a given area of ground.

Below: For staked indeterminate tomatoes, pinch out side shoots with your fingers to train the plants to a single central stem.

on the plant as a whole. A shoot that has made 2 ft. of growth is easily overlooked as you concentrate on small shoots just beginning to grow from leaf axils.

As the main stem grows, tie it to the stake at 12-in. to 18-in. intervals. First make a loop with tying material around the stake, and knot it tightly. Then knot the material loosely around the tomato stem.

You might want to try pinching out the tip of the single stem as soon as a few fruit clusters have set, or when the stem reaches the top of the stake. Continue to remove any new leaves or flowers that form. This pinching carries tomato pruning to the extreme, and is chancy because its success depends on the maturity of a plant's leaves and fruits. At worst, you reduce yield to a few clusters of fruit. At best, you harvest the earliest and largest tomatoes possible for that variety.

PART 3

SPECIAL PRUNING TECHNIQUES

CHAPTER ELEVEN   POLLARDING

Y ou either like pollarding or you do not. Pollarding is not a natural look: in winter, the trunk or short scaffold limbs are terminated by a clubbed head or heads; in summer, a mass of vigorous shoots bursts wildly out of that head or heads. Pollarding is useful for lending a formal appearance to a tree (those wild shoots originate from one or just a few points, so are well contained), and for controlling the size of an otherwise large-growing tree.

Pollarding seems to have isolated but diverse appeal. You find pollarded trees lining streets in San Francisco and some European cities, as well as standing sentinel in front of homes in rural Delaware. The technique originated out of need, centuries ago in Europe, as a means of harvesting firewood without killing a tree. Regularly cutting a tree to

the ground—coppicing—accomplishes the same thing on those trees that can tolerate such treatment, but sprouts growing up near ground level were prey to grazing animals.

Fast-growing deciduous trees that do not mind being cut repeatedly are ideal candidates for pollarding. Among such trees are tree-of-heaven (*Ailanthus altissima*), black locust (*Robinia Pseudoacacia*), catalpa (*Catalpa bignonioides*), chestnut (*Castanea* spp.), horse chestnut (*Aesculus Hippocastanum*), linden (*Tilia* spp.), London plane tree (*Platanus* × *acerifolia*), princess tree (*Paulownia tomentosa*), sycamore (*Platanus occidentalis*), and willow (*Salix* spp.). Vigorous shoots on some of these trees bring along other special effects, such as the monstrous leaves of princess tree, or the bright red bark of the 'chermesina' variety of white willow (*Salix alba*).

Nothing special needs to be done for the young tree to be pollarded except to give it a high head, with at least 5 ft. or 6 ft. of clear trunk. This high head is only for appearance's sake. While the tree is young, leave some branches on the trunk to help thicken it and to shield it from direct sunlight. But keep these branches pinched back so that they do not grow more than 1 ft. in a season, and remove them completely after a few years. For the plant that will be merely a trunk with a clubbed head, cut back the trunk in winter to the height you want for that head.

If your pollarded tree is to have stubby scaffold limbs growing off the trunk, train the tree so that these limbs are spirally arranged around the trunk, spaced 6 in. to 18 in. apart vertically, and radiating out at wide angles. Again, you are designing your tree for appearance; strength is not a concern for a tree never allowed to achieve great height or to grow limbs that are both long and thick. Once scaffold limbs develop, shorten them each winter to a point 2 ft. to 5 ft. from the trunk. Also remove any side branches growing from the scaffold limbs. The eventual size of the tree should determine what will look best as far as the spacing and length of the scaffold limbs. Do not allow the trunk to keep growing upward. Before it grows too thick or too far out of reach, lop it back to the topmost scaffold.

Once the trunk and scaffold limbs are in place, the pollarded tree needs pruning every winter, or at least every second or third winter. Pruning is easy: Just lop all young stems back to within ½ in. or so of where they began growing the previous season. Repeatedly lopping stems back to that point is what makes the knob atop the trunk or at the end of a scaffold limb.

So there you have it, a high head capped by a knobby stub, or by short scaffold limbs ending in those knobby stubs. Prune early enough in the dormant season so that you can enjoy the curious look of your pollarded tree when it is leafless. Interesting.

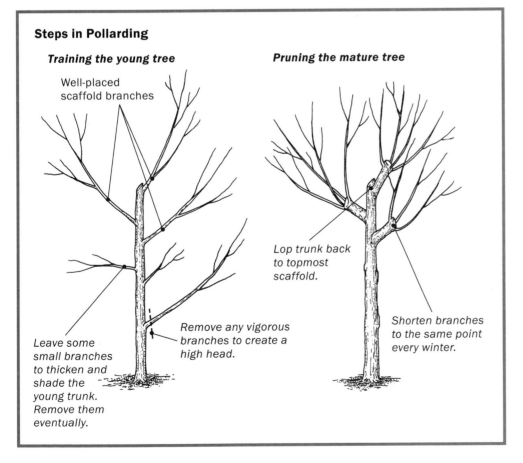

Steps in Pollarding

Training the young tree

Well-placed scaffold branches

Leave some small branches to thicken and shade the young trunk. Remove them eventually.

Remove any vigorous branches to create a high head.

Pruning the mature tree

Lop trunk back to topmost scaffold.

Shorten branches to the same point every winter.

CHAPTER TWELVE

PLEACHING

Pleached beeches form an inviting tunnel in Williamsburg, Va.

The word "pleach" derives from the old north French word *plechier*, meaning "to braid," and this is exactly what you do when you pleach trees. You informally weave together their branches. A row of pleached trees is a two-dimensional planting, a thin, horizontal wall of greenery. Plant a row of trees on either side of a walkway, then train stems from the top of each wall over the center, and you have a shady tunnel of greenery—with fruit for the picking if the trees are, for example, apple trees. Or plant trees to enclose an area, clear their trunks of branches to "roof" height, then train a roof of greenery over this living summer house.

Choose your trees for pleaching with care. Species suitable for pleaching have strong yet flexible branches. Good choices include apple *(Malus sylvestris)*, beech *(Fagus* spp.), hornbeam *(Carpinus* spp.), linden *(Tilia* spp.), pear *(Pyrus* spp.), and sycamore *(Platanus occidentalis)*. All trees in a pleached row or "room" should be not only of the same species, but also of the same variety and of similar size, so that growth is uniform. Planting distances within the row depend on how large you are going to let the trees grow, and might range from as little as 3 ft. to as much as 10 ft. or more. Rows that stretch from north to south receive sunlight more uniformly on either side than rows that run east to west.

Although a row or a bower of pleached trees is eventually self-supporting, some sort of framework is needed to direct growth into the desired form. This support might be built of metal or wooden posts and crosspieces, or posts with horizontal wires or bamboo canes between them.

The goal in training the young planting is to force growth upward and outward. Cut plants back right after planting to stimulate vigorous regrowth of a single stem. Allow a single stem on each plant to climb upward, but periodically interrupt growth with a heading cut to promote branches, which you train horizontally in one plane. Tie the main stem and side branches to the support as growth proceeds. Even if you want a length of clear trunk from the ground up to the first branches, allow some temporary low branches to grow on the young plant to help thicken the trunk. Pinch the temporary branches back so that they never get more than about 1 ft. long, and cut them off after a few years. Completely cut back any stems growing out perpendicular to the plane of the pleached trees.

As branches from adjacent trees reach each other, informally weave them together. You could even temporarily tie them together—temporarily because the tie will eventually strangle the branches unless it decays or is removed.

Once pleached trees have filled their allotted area, they need annual pruning from top to bottom. (Keep the "top" part in mind when you plan a row of pleached trees—you'll have to reach up there for regular pruning.) Remove any vigorous upright stems growing near ground level or along branches. Thin out growth where it is too dense. This thinning gives an airy look (if desired) to the row, and also lets light penetrate to avoid a buildup of dead, leafless wood. Cut back any unruly stems, especially those growing out perpendicular to the flat surface.

Eventually, you can remove the supporting frame. A planting of pleached trees grows sturdier with age, as the woven branches naturally graft together.

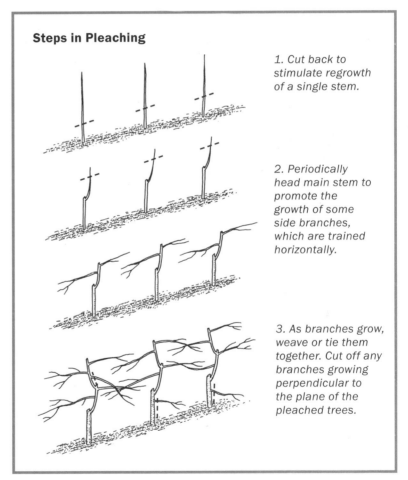

Steps in Pleaching

1. Cut back to stimulate regrowth of a single stem.

2. Periodically head main stem to promote the growth of some side branches, which are trained horizontally.

3. As branches grow, weave or tie them together. Cut off any branches growing perpendicular to the plane of the pleached trees.

CHAPTER THIRTEEN TOPIARY

A topiary requires constant attention.

Topiary is the art of growing trees and shrubs as living sculptures—cubes, spheres, obelisks, animal shapes, even combinations of these shapes nestled side by side or piled on top of one another. The art originated in ancient Rome, where *topiarius* meant ornamental gardener, and has progressed, or at least endured, to the present day. The tradition survived the Dark Ages in monastery gardens, then resurfaced in Renaissance Italy. The French and the Dutch, and occasionally the British, have been fond of topiary. In modern gardens, topiary is rare unless you count the pervasive American foundation plantings of clipped yews and junipers—derisively labelled "gumdrop" or "dot-dash" landscaping by some people—as topiary.

(Note that we are not considering here topiaries made from mesh frames filled with wet moss, then "plugged" with hens-and-chickens, or made from wire frames on which twine vining plants such as English ivy. Neither of these topiaries requires pruning for their development or maintenance.)

Only certain plants are suitable for topiary. The ideal plant is slow growing, tolerant of repeated pruning, and able to resprout from older wood. Especially for smaller topiary viewed at close range, small leaves are needed to create a surface with a crisp edge. Winter damage to a topiary tree or shrub that is years or even decades old is a disaster, so the plant also must be cold hardy for the site. If possible, select a species or variety whose natural shape approximates its intended shape: 'Brownii' yew for a sphere, 'Sentinalis' yew for a obelisk, and 'Hillii' yew for a pyramid. (Other plants, admittedly, do not exhibit such variety of form as does yew.)

Evergreens generally are used for topiary, but occasionally a deciduous plant such as English hawthorn (*Crataegus monogyna*) or European beech (*Fagus sylvatica*) is used. California privet (*Ligustrum ovalifolium*) also makes nice topiary, and is evergreen where winters are not too cold. A drawback to a deciduous topiary, of course, is that it is bare in winter (although beech does not shed its dead leaves until spring). Deciduous plants generally grow more exuberantly than do evergreens, so they also require more diligence to keep growth in check.

Many species of evergreens have been used for topiary. The quintessential plants for topiary are yew (*Taxus* spp.) and boxwood (*Buxus* spp.). Other suitable plants include arborvitae (*Thuja* spp.), bay laurel (*Laurus nobilis*), hemlock (*Tsuga* spp.), holly (*Ilex* spp.),

holly oak (*Quercus Ilex*), Italian cypress (*Cupressus sempervirens*), juniper (*Juniperus* spp.), Leyland cypress (×*Cupressocyparis Leylandii*), *Lonicera nitida*, Monterey cypress (*Cupressus macrocarpa*), myrtle (*Myrtus communis*), Portugal laurel (*Prunus lusitanica*), and rosemary (*Rosmarinus officinalis*).

In most cases, begin shaping your plant while it is young. You could, however, carve a shape out of an old overgrown yew much as you would out of wood or stone, because yew grows so densely and sprouts so freely from old wood. Or a growing plant might suggest a form that you could then develop. You might even juxtapose two plants, or let one grow up through the other to create, for example, a pedestal on which sits a verdant animal. In any case, topiary lends itself more to

A privet 'chair.'

bold shapes than to intricate designs whose details are swallowed up between prunings. Site your topiary so that it receives good light on all sides, for dense growth throughout.

Most young topiary plants that are still in their formative stage need nothing more than frequent shearing or clipping off of the ends of stems in order to encourage dense branching. Clipping individual stems is the preferred method for plants with large leaves because shearing would mangle individual leaves. Obviously, if a stem protrudes in the direction where you want growth, leave it.

For a more complex shape, such as that representing an animal, use a frame on which to train stems. Make the frame of heavy wire and make sure that it is firmly anchored to a stake. To avoid eventually choking the stems, tie them to the frame with string that will decompose with time. As you encourage growth along the wire frame, also frequently head back side shoots to promote bushiness.

Once a topiary is fully grown and shaped, it will need pruning at least once a year, two or three times a year in some cases. Where a plant is reliably cold hardy, prune just after midsummer. By then, the spring flush of growth has ceased, and there is less chance that pruning will stimulate regrowth before the following spring. Cut freehand, or use a guide to make sure your topiary is not gradually changing shape over the years. A guide is also useful when you have matching topiaries—without the guide, you may one day look up to find that they no longer match. If you cut freehand, step back frequently to check and admire your work.

What is to be done with a neglected topiary? Severe cuts may be needed to stimulate growth within the plant. Repair a leafless hole by widening it, cutting old wood around the hole back to healthy wood. If severe cuts are needed, renovation is possible only if the plant is capable of sprouting from old, perhaps leafless, wood. Otherwise, start again with a new plant.

Using a Frame to Form Topiary

Wire frame

Tie growing shoots to the frame; head back side shoots frequently to promote branching.

In the world of gardening, people are divided over how they feel about "standards." Some gardeners love them, others will have nothing to do with them. "Standard" has many meanings both in and out of horticulture, so let's first get straight which kind of "standard" we are dealing with: Here, I mean a naturally bushy plant trained to have a clear, upright stem capped by a mop of leaves. A miniature tree. I count myself among standardophiles and, if I may speak for the group, we like standards for their neatness and because they have the lollipop shape of storybook trees. "Standard" does seem like an odd word to describe such a plant until you realize that the "stand" in "standard" does indeed mean just that. ("Standard" comes from the Old English words *standan*, meaning to stand, and *ord*, meaning a place.)

A plant may set off on the road to standard-dom by several routes. One way to create a standard is to graft a bushy plant atop a straight trunk of another plant. The rootstock, then, is a plant with a naturally vigorous, upright growth habit and must of course be closely related to the plant grafted to it. A rather unique way to create an English ivy *(Hedera Helix)* standard is to use mature English ivy, an upright shrub, as a rootstock upon which you graft juvenile English ivy, a vining plant. But this is not a book about grafting, so here we will explore the ways you can make standards by pruning.

Rosemary, grown as a potted standard, provides fresh flavor and beauty all year round.

Begin, for example, with a seedling, a rooted cutting, or an established bushy plant. With the established bushy plant, start off by lopping all stems down to soil level.

From here on, the seedling, the rooted cutting, and the plant that has been lopped back can be treated in the same way. The lopped-back plant will grow faster than the others, but in any case it is important to provide excellent growing conditions for vigorous growth in developing the main stem. And you will allow only one main stem—the trunk-to-be—to develop. Set a stake in the soil and tie the growing stem to the stake every few inches. Keeping the stem upright and straight does more than just create a straight trunk. Upright growth is inherently most vigorous and naturally suppresses the growth of lower buds—just what you want in the developing standard.

Other buds will still grow, though, more or less depending on the natural bushiness of the plant. Diligently remove any shoots growing up near ground level. If you get to them while they are young, just snapping them off, they will be less inclined to regrow. Branches may also try

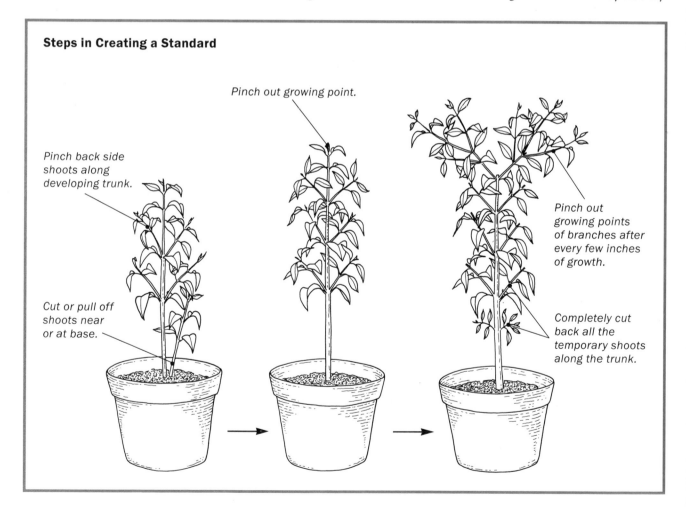

Steps in Creating a Standard

Pinch out growing point.

Pinch back side shoots along developing trunk.

Cut or pull off shoots near or at base.

Pinch out growing points of branches after every few inches of growth.

Completely cut back all the temporary shoots along the trunk.

to grow from the main stem. These branches do contribute to the total growth of the plant and thicken the developing trunk, but they also take away from the vigor of the main stem. Pinch back branches to weaken them. Some judgment is needed here. A seedling or a weak plant needs all the energy it can garner, so you might allow a couple of inches of growth on its branches. On a vigorous plant, pinch branches back to a single leaf or pair of leaves.

Once the main stem reaches full height, it is time to form the mop head. The length of the main stem is going to depend, artistically, on the density and size of the leaves, and, physiologically, on the vigor of the plant. You would have trouble getting a very long trunk on a weak-growing, weeping plant. The thin, dense leaves of my rosemary *(Rosmarinus officinalis)* look just right filling the 12-in. wide ball capping an 8-in. long trunk. (At three years old, it is indeed a trunk!) But an 18-in. mop head on a 2½-ft. long trunk is more suitable to accommodate the large, broad leaves of my potted bay laurel *(Laurus nobilis)* standard.

Begin forming the head by pinching out the growing point of the main stem. This pinch takes out the bud that made hormones that inhibited growth of lower buds. The most vigorous new branches will be those near the top of the main stem, and that's where you want them. Create a dense head, now, by pinching those branches after every few inches of growth. You also can now completely cut away any temporary branches or leaves lower down along the trunk.

Once your standard is fully grown, periodic maintenance pruning is required. Continue to snap off or cut away any shoots growing from the trunk or from ground level. As for the head of the plant, treat it just as if it were a bush. Refer elsewhere in this book for specific pruning directions for any of the many plants that can be grown as standards.

Just about any bushy plant can be trained as a standard. Upright, vigorous varieties, when they exist, are easiest to train this way. Hence, the use of 'Annabel', 'Tennessee Waltz', and 'Hidcote Beauty' for fuchsia *(Fuchsia × hybrida)* standards. On the other hand, if you want a standard with a languorous weeping head, you will have to force a weeping variety up to head height, or graft the weeping variety atop a trunk of an upright variety. (The latter method does sometimes results in an unnatural-looking juncture at the graft.) Besides fuchsia, rosemary, bay laurel, and English ivy, other plants commonly trained to standards are coleus *(Coleus × hybridus)*, geranium *(Pelargonium* spp.), flowering maple *(Abutilon* spp.), heliotrope *(Heliotropium arborescens)*, marguerite *(Chrysanthemum frutescens)*, and verbena *(Verbena × hybrida)*. You may be surprised to see in this list some plants usually grown as annuals. They can, in fact, develop woody trunks when grown as perennials, in which case they need protection from cold where winters would kill them.

For us standardophiles, artistic restraint rather than a shortage of plant candidates for treatment limits the number of standards we grow. Standards are accent plants, and too much accent becomes disturbing or ceases to be an accent at all. (But hmmm: How about forgetting about accent, and creating a forest of storybook trees?)

A bay laurel standard.

owing the lawn is at once the most mundane and the most unique form of pruning. Everyone does it, yet what other kind of pruning calls for cutting off only a part of the leaf blade—and thousands at a time! The growing point of a grass plant is nestled down near ground level, below the reach of mower blades, so it is able to go on making new growth.

Even though the growing point remains unscathed, mowing, like any other form of pruning, weakens a plant, so you have to strike a balance between what looks nice and what keeps the plants healthy. As a general rule, mow frequently enough to remove no more than one-third of the length of the grass blades down to a maximum acceptable height. So if you want your lawn at 2 in., mow 1 in. off when the leaves reach 3 in. Keep in mind that uniformity of cut (rather than just closeness of cut) plays a large part in making an elegantly beautiful lawn. Longer grass also needs less frequent mowing than does grass kept short, and creates shade which interferes with the germination and growth of lawn weeds such as crabgrass.

The optimum mowing height varies with the grass species and the growing conditions. Stress such as as shade or drought calls for longer grass. Also, let a newly seeded lawn grow a little longer than an established lawn. Recommended lengths, after mowing, for various types of grass are given in the chart on the facing page.

Ideally, all grass blades are dry and standing upright like soldiers when you go out to mow. By mowing down to the recommended lengths without removing more than one-third of the blades, the grass will not be so long that it is flopping over under its own weight. One advantage of a rotary mower over a reel mower is that the rotary mower's cutting blade acts like a propeller to suck the grass blades upright. Timely mowing dispenses with the need to rake up the clippings; left on the soil, they add valuable nutrients and humus. If you have been remiss in mowing, lower the grass in stages to avoid shocking it, and collect the clippings after each mowing.

As with any type of pruning, sharp cutting blades make cleaner cuts—important for plant health and appearance in the case of lawns. Reel-type mowers make the cleanest cuts, but rotary mowers can cut longer grass. No matter what type of mower you use, vary your mowing pattern each time you mow if you want to avoid the development of permanent ruts in the ground and create a uniform surface.

On the other hand, you may not want to create a perfectly uniform surface. Notice that just after you mow, the grass is a slightly different hue of green depending on the direction that the mower traveled. This effect is most dramatic when a lush lawn has been cut with a reel-type mower. In Great Britain, land of perfect lawns, lawn mavens create striped patterns in their lawns by directing their mowers back and forth across the greensward in neat parallel lines. For the British, it seems, "Regular stripes emphasize the calm and orderliness of a well-kept lawn. To a lawn fanatic the process of mowing is a pleasure in itself: the noise of the mower,

OPTIMUM MOWING HEIGHT OF GRASSES	
Plant	Height (in inches)
Bahia Grass (*Paspalum notatum*)	2.5 – 3.5
Bent Grass	
Colonial (*Agrostis tenuis*)	0.5 – 1.25
Creeping (*A. stolonifera*)	0.25 – 1.0
Bermuda Grass (*Cynodon Dactylon*)	0.25 – 1.5
Buffalo Grass (*Buchloe dactyloides*)	1.0 – 2.5
Carpet Grass (*Axonopus affinis*)	1.5 – 2.5
Centipede Grass (*Eremochloa ophiuroides*)	1.5 – 2.5
Fescue	
Chewing (*Festuca rubra* var. *commutata*)	1.5 – 3.0
Red (*F. rubra*)	2.0 – 4.0
Tall (*F. elatior*)	2.0 – 4.0
Kentucky Bluegrass (*Poa pratensis*)	1.5 – 4.0
Ryegrass	
Italian, or Annual (*Lolium multiflorum*)	1.5 – 3.5
Perennial (*L. perenne*)	1.5 – 3.5
St. Augustine Grass (*Stenotaphrum secundatum*)	2.0 – 4.0
Wheatgrass (*Agropyron* spp.)	2.0 – 4.0
Zoysia Grass (*Zoysia* spp.)	0.5 – 2.0

The British love their stripes, and perhaps you do too.

the smell of the exhaust and the oil and the warm green cuttings. For the richest green and the most pronounced stripes three-quarters of an inch is best." (Hugh Johnson, *The Principles of Gardening*, 1979). Each to his own.

For myself, I prefer a bolder effect, possible even on a less than perfect lawn, created by sculpting out two tiers of grassy growth. I like to call this "Lawn Nouveau," and I admit that the idea sprung from my lack of time and enthusiasm for mowing the lawn.

The low grass is just like any other lawn, and kept that way with a lawn-mower. The taller portions are mowed with a scythe. Clippings from the tall grass portions must be raked up after mowing or else they would leave unsightly clumps and smother regrowth. A crisp boundary between tall and low

grass keeps everything neat and avoids the appearance of an unmown lawn.

Lawn Nouveau saves me time because the tall grass needs infrequent mowing, even less than once a month, and there's no rush to get it done. The "tall grass" becomes more than just grass as other plant species gradually elbow their way in. Which ones gain foothold depend on the weather and frequency of mowing. An attractive mix of Queen Anne's lace, chicory, and red clover might mingle with the grasses in a dry, sunny area, with ferns, sedges, and buttercups mixing with the grasses in a wetter portion. Design flaws are easily and quickly corrected with the help of the scythe and rake. And you can maintain or change your design at any hour you wish, without bothering your neighbors. The only sound a scythe blade makes is a

The juxtaposition of tall and short grass adds interest to the lawn.

A lawnmower carves a design for Lawn Nouveau.

The author, happily scything.

whispering swoosh, a "sound to rout the brood of cares, the sweep of the scythe in morning dew" (Alfred, Lord Tennyson, *In Memoriam*, 1850).

In addition to carving fancy designs in a lawn, tall and short grass can help define areas—"garden rooms," you might say. And rather than straight edges and 90° corners, curves in bold sweeps can carry you along, then pull you forward and push you backward, as you look upon them. These undulations are more than just imagination, for they really can change position with each mowing. Avenues of low grass cut into the tall grass invite exploration, and, like the broad sweeps, can be altered throughout the season. Such is the fluidity of Lawn Nouveau.

Root and shoot pruning have coaxed this Chinese elm into a diminutive size.

A bonsai planting portrays, in miniature, a natural theme—the rugged beauty of a gnarled pine on a windswept slope, the tranquility of a grove of larches, the joyousness of spring in the cascading branches of an old fruit tree bursting into bloom. To evoke such a mood, the pot must be chosen with an artistic eye; likewise for the manner in which branches are shaped and the choice of groundcover. And in addition to all this, the plant must also be kept healthy with careful attention to soils, fertilizers, watering, and the provision of winter quarters.

Pruning plays a role in creating the artistry of bonsai, and also is needed to keep a plant healthy and, of course, small. Most bonsai are created from plants that, given their way, could grow into towering trees or billowing shrubs.

You first prune a bonsai before even potting it up, beginning with the roots. Wild plants, even small wild plants, often have surprisingly far-reaching roots, and these roots must be untangled and shortened in order to fit the plant into its pot. Certain trees have taproots in addition to shallow feeder roots. The taproot must be cut off if the plant is to grow in a shallow tray.

The top of a new bonsai also might need to be cut back to bring it down to bonsai size, which is usually under 4 ft. (Bonsai are classified according to form and size, and the smallest bonsai are less than 7 in. high.) But you cannot simply

Bonsai (pronounced BONE-sigh) is the growing of plants, usually woody plants, in shallow trays or pots. Pruning is what makes a bonsai plant small, but pruning is only a small part of the art of bonsai. The art began in China almost 2,000 years ago, then was carried to Japan during the Kamakura period (1180-1333), where it was brought to a high state of perfection.

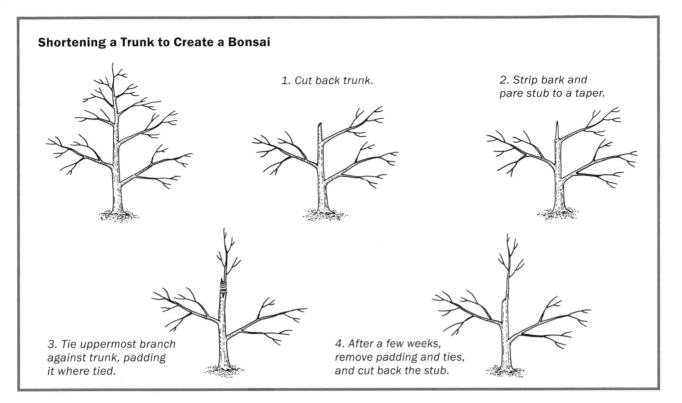

Shortening a Trunk to Create a Bonsai

1. Cut back trunk.

2. Strip bark and pare stub to a taper.

3. Tie uppermost branch against trunk, padding it where tied.

4. After a few weeks, remove padding and ties, and cut back the stub.

lop back a stem or trunk; the plant will look like a lopped-back plant instead of an ancient tree in miniature.

To shorten a trunk, cut it back to a few inches above its desired height—no need to cut to a node, as you would with most other pruning. Trim the bark from the portion of trunk above the highest remaining node, then pare the stub to a taper. Take a branch growing from that highest node, bend it upward, and tie it right up against the tapered stub with some padding to prevent the string or wire used for tying from marring the branch. After a few weeks, when the branch can hold the upright position without assistance, remove the ties and cut back the stub, with a sloping cut, to the base of the branch that has now become the new leader—and which you will keep pruned to prevent it from growing tall.

Another way to shorten a trunk is to create a "broom" style bonsai, a trunk capped by a fan of stems (see the photo and drawing on p. 210). Begin by cutting the trunk back to where you want the branches to begin. Rather than a flat or slanted cut, leave the cut surface of the decapitated plant looking like an asymmetrical V, something like a saddle. Next, wrap rubber strips tightly around the trunk at the top to prevent it from swelling and ruining the form. Many new shoots may attempt to grow from where you cut, but rub off all but perhaps a half-dozen of them. As the shoots grow, pinch their tips to promote branching. This broom style is especially suited to the growth habits of elm and zelkova.

To create an "old" snag of wood on your young bonsai, snap off the trunk or a branch. Pull down a strip of bark from the snag as far as you want. Let the exposed wood dry out, then paint it with

A broom-style bonsai.

Creating a Broom-Style Bonsai

Make a saddle cut back to the desired height, then bind the trunk just below the cut with rubber strips.

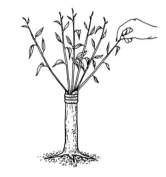

Many new shoots will grow at the cut.

full-strength lime-sulfur solution three or four times every two weeks to preserve it.

Bonsai need regular pruning both above and below ground throughout their life. The frequency of pruning depends on the inherent growth rate of the particular plant, the size of the container, and the growing conditions.

Roots eventually fill the soil in the container, so root pruning is needed to make room for fresh new soil. Root-prune deciduous bonsai in early spring or late autumn, evergreen bonsai in early spring or late summer. Cut the root ball

Rub off all but about six of the shoots, then pinch their tips to promote branching.

Creating an 'Old' Snag on Bonsai

1. Snap back branch, pulling off a strip of bark.

2. After the wound dries, paint it with lime-sulfur solution.

back with a sharp knife and tease roots on the outside of the ball outward, then put the plant back in the pot, packing new soil among and around the roots.

Prune the top portion of a bonsai both while it is dormant and while it is growing to keep the plant small and to develop or maintain its form. Response to pruning is the same as for full-size plants: Pinch shoot tips to slow growth; shorten a stem where you want branches; rub off buds where growth is not wanted; pinch back "candles" of pines; pinch back expanding new growth on spruces and junipers; etc. With bonsai, though, even your fingernails might be too coarse a pruning tool. So, to avoid damaging the remaining leaves when you shorten expanding growth on spruce, for example, reach within a tuft of foliage with a pair of tweezers to tweak off all but a few new leaves.

Some bonsai benefit from having all their leaves pruned off just after they fully expand. Timed correctly, such leaf pruning forces a second flush of leaves which are smaller and hence better

proportioned to the size of the plant. You can get two seasons of development in one season with this trick, and, as an added benefit, that second flush of leaves often gives more dramatic autumn color than the first flush would have. On some trees, such as maples and elms, you can leaf-prune twice each season, as the first and second flushes of leaves fully expand. With trees such as ginkgo, beech, and oak, timing is critical for getting even a second flush of leaves. If there is any chance of injuring buds at the bases of the leaf stalks, just cut off most of each leaf with a scissors. The stalk will come off, perhaps needing some help from you, as new leaves appear.

Leaf pruning is not for every bonsai. Don't do it on evergreens or on fruiting bonsai that are bearing fruit. And leaf pruning is stressful, so avoid this practice on any tree that is weak or sick. The rigorous root and shoot pruning needed for bonsai is itself weakening, which is a good reason to take extra care in giving bonsai perfect growing conditions in every other respect.

An old snag gives this bonsai a wizened appearance.

CHAPTER SEVENTEEN   ESPALIER

**A well-grown espalier
offers food and beauty.**

E spalier (es-pal-YAY) is the training of a plant, usually a fruit plant, to an orderly two-dimensional form. The word is derived from the Old French *aspau*, meaning a prop, and most espaliers must, in fact, be propped up with stakes or wires. Espalier had its formal beginnings in Europe in the 16th century, when fruit trees were trained on walls to take advantage of the strip of earth and extra warmth near those walls. Strictly speaking, an espalier grown on a trellis in open ground is termed a *contre-espalier* of an *espalier-aere*. But no need to be a stickler for words. The definition of espalier is as lax as the plant is formal: The British reserve the term for a specific two-dimensional form; and some fanciful, yet well-ordered, shapes which might be called "espalier" by some gardeners, are, in fact, three-dimensional.

Why go to all the trouble of erecting a trellis and then having to pinch and snip a plant so frequently to keep it in shape? Because a well-grown espalier represents a happy commingling of art and science, resulting in a plant that pleases not only the eye, but also the palate. You apply this science artfully (or your art scientifically) by pulling exuberant stems downward to slow their growth, by cutting notches where a stem threatens to remain bare, by pruning back stems in summer to keep growth neat and fruitful—more on all of this later. The result: Every stem on a well-grown espalier is furnished throughout its length with fruits, and these fruits, bathed in abundant sunlight and air, are luscious, large, and full colored.

Despite the constant attention demanded by an espalier, caring for it is not really a great hardship. The trees never grow large, so they can be pruned, thinned, and harvested with your feet planted squarely on terra firma. And while pruning must be frequent, the cuts are small and quickly done, in many cases requiring nothing more than your thumbnail.

Espalier need not be restricted to plants bearing edible fruits. A purely ornamental espalier is in keeping with a formal setting (and so is an edible-fruited espalier). Maintenance of a purely ornamental espalier, especially when such a plant does not bear even flowers or ornamental fruit, entails nothing more than repeated clipping of wayward stems. When fruit, especially edible fruit, is a goal, however, you must carefully consider the response of the plant before you cut back stems: Are there enough leaves to nourish each fruit adequately? Will a new stem defiantly replace the one that you just cut off? Will your pruning restrict growth and keep stems furnished with fruit buds throughout their length?

Forms for an espalier

An espalier consists of one or more main stems, called leaders, which grow from the trunk. Permanent stems, called arms or ribs, may or may not arise from the leader(s). Arms usually are horizontal, or nearly so. Ribs usually refer to the herringbone pattern of stems that grow off the leaders of a fan-type espalier, which I will describe soon. Temporary stems, referred to as branches, grow directly from the leaders or, if present, arms or ribs. The trick in growing an espalier is minimizing branch growth while maximizing fruiting.

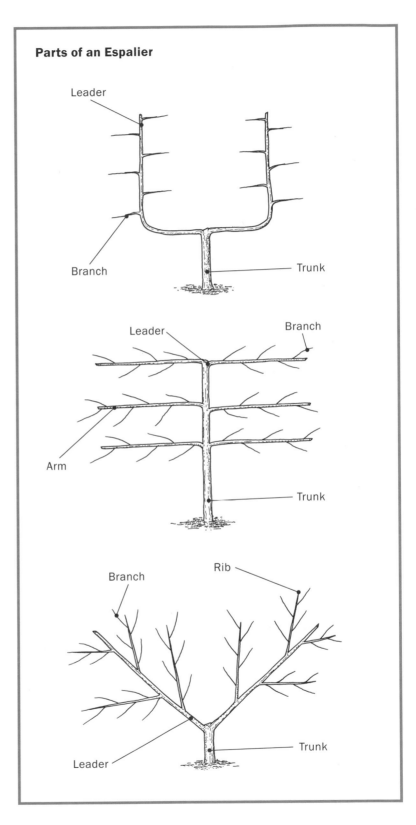

Parts of an Espalier

The simplest form for an espalier is that of a single leader (which some people choose to call a "cordon" rather than an "espalier"). Vertical cordons can be set a mere 18 in. apart in a row, so they are useful, for example, for growing many varieties of apple in a small space. Or a cordon can be trained horizontally to border a path or to edge a garden.

The cordon is best suited to plants that bear fruits on short growths, called spurs, so that the cordon looks like a cordon, rather than a porcupine. Among common fruits, apples and pears, and, to a lesser extent, plums, make good cordons. To counteract the tendency to top-heavy growth due to apical dominance of a vertical leader, single

Various Forms of Espalier

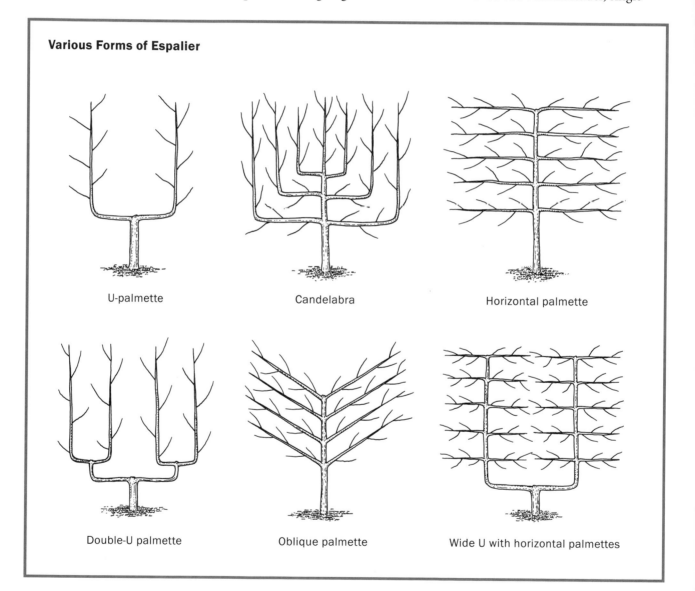

U-palmette

Candelabra

Horizontal palmette

Double-U palmette

Oblique palmette

Wide U with horizontal palmettes

cordons are commonly planted and grown at an angle, rather than vertically. This practice encourages uniform budbreak and growth up and down the cordon.

Terminate that single stem of a vertical cordon near ground level and split it into two stems, which you turn away from each other before letting them grow vertically again, and you have a U-palmette. Split those two vertical leaders of the U again and you have a double-U palmette, increasing the spread and yield from a single plant—and also changing the design, of course.

Just imagine how many variations can exist on this theme! The central stem could have two of its laterals grow out, then up, into leaders forming a wide U, then continue upward to have another two of its laterals growing out, then up, into a less wide U, and so on, candelabra fashion. Or, the central stem could grow up to the top of the plant, along the way sending out tiers of horizontal arms growing off to the left and to the right. (This latter form is what the British choose to call espalier; others call it a horizontal palmette or, if the side arms angle upward, an oblique palmette.) Or the central stem could split into a broad U with horizontal tiers of arms growing outward in two directions from each of the two leaders.

All these forms are prey to a common problem: excess growth near the tops of their upright leaders. This is the result of apical dominance, which is the tendency for the buds and shoots highest on a plant to grow most strongly. (A hormone called auxin, produced in the uppermost growing tips and buds, suppresses growth and budbreak farther down a stem.) To quote M. Gressent (*Arboriculture Fruitière*, 1869), a vertical growth "throws trouble into the whole economy of the tree and paralyzes its production and compromises the very existence of the horizontal branches." Well, not always, but those verticals do have to be watched.

Other shapes of espalier have been developed to overcome the potential hazard from vertical leaders. One popular form is the "fan," in which the

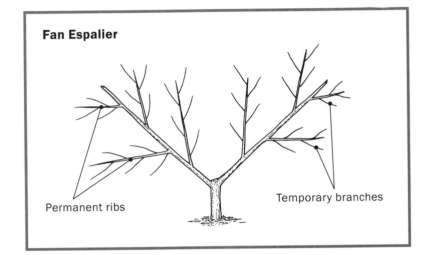

Fan Espalier

Permanent ribs

Temporary branches

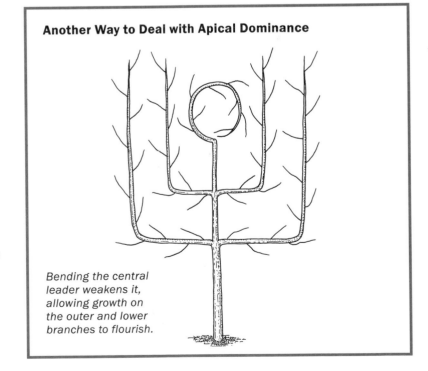

Another Way to Deal with Apical Dominance

Bending the central leader weakens it, allowing growth on the outer and lower branches to flourish.

central stem terminates low in the plant, dividing into two leaders that angle upward and outward. Off each of these leaders, above and below, grow ribs, with fruiting spurs or temporary branches growing from them. The number of ribs, and just how vertically they are allowed to grow, depend on the inherent vigor of the plant. Building up the lower and outside parts of the fan first keeps the potentially most vigorous part—that which is highest and in the center—from overtaking the rest. In other designs, the central leader is purposely weakened as it is bent around in a decorative curve, rather than allowed to grow straight upward.

Then there are espaliers composed of plants lined up and overlapping in a row. Among the most popular of such designs is the Belgian fence, a living latticework of stems. With some designs, adjacent stems graft together so that the espalier eventually becomes self-supporting.

Training

Training an espalier is just like training any other plant. Use heading cuts into young wood where you want branching, and thinning cuts when you want to get rid of unwanted growth (which includes stems growing perpendicular to the plane of the espalier). The differences between training a conventional fruit plant and an espalier lie in the goals: With an espalier, you want to develop stems having near perfect symmetry and furnished with live buds throughout their length.

No matter what your design, allow sufficient space (about 12 in.) between leaders. Where you want to bend a developing leader to change its direction of growth, lessen the chance of breakage by twisting the stem slightly as you bend. Where you want a leader to divide into a Y or a U, choose for those side arms stems that are growing as nearly as possible opposite and close to each other along the leader. The plant might already have some suitably positioned stems, or you might make a heading cut just above where you want them. Because laterals originate some distance apart along any stem on plants with alternate rather than opposite leaves, arms resulting from heading back a dormant shoot on such plants will never emerge *exactly* opposite each other.

The espalier maven, however, wants perfect symmetry (even in alternate-leaved plants), and there are two ways to put arms directly across from each other. One way is merely to graft a shoot opposite an existing shoot, or a bud opposite an existing bud, where you want the arms. The other way is to cut the stem back to the level where you want it to divide, while the plant is dormant. A vigorous shoot will grow vertically from the top of that cut stem, and at the base of that shoot will be a whorl of buds close

When mature, this apple trained as a Belgian fence will become a decorative screen producing luscious fruit.

together. When the vertical shoot is about 1 ft. long, cut it back to the whorl (leaving about ¼ in. of new growth) and you should get two new shoots originating from buds within that whorl—at almost exactly the same level. Aesthetics aside, shoots originating at the same level are more likely to keep in step as they grow.

Shorten the leader or leaders of an espalier each year, while the plant is dormant. Until a leader reaches its full length, cut back one-quarter to one-half of the previous season's growth, with the more severe cuts on weaker shoots. The purpose of this annual shortening is to keep the buds along the stem active. Upon reaching full length, the leader or leaders are cut back each year to within an inch or so of the previous season's growth.

Make free use of your thumbnail to pinch the tips of growing shoots as you train an espalier. Where any shoot is trying to outgrow its brethren, maintain symmetry by pinching back its tip. Pinching back the tips (just the tips, no more) of developing leaders every foot or so also keeps buds lower on the shoot active so that you do not get blind wood, possibly reducing or even eliminating the need for dormant heading of the leader or leaders.

You will need to erect a framework—commonly of wood, wire, or metal—to support your espalier and make sure its leaders are ramrod straight and at the desired angles. (All this rigidity is more a matter of aesthetics than plant physiology.) Once you have a framework erected, tie a leader as it grows to a bamboo cane that follows the desired direction of the shoot, then tie the cane to the framework.

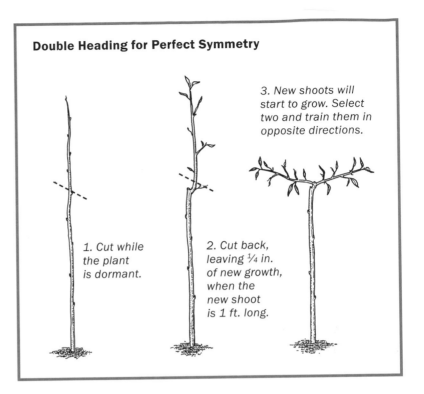

Double Heading for Perfect Symmetry

1. Cut while the plant is dormant.

2. Cut back, leaving ¼ in. of new growth, when the new shoot is 1 ft. long.

3. New shoots will start to grow. Select two and train them in opposite directions.

There are two reasons for tying a leader to the cane rather than directly to the framework. First, even though trellises are most easily constructed with horizontal and vertical members, and wires are most easily strung horizontally between end posts, the bamboo cane—with the attached leader—can be fixed at any desired angle. And second, tying a shoot to a cane rather than directly to the trellis also keeps a stem straight even if you have to raise or lower it as it grows. In this, we can befriend our old bugbear, apical dominance. For example, if your espalier will have two horizontal arms, you might want to train those arms initially at an upward angle to keep growth moving along—the more upward pointing, the faster the growth. As the arms approach full length, gradually bring them down to horizontal to slow growth. To do this, it is necessary only to untie the cane, and then, with the branch still firmly lashed to it, retie it at the desired angle.

Another way you can make use of apical dominance to build up horizontal arms while keeping growth active is to lash all but the ends of the shoots to horizontal supports. The free ends of the shoots then do what they are naturally inclined to do, turn upward, and that upward orientation keeps the growing tips vigorous. As the shoot elongates, keep tying the older portions down to the horizontal support.

Plants never follow rules exactly, and delinquent buds and shoots require special treatment. Use your knife to cut a notch just beyond a bud that needs awakening (see the photo on p. 29), or

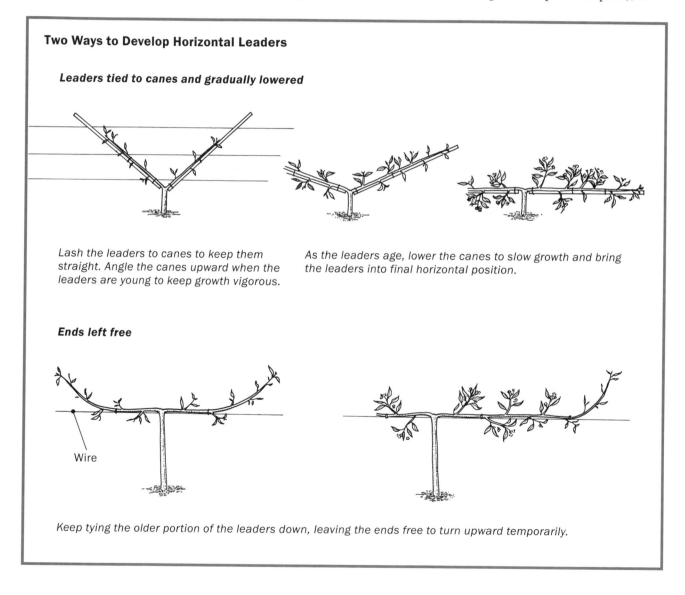

Two Ways to Develop Horizontal Leaders

Leaders tied to canes and gradually lowered

Lash the leaders to canes to keep them straight. Angle the canes upward when the leaders are young to keep growth vigorous.

As the leaders age, lower the canes to slow growth and bring the leaders into final horizontal position.

Ends left free

Wire

Keep tying the older portion of the leaders down, leaving the ends free to turn upward temporarily.

just below a shoot that needs restraint. A direct way to fill in a bare spot on a branch is to graft a bud, even a fruit bud, wherever it is needed. Deal with strong vertical shoots that are not wanted for extension growth either by cutting them away completely or by shortening them to a few buds, which may turn into fruit buds. But this latter pruning is the specialized pruning that is at the core of the next phase of pruning an espalier…

Maintenance pruning

Even before an espalier is fully trained, the older parts of the plant will need strict pruning to control branch growth and so maintain the neat shape of the plant—all the while avoiding sacrifice of fruit yield or quality. How pruning can help reach this goal depends on a particular plant's fruiting habit.

No matter what the plant, though, always keep shoots growing perpendicular to the plane of the espalier in check. Cut them cleanly away or pinch them back to a single leaf. And thin out branches if they become overcrowded. The stems of the perfect espalier will be solidly clothed with fruit, and if this goal is realized, make sure also to thin out some of the developing fruits. Some plants fruit on spurs, which eventually grow old and overcrowded and need to be thinned out and rejuvenated.

Now, on to some specifics, which, I caution you, must in some cases be varied to account for differences in varieties and climates.

Apple and pear espaliers

Apple and pear trees have similar growth and fruiting habits (fruits are borne on long-lived, stubby spurs) that are ideally suited for many different shapes of espalier, and made more so by the range of dwarfing rootstocks available for each of these fruits. But especially with these two fruits will you have to tailor your system of pruning to the variety and the location.

Apple 'Egremont russet' in an English garden in September.

In Lorette pruning, a half-woody shoot is cut back to the whorl of leaves at its base.

Let's start with one of the most elegant systems for pruning apple and pear espaliers, which was devised at the end of the 19th century by Louis Lorette, curator and professor of the Practical School of Agriculture at Wagonville, France. According to the Lorette system, which produces spectacular results in terms of beauty and fecundity, trees are pruned only during the growing season.

The first pruning, that of the extension growth from the tip of the leader (or tips of leaders), takes place when side shoots are about 2 in. long (the end of April in Wagonville). If a leader has not yet attained its full length, you cut back the previous season's growth by one-quarter to one-half, the lesser amount if growth was weak and the greater amount if it was strong. Shortening a developing leader keeps the lateral buds on this year-old wood active enough to prevent blind wood. The new shoot that grows from the end of a shortened leader is then allowed to grow unfettered for the whole season, thereby extending the leader. If a leader has reached its full length, cut it

back each year to where it began growing the previous season.

Pruning of branches growing off leaders begins later in the season (the middle of June in Wagonville), when they are pencil thick, about 1 ft. long, and becoming woody at their bases. Cut each branch that fits this description back to the whorl of leaves at its base, leaving a stub about ¼ in. long. Do not touch any branches that have not yet reached the proper growth maturity. Repeat this cutting back of properly mature branches at monthly intervals throughout the summer. Where regrowth has occurred following the previous pruning, also cut it back, but only if regrowth is at the proper stage of maturity. At the last pruning, in late summer, cut any immature branches back to three buds. Never shorten branches that are long, but insufficiently thick; instead, bend them over, then tie down their tips in order to furnish them with fruit buds. That's the bare bones of Lorette pruning; for more detail I refer you to *The Lorette System of Pruning* by Louis Lorette, revised edition in English published by John Lane The Bodley Head, Ltd., 1946.

Where the Lorette system works, buds at the bases of side shoots that have been cut back eventually become fruit buds hugging the leaders. And there's the rub: Lorette pruning is not effective everywhere. It seems to work where the climate is equable year round, with regular rainfall throughout summer and a long period of warmish weather in autumn. This is just the climate you find in northeastern France, but not over much of North America. My experiences in northeastern America with Lorette pruning concur with those of many others who have tried it. Variable summer rainfall, with intense sunlight, and wet autumns result too often in either rampant regrowth that is susceptible to winter injury or in dead stubs.

Across the English Channel from M. Lorette's France, the British had their own system of pruning pear and apple espaliers: the "three-bud" system. This method entails both summer and winter pruning, and also has its share of special wrinkles. In winter, the previous year's extension growth on a leader is shortened by about one-third to stimulate lateral growth for the coming season, or cut back completely if the leader is already full length. Also, at this time, young branches are cut back to three buds, and older branches are trimmed to a single stem and/or shortened to three buds beyond any fruit buds.

Subsequent pruning with the three-bud method takes place throughout the growing season. Pinch the tip of any side shoot when it has grown three leaves beyond the whorl of leaves at the base of the shoot. Shoots may also develop from older fruiting branches, and the time to pinch these shoots depends on the vigor and activity of the lower buds. If you pinch too early, those lower buds are jarred awake and grow out into shoots. But if your pinch is just right, those lower buds plump up into fat fruit buds. Close observation and the ability to predict the weather improve results, and I refer you to the previously cited edition of the Lorette book for more details.

Soon after becoming familiar with the beauty and effectiveness of the Lorette system, the British modified it to their conditions and inclinations (they weren't so keen on having to prune their trees throughout the summer). "Modified Lorette" pruning requires that the trees be pruned only twice a year. The timing of the first branch cut corresponds with that of M. Lorette's first branch cut, except that half-woody shoots are shortened to the second leaf (not counting the basal cluster of leaves), perhaps to the third leaf if growth is very strong.

The next time to cut is in winter, when you shorten regrowth from your summer cuts. If one stem grew from that two-bud stub, shorten it to two buds. If new stems grew from both those buds, shorten the one farther out to one bud and the one closer in to two buds. Either way, the branch is left with a total of three buds. The following summer, prune shoots when half woody to leave a total of three buds on any of these branches.

Other pruning methods also have proved successful for apple and pear. Pinching the tips of lateral shoots when they are half woody and about 1 ft. long, then shortening them to about 1 in. two weeks later, has quelled growth and set up fruit buds in New Zealand. In northeastern America, a similar result has been achieved by shortening any shoots longer than 1 ft. back to 1/4 in. in the middle of August. This latter pruning is supplemented by winter pruning, when regrowth and all vertical sprouts are cut back. Of course, an espalier spending the bulk of the summer spiky with relatively long lateral shoots off the leaders is not particularly neat, designwise. In Australia, a technique called "twice-heading" is used to make fruiting spurs from vigorous shoots. A shoot is shortened early in the season, and then, when the resulting regrowth of two or three shoots is 3 in. to 4 in. long, a second cut is made just below where this regrowth occurs. Where summer sun is intense and hot, as in California, whether or not you can clothe a leader in fruits rather than shoots becomes a moot point, because longer shoot growth might be needed to shade and prevent sunburn of the fruits. Obviously, climate is an important factor in determining the response of apple and pear to summer pruning.

In addition to climatic influences, you also have to take varietal differences into account. For example, quite a few apple varieties—'Rome Beauty', 'Cortland', 'Bramley's Seedling', and 'Idared', to name a few—bear their fruits at the ends of thin stems rather than on spurs. To espalier such "tip-bearers," you must promote the development of these fruit-bearing stems by moderate heading of leaders during training. And you obviously cannot stub shoots or you will be cutting off fruit buds.

Espaliers of other fruits

Less elaborate systems have been devised for pruning espaliers of fruits other than apple and pear. With any of these fruits, choose a form of espalier that takes into consideration the growth and fruiting habit of the plant, and then prune to maintain lateral fruiting wood close to the leader or leaders. Below is a summary of how this has been accomplished for various fruits (again, mostly in Europe and the British Isles, where espalier has been most popular).

Apricot   Apricot trees are best trained as fans. To induce the formation of spurs, pinch out the tips of branches when they are 3 in. to 6 in. long, reserving the latter length for the more vigorous branches. The spurs are not long-lived, so periodically cut away old ones and develop replacements.

Cherry   Although sweet, tart, and duke cherries are all best trained as fans, summer-pruning tactics vary with the type of cherry. With sweet and duke cherries, pinch out the tips of side shoots when they have six leaves, then cut those shoots back to three buds in early autumn. This pruning promotes the formation of fruiting spurs. The twice-heading technique mentioned for apple and pear espaliers also has been effective (in Australia and South Africa, at least) on sweet cherry trees, with the first cut just as the cherries are coloring up, and the second cut just after harvest.

On sweet and duke cherry trees, the fruiting spurs are not long-lived, so they need periodic replacement. On tart cherry trees, thin out the branches so that they are 3 in. apart along the ribs of the fan. These branches will bear both fruits and secondary branches. Allow only one of those secondary branches, near the base of the primary branch, to grow. After harvest, cut the primary branch back to the secondary branch, which will bear fruits the following season. Eventually, any of these cherries needs to be cut back more drastically to bring fruiting wood back toward the leaders.

Currant and gooseberry   Red currant, white currant, and gooseberry can be trained as a fan, cordon, or U-palmette. Shorten branches in early July to about 5 in. During the winter, cut these shortened branches farther back, to about 2 in.

Fig   The fig—now here's a plant that does not take all that kindly to the rigidity of espalier. (Such is the temperament of a plant with Mediterranean heritage, perhaps.)

PRUNING A RED CURRANT ESPALIER

1. Summer pruning of a red currant espalier consists merely of shortening the branches in July to about 5 in.

2. In winter, further shorten the branches to about 2 in.

3. The espalier after winter pruning.

4. Dangling daintily from the branches, these red currant fruits look almost too pretty to eat.

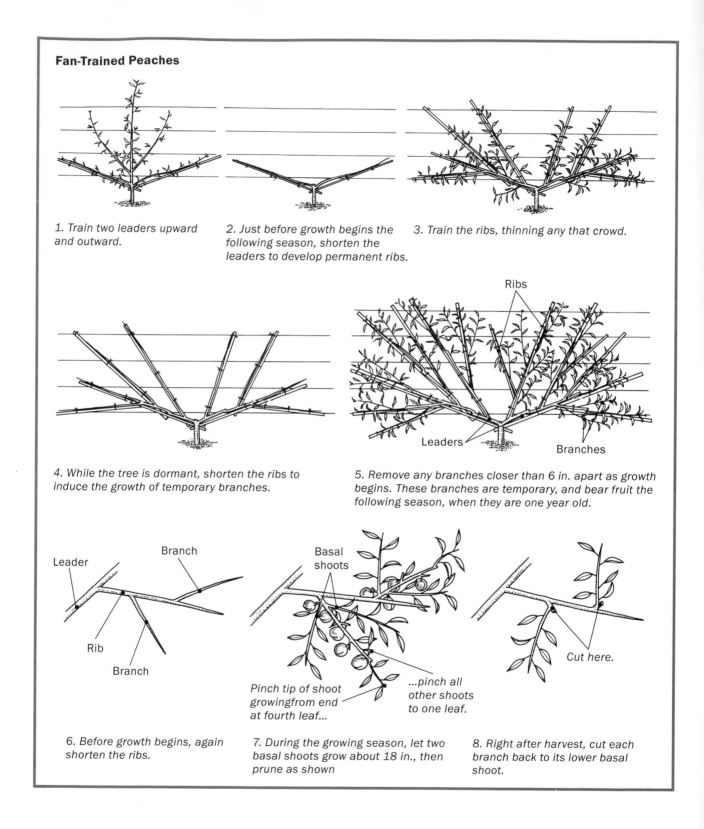

Fan-Trained Peaches

1. Train two leaders upward and outward.

2. Just before growth begins the following season, shorten the leaders to develop permanent ribs.

3. Train the ribs, thinning any that crowd.

4. While the tree is dormant, shorten the ribs to induce the growth of temporary branches.

Ribs

Leaders

Branches

5. Remove any branches closer than 6 in. apart as growth begins. These branches are temporary, and bear fruit the following season, when they are one year old.

Leader

Branch

Rib

Branch

Basal shoots

Pinch tip of shoot growing from end at fourth leaf...

...pinch all other shoots to one leaf.

Cut here.

6. Before growth begins, again shorten the ribs.

7. During the growing season, let two basal shoots grow about 18 in., then prune as shown

8. Right after harvest, cut each branch back to its lower basal shoot.

Nonetheless, even if the fig cannot be coerced into rigid symmetry, it can at least be kept two-dimensional, preferably as a fan. Varieties such as 'Beall', 'Flanders', 'King', 'Mission', 'Osborne', 'Pasquale', 'Tena', 'Ventura', and 'Verte', which crop on one-year-old wood, make neater espaliers than do varieties that crop mostly or only on new shoots. Manage a fan-trained fig by cutting back, in alternate years, every other fruiting branch growing from main stems to one bud. As a main stem grows old, drastically shorten it so that a young shoot can grow as a replacement; this it will do readily, reflecting the fig's naturally bushy tendency.

Peach and nectarine   Train peach or nectarine as a fan, with one-year-old stems, which bear fruit, spaced 6 in. apart and growing from the ribs. In spring, side shoots will grow from these one-year-old stems. Pinch to a single leaf all side shoots except the two at the base, and pinch back the shoot growing from the end of that one-year-old stem back to four leaves, unless there is sufficient space to let it grow freely. Depending on the space available, let those two basal shoots grow to 18 in. or less before pinching out their tips. Right after harvest, cut the one-year-old stem (which bore fruit) back to the lower basal side shoot, which will bear fruit the next season. (The other basal shoot was there only for insurance, to be left in case the lower one was damaged.)

Plum   Grow plums as fans or, less satisfactorily, as cordons. Thin branches so that they are 4 in. apart, and keep pinching them back to six leaves. After harvest, shorten the branches to three leaves.

And so we come to the close of "espalier." As you can see, it is the commonly grown fruits of Europe, the home of espalier, for which most details of training and maintaining an espalier have been devised. I repeat my earlier caution that pruning may have to be varied to suit the length of the growing season, autumn temperatures, day length, rainfall, and intensity of sunlight at any particular location. But armed with an understanding of how plants respond to pruning, as well as the fruit plants' specific growth and fruiting habits, you are now in a position to devise your own method for pruning any fruiting espalier, no matter where your plants grow.

Espalier is a fitting finale to this book, for no other aspect of plant growing requires more constant and close attention to pruning. But rest assured: All this snipping and pinching, this almost daily fussing over the plants, is rewarding work.

And the rewards of pruning are not only limited to espalier. Any pruning—whether it is to shape a rose bush, to grow a sturdy maple tree, or simply to mow a handsome lawn—is most satisfying and produces the best results when done intelligently and with attention to necessary detail.

GLOSSARY OF PRUNING TERMS

APICAL DOMINANCE
The natural tendency for strongest growth from the highest buds on a stem, along with the suppression of growth from buds or branches lower down.

BARK RIDGE
A fold of bark on the upper side of a branch near its origin.

BLIND WOOD
A portion of stem bare of either branches or flowers.

BONSAI
A plant, usually a woody plant, grown as a dwarf in a shallow pot.

BRANCH
A secondary (lateral, subordinate) shoot or stem growing off a more major shoot or stem.

BRANCH COLLAR
A swollen ring of bark on the lower side of a branch near its origin.

CANE
Usually a vague term referring to a plant stem, but in the case of grapes, a stem that made its growth the previous growing season.

CANOPY
The sum total of the branches of a tree.

CENTRAL LEADER
The central axis of a tree, growing as a continuation of the trunk and off which grow scaffold limbs. Not all trees have a single central leader.

CORDON
A woody plant grown as a single, permanent stem, or that part of a woody plant that is a single, long, permanent stem. Every year, temporary branches growing off a cordon are cut almost back to where they originated. Cordon comes from the same root as the word "cord."

CROWN
Oddly, this term can mean either the part of any plant just below the ground or the sum total of the branches—the canopy—of a tree.

DEADHEADING
Removing spent flowers from a plant to make it more tidy and prevent seed formation.

ESPALIER
A plant, usually a fruit plant, trained to an orderly two-dimensional form.

FEATHERED TREE
A young nursery-grown tree with branches.

GIRDLING
Removing a strip of bark from around the trunk or a limb of a woody plant.

HEADING CUT
A pruning cut that removes only part of a stem.

LEADER
A stem that is the main axis of a woody plant. A plant may have a single central leader or multiple leaders.

LEG
A very short length of trunk on a woody plant.

NODE
The point on a stem where a leaf was or is attached.

PINCHING
Nipping out the tip of a growing shoot with your fingernail.

PLEACHING
Informally weaving together the branches of trees to form a living wall or roof.

POLLARDING
Stubbing back all the growth of a tree each year to the same point on either the trunk or scaffold limbs, thereby creating a knobbed trunk or limb that will sprout again in the growing season.

RENOVATION
Revitalizing a plant or planting.

RINGING
Another term for girdling.

ROOT SUCKER
A shoot growing from the base of a woody plant.

SCAFFOLD LIMBS
Major branches of a woody plant.

SCORING
Making a single knife cut into and around the bark on the trunk or a limb of a woody plant.

SPUR
A naturally stubby flowering branch that grows only a fraction of an inch each year.

SHOOT
A stem in active growth.

STANDARD
This term can mean either a full-size (as opposed to a dwarf) tree, or a plant, usually one that is naturally bushy, trained to have a length of clear trunk capped by a leafy head.

STOOL
A plant periodically renewed by cutting old stems down to the ground to be replaced by new stems that grow up.

THINNING CUT
A pruning cut that removes a stem right to its origin or to a large branch.

TOPIARY
The practice of pruning a tree or a shrub to create a living sculpture.

WATERSPROUT
A very vigorous vertical shoot growing from a branch of a tree.

WHIP
A nursery-grown tree consisting of an unbranched single stem.

INDEX

A

Aaron's Beard. *See* St.-John's-Wort
Abelia (*Abelia × grandiflora*), 47
 as hedge, 66
Acacia spp., 96
Acerola cherry (*Malpighia glabra*), 141
African Boxwood. *See* Cape Myrtle
African Hemp (*Sparmannia africana*), 105
African Tulip Tree (*Spathodea campanulata*), 106
Alder (*Alnus* spp.), 80
 growth habits of, 77
 pruning, tolerance for, 79
Allamand (*Allamanda cathartica*), 114
Almond (*Prunus* spp.):
 Dwarf Flowering (*P. glandulosa*), 45
 Dwarf Russian (*P. tenella*), 47
 Flowering (*P. triloba*), 45
 P. dulcis var. *dulcis*, 141
Alyssum (*Lobularia maritima*), 182, 183
Ampelopsis spp., 114
Andromeda. *See* Pieris
Anemopaegma Chamberlaynii, 114
Angel's-trumpet (*Brugmansia* spp.), 96
Anise Tree (*Illicium* spp.), 101
Annuals. *See* Herbaceous plants
Apple (*Malus* spp.):
 crab, 82
 dwarf, 9-10
 for espalier, 214, 216, 219-222
 for pleaching, 196
 pruning, 141-144
 to dwarf pyramid, 125, 141
 for earliest bearing, 142-144
 of fruits, 144
 of mature tree, 141-142
 of roots, disadvised, 28
 to slender spindle, 142-144
 of spurs, 142, 143
 summer, 142
 timing of, 26, 142
 of tip bearers, 142
 size control of, 11
 spurs on, fruit-bearing, 133
Apricot (*Prunus Armeniaca*), 144
 espaliering, 222
Aralia Ivy (× *Fatshedera Lizei*), 99
Arborvitae (*Thuja* spp.), 92
 dwarf, 9
 for topiary, 199

B

Argentine Trumpet Vine (*Clytostoma callistegioides*), 114
Aristolochia spp., 114
Artemisia (*Artemisia* spp.), crown division for, 184
Ash (*Fraxinus* spp.), 81
 pruning, tolerance for, 79
Aspen. *See* Poplar
Aster (*Aster novi-belgii*):
 crown division for, 184
 pruning, 181-182
Athel Tree (*Tamarix aphylla*), 82
Australian Bluebells. *See* Bluebell Creeper
Autumn Olive (*Elaeagnus umbellata*), 39
Auxin, effects of, 29-30
Australian Umbrella Tree (*Brassaia actinophylla*), 96
Avocado (*Persea americana*), 144
Azalea (*Rhododendron* spp.):
 deciduous, 45
 evergreen, 104-105
Azara, Boxleaf (*Azara microphylla*), 96

Baby's-breath (*Gypsophila* spp.), crown division for, 184
Bald Cypress (*Taxodium distichum*), 82
 branching in, encouraging, 75
Bamboo, 108-109
Banana (*Musa acuminata*), 144-145
Barbados-pride (*Caesalpinia pulcherrima*), 96
Barberry, Japanese (*Berberis Thunbergii*), 39, 96
 as hedge, 66
Bark:
 notching, 29, 130, 131
 removing, 29
 ringing, 29
 of *Prunus*, disadvised, 135
 to stimulate fruiting, 135
 scoring, 29
Bark cankers, pruning against, 8
Barometer Bush. *See* Ceniza
Basket-of-gold (*Aurinia saxatilis*), 183
Basswood. *See* Linden
Bearberry (*Arctostaphylos* spp.), 96
Bearing, biennial, causes of, 27
Beautybush (*Kolkwitzia amabilis*), 44
Bee balm (*Monarda didyma*), crown division for, 184

Beech (*Fagus* spp.), 81
 as bonsai, 211
 European (*F. sylvatica*),
 as hedge, 66
 for topiary, 199
 as hedge, 37
 for pleaching, 196
 pruning, tolerance for, 79
Birch (*Betula* spp.), 80
 growth habits of, 77
 pruning,
 timing of, 26
 tolerance for, 79
Bird-of-paradise Shrub (*Caesalpinia Gilliesii*), 96
Bittersweet (*Celastrus scandens*), 112, 113, 114
Black knot disease, pruning against, 8
Blackberry (*Rubus* spp.), 145-146
Bladder Nut (*Staphylea* spp.), 45
Bladder Senna, common (*Colutea arborescens*), 39, 43
Bleeding Glory-bower (*Clerodendrum Thomsoniae*), 97-98
Bleeding-heart (*Dicentra spectabilis*), crown division for, 184
Blossoms, thinning, with garden hose, 15
Bluebeard (*Caryopteris* spp.):
 C. × clandonensis, 49
 C. incana, 49
Bluebell Creeper (*Sollya heterophylla*), 116
Blueberry (*Vaccinium* spp.), 147
Blue-mist Shrub. *See* Bluebeard
Blue Sage (*Eranthemum pulchellum*), 99
Blue-spiraea. *See* Bluebeard
Bog Myrtle. *See* Sweet Gale
Bonsai:
 broom-style, 209, 210
 described, 208
 pruning, 210-211
 pruning for, 11
 "snags" on, 209, 211
 trunks of, shortening, 209
Borers, pruning against, 8
Bottlebrush (*Callistemon* spp.), 96
 See also Buckeye, Bottlebrush; Honey Myrtle
Bottle Tree (*Brachychiton* spp.), 96
Bougainvillea (*Bougainvillea* spp.), 96
Box (*Buxus* spp.), 96
 hedges of, 36
 for topiary, 199

Branch collar, cutting to, 32-33
Branches:
 distance between, optimal, 73
 for fruit trees, 125-126
 growth of, suppressing, 76
 large, removing, 30
 pruning, of bare-root trees, 127-128
 scaffold, 73-75, 94
 side, cutting to, 32
 sucker, removing, 77
 temporary, 76-77, 95
 upright vs. horizontal, 74, 75
 watersprout, removing, 77, 131
 wide-angled, training for, 129-131
Branching:
 in conifers, inducing, 75
 in fruit trees, encouraging, 128
Breath-of-Heaven (*Diosma ericoides*), 98
Broadleaf evergreens:
 listed, 96-107
 pruning, 93
 maintenance, 95
 for renovation, 95
 for training, 94-95
Broom (*Cytisus scoparius*), 43, 60
Buckeye (*Aesculus* spp.), 80
 Bottlebrush (*A. parviflora*), 39
 pollarding, 194
 pruning, tolerance for, 79
Buckthorn (*Rhamnus* spp.), 40
Buddhist Pine. *See* Southern Yew
Buds:
 cutting to, 31-32
 hormones in, 72, 128, 215
 notching to, 130, 131
 stimulating, 26
Buffalo berry (*Shepherdia* spp.), 147
Burning bush (*Euonymus* spp.), as hedge, 66
Bushes:
 broadleaf evergreen,
 listed, 96-107
 pruning, 93-95
 coniferous evergreen,
 listed, 90-92
 pruning, 84-89
 deciduous,
 as hedges, 36
 as shrubs, 36-38
 defined, 36-37
 fruit, pruning of, 123
 maintenance, 138
 for renovation, 138
 for training, 137-138
 pruning, by flowering type, 37-38
 See also Hedges; Shrubs; *specific plants*

CREDITS

COVERS

front, Peter Vitale
back, Susan Kahn

CHAPTER 1

p. 4, Scott Phillips
pgs. 6, 7 top, 8 left, Lee Reich
pgs. 7 bottom, 8 right, Susan Kahn
p. 9, William Talarowski/New England
    Stock Photo
p. 10, Ken Druse
p. 11 top, © Alan and Linda Detrick
p. 11 bottom, Montreal Botanic Garden,
    © Mick Hales

CHAPTER 2

pgs. 13, 16, 17, 18, 19, 20, Susan Kahn
p. 14, Lee Reich

CHAPTER 3

p. 22, Ken Druse
p. 27, Charles Kennard
p. 28, Susan Kahn
p. 29, Lee Reich

CHAPTER 4

p. 34, Mick Hales
p. 36, Howard Rice/Garden Picture
    Library
pgs. 37 top, 53, © Alan and Linda
    Detrick
p. 37 bottom, John Glover/Garden
    Picture Library
p. 39, Susan Roth
p. 44, © Alan and Linda Detrick
pgs. 46, 48, 59, Susan Kahn
pgs. 49, 57, Ken Druse
pgs. 54, 67, Derek Fell
pgs. 56, 61, Lee Reich
p. 62, Charles Mann
p. 64, Michael Shedlock/New England
    Stock Photo

CHAPTER 5

p. 68, Ken Druse
pgs. 69, 70, 75, Lee Reich
pgs. 77, 78, 81, 82, Derek Fell

CHAPTER 6

pgs. 83, 91, 97, 98, 108, 109, Derek Fell
pgs. 84, 101, 104 top, Lee Reich
pgs. 87, 88, 89, 104 bottom, Susan Kahn
p. 93, Lamontagne/Garden Picture
    Library

CHAPTER 7

p. 110, Karen Bussolini
pgs. 111, 115, 117 top, Ken Druse
pgs. 113 top, 117 bottom, © Alan and
    Linda Detrick
p. 113 bottom, Derek Fell
p. 118, Susan Kahn
p. 120, Lee Reich

CHAPTER 8

pgs. 122, 137, Derek Fell
pgs. 130, 131, 133, 141, 161, 166, 167,
    170, 175, Lee Reich
pgs. 132, 135, 136, 147, 151, 153, 155,
    173, Susan Kahn
p. 142, Bruce H. Barritt
p. 145, Dodge Photography/New
    England Stock Photo
p. 149 top, W. J. Kender
p. 149 bottom, David Goldberg/David
    Goldberg Photography
p. 157, Lon J. Rombough
p. 160, David Askham/Garden Picture
    Library
p. 163, Pamela K. Pierce/David Goldberg
    Photography

CHAPTER 9

p. 177, Karen Bussolini
pgs. 178, 179, Susan Kahn

CHAPTER 10

p. 180, Ken Druse
p. 185, © Alan and Linda Detrick
p. 187, Karen Bussolini
pgs. 183, 189, 191, Lee Reich

CHAPTER 11

p. 192, Clive Boursnell/Garden Picture
    Library
p. 194, Marijke Heuff/Garden Picture
    Library

CHAPTER 12

p. 196, Derek Fell

CHAPTER 13

pgs. 198, 199, Ken Druse

CHAPTER 14

pgs. 201, 203, Lee Reich

CHAPTER 15

pgs. 204, 205, Ken Druse
pgs. 206, 207, Lee Reich

CHAPTER 16

p. 208, © Alan and Linda Detrick
pgs. 210, 211, Herb Gustafson

CHAPTER 17

p. 212, © Mayer/Le Scanff/Garden
    Picture Library
p. 216, Derek Fell
p. 219, John Glover/Garden Picture
    Library
p. 220, Susan Kahn
p. 223, Lee Reich

GLOSSARY

p. 227, Derek Fell